Lanford Wilson

Collected Plays
1965-1970

Lanford Wilson

Collected Plays
1965-1970

Contemporary Playwrights Series

SK

A Smith and Kraus Book

A Smith and Kraus Book
Published by Smith and Kraus, Inc.
One Main Street, PO Box 127, Lyme, NH 03768

Copyright ©1996 by Smith and Kraus
All rights reserved
Manufactured in the United States of America
Cover and Text Design by Julia Hill
Cover Photo by Frederick Eberstadt ©1965

First Edition: September 1996
10 9 8 7 6 5 4 3 2

Library of Congress Cataloging-in-Publication Data
Wilson, Lanford, 1937 –
[Plays. Selections]
Lanford Wilson: collected plays, 1965-1970. --1st ed.
p. cm. -- (Contemporary playwrights series, ISSN 1067-9510)
Contents: Balm in Gilead — The Sand Castle — The Rimers of Eldritch —
The Gingham Dog — Lemon Sky
ISBN 1-57525-026-8 (cloth). — ISBN 1-57525-025-X (paper)
I. Title. II. Series.
PS3573.I458A6   1996
812'.54--dc20   96-1909
CIP

Contents

Introduction
by Michael Feingold

Before sitting down to write this, I pulled out my World Atlas and found Lebanon, Missouri on the map, just to be sure I wouldn't say anything stupid about it. Lebanon, where Lanford Wilson was born, is the county seat of Laclede County in central Missouri, southeast of the Lake of the Ozarks; when my old atlas was printed, it had a population of about 8600. I have no idea what it looks like, but I know the people. I know them from many productions of *The Rimers of Eldritch* and any number of other Lanford Wilson plays set in Lebanon or in towns a lot like it.

Now I'm thinking of other places. I'm thinking of ramshackle, sand-tracked beachfront houses in southern California; of tidy, glossy suburban homes both east and west; of tacky, funny-angled Greenwich Village apartments. And of an all-night greasy spoon that doesn't exist any more, on Broadway below 72nd Street, when that intersection was nicknamed Needle Park, (realtors now call it Sherman Square). I used to get nervous walking past that diner at night. Lanford apparently went in—isn't that the difference between critics and playwrights?—and stayed long enough to "get" the material for *Balm in Gilead*, just as he's stayed in each of the places where his plays are set. Think of how often in his plays the action takes its tone from the place. I'm not talking about regionalism and accents and folkways; I mean the tone of a *place*. A place has its own particular voice, no matter how much we Americans try to sterilize it and level it and build over it; and in Lanford Wilson's plays, American places speak.

As do the people. Now I'm not thinking of the real people on whom Lanford's characters are based. Every playwright has models, conscious or unconscious; Shaw used to send his the rough drafts and ask them to correct what he'd made them say. I'm thinking of the actors I've seen in Lanford's plays over the years, close friends, acquaintances, and strangers; actors for whom he's written time and again, actors he's taken on trust, and actors he's sighed and accepted because the producer assured him that so-and-so was *perfect* for the role. Sometimes the producer turns out to be right, too, because Lanford writes for actors—a virtue rarer than you might think in today's theatre. Actors often find his characters speaking with their inner voice. *How did you know that,* they ask, *Where did you get that phrase, that rhythm, that tic of behavior, that half-formed thought?* When audiences feel it, too, as they often do, it's called the shock of recognition. *Yes,* they think, *this is who we are.* And the smarter or braver ones may add, *What terrible people, and what awful situations they get into. What things life does to us!*

Not that Lanford has a specially terrible or gloomy view of the world; it's just the way the world is. Things turn out terribly; people faced with awful situations make terrible choices. Not all the time and not without some show of courage or honor or fairness. But things turn out terribly, for the most part, and we go on living; that's reality. And I think of the actors I've seen in Lanford's plays, of their faces and voices and physical presence, because it's the special reality of human beings that I mean, the thing that makes them so remarkable and so horrible compared to everything else on this planet. Lions don't worry about whether their wives are faithful or their kids are acting weirdly; they just pounce when they scent an intruder. Even at their freest and happiest, Lanford's characters carry the pain of being human.

And they carry it onto the stage, because if this volume proves one thing, it's that Lanford Wilson is not a naturalist, not a writer who sees a place or person and tries to reproduce literally what he sees onstage. Just as you can only hear a place's voice by steeping yourself in its reality, you can only communicate what you hear by refracting that reality through art. Lanford's places and times intersect and criss-cross onstage; his people are real, but they also know that they're in a play. They work hard, even outside their reality, to make the play turn out well. They talk to the audience, they prompt each other, they time-jump to favorite moments. But the play turns out badly anyway, like reality; the climactic violence gets obsessively repeated, as at the end of *Balm in Gilead,* or a flood of climaxes piles in at once, as in *Lemon Sky* and *Serenading Louie.* All anybody wanted was for things to turn out well, but things don't.

Maybe if the characters had their way, these would be well-made naturalistic plays with tidy endings. But life's untidy, this society's untidy (not to say falling apart), and Lanford's plays track its untidy graph. When small-town sentiment was big in popular entertainment, he wrote *The Rimers of Eldritch,* in which a small town is a nasty mess of misunderstandings and gossip. When everyone was swallowing platitudes about the Great Society ending discrimination and poverty, he wrote *The Gingham Dog,* in which a black-white relationship becomes a shouting match that leaves love dead on the floor. And when affluence and a lavish lifestyle were the operative notions, he wrote *Serenading Louie,* in which the comforts you buy never equal the pleasures you recall from your impoverished youth and may ultimately become what destroys you.

I don't believe, knowing Lanford, that he thought consciously about these themes or about countering the trend of the times. I think he thought about people he knew, and places, and the themes came along willy-nilly. And because he thought so clearly and deeply, the themes turned out to be the most truthful ones for the times. Because people and places live in time, and change with it; when you have two or three people and a place, you have a play, a thing that moves through time. The past doesn't disappear in real life any more than it dies in Lanford's theatre; it hovers and recurs, changing its facets in retrospect as the people change. And Lanford, off in Sag Harbor, cultivates his garden—a place that, like people, requires nurture and attention, and changes over time, in big ways and small. It's the same with plays as with gardens: You can't assume that, because there are so many small changes, the big ones won't be very big and violent when they come. Gertrude Stein—a writer Lanford owes absolutely nothing to, as far as I can tell—said my favorite thing about it: "A landscape is such a natural setting for a battlefield or a play that one must write plays." Lanford's plays, so transfused by their places, are really battles. Don't be misled by the myriad little details of the characters' humanity. Underneath, they're lions waiting to pounce. Lanford knows. In the Ozarks, where he comes from, they still have mountain lions.

Michael Feingold, chief theatre critic of New York's weekly The Village Voice, *is also well known as a translator, playwright, and director.*

Balm in Gilead

To Tanya

INTRODUCTION

It was a fairly logical path: High School in Ozark, Missouri, where I had a great mother who said, Get out of this town there's nothing for you here (and a stepfather I was eager to remove myself from), to one term at Southwest Missouri State in Springfield, Mo., to one year of college in San Diego, California, where my father lived with his new wife and two new sons (see *Lemon Sky*), back to Chicago for a one week visit with friends from high school, where I stayed for six years and discovered I was a playwright. So. On to New York City's cheap (then) Upper West Side, smack in the middle of Drug City.

I always thought I was going to be a painter. Painter or graphic designer, I'd have been happy with either. All my friends after high school knew me as an "artist." In Chicago I worked at an advertising agency: art department, apprentice, lowest of the low, mounting photographs and pasting-up type, writing stories during all my breaks. It was my intention to support my painting habit by selling stories to the Better National Magazines. I'd finish a story, send it out, start another—they were terrible, none was published, thank you God. I got an idea for my next opus and thought, That's more like a play than a story. I had been in two plays in high school, had been an assistant stage manager my only term at S.M.S., had read plays regularly since and seen the national touring companies when they came to Chicago. Why not write a play? By the middle of page two it was clear to me that I was, of all things, a playwright. All my life, all of twenty-one years, I had expected to be a painter: If anyone had asked me what I did that evening, I would have said, I'm a playwright, I write plays. No one was producing new plays in Chicago—if you can believe it, considering the great theater energy that has come from there since. But we had no model, we didn't know we could start our own theater company there, it wouldn't have entered our heads. Second City was an important breeding ground for comics, Goodman Theater and Northwestern excellent schools for actors, but no one was doing new plays outside of New York. I came to New York to write.

That's the title of a Robert Patrick play: *I Came to New York to Write*. It would work as the title for the autobiography of about half the American playwrights of my generation (the other half already lived in the New York area). In the early 1960s new American plays simply were not being produced anywhere else, or so rarely as to make no difference. What has happened since then is amazing. The proliferation of small theater companies, in every state, in every city of any size, doing new work by American playwrights, many of them local playwrights in residence, is one of the more important (largely unrecognized and unheralded) cultural changes of the last quarter century. It wasn't like that when I came to New York to write.

But I didn't come to New York immediately. I've had two butt-saving days in my life. The first when I discovered I was meant to write for the stage, the second when I decided to check out New York City before I moved there. The city would have eaten me for breakfast. I earned my two weeks vacation and took a bus to New York. In the Greyhound station the first sound I heard came from the mouth of a man with the thickest Brooklyn accent in the city. It was music. The sidewalks were crowded with people. The chorus of, *clash* of, accents and languages, I couldn't begin to guess which, thrilled me. I walked under the lights of Broadway theaters; they were incubator lights to a young chick. They warmed me. I felt my shoulders drop four inches. I had been tense for over twenty years and hadn't known it. I relaxed for the first time in my life. And, this is strange, the city still terrified me. It shocked me. The city is a crucible. I was not ready for New York. It excited me as the place I would be coming to, this is where I would live one day, when I was ready. My first subway ride: Forty Second Street. The platform was crowded. The train came, the doors opened right in front of me. I stood there. People pushed out, *pushed* out. I was carried back to the middle of the platform. People around me had to elbow their way past me to get on the train. The doors closed, the last people squeezing in through the doors that had them in their grip, the train pulled out, and I was left standing there, the only person in the station.

All I knew of New York Theater was Broadway and the plays I'd read in anthologies and magazines. Yes, magazines used to publish plays. I imagined *Death of a Salesman* playing next to *The Children's Hour* next to *A Streetcar Named Desire* next to *Long Day's Journey into Night* next to some classic. Fat chance. Even then Broadway was The Broadway Musical and British plays. I saw them all in two weeks. Let's just say I judged them harshly. It's the nature of youth to judge the establishment harshly. I went to Greenwich Village to check out the intellectuals (Beatniks back then, not hippies) and the gay bars. I weighed one hundred and twenty-seven pounds. A man six-five followed me all over the village, I thought I'd never lose him. I wasn't ready for New York. I went back to Chicago to grow the tough hide Harper Lee said you needed to be a writer in America. A year and a half later I moved to New York.

I came with Michael Warren Powell and Dean Morgan. We shared a large room with three beds. The bathroom was down the hall. You often stepped on a disposable syringe on the way to the john. The all-night coffee shop on the corner, just four stories below our room, was the hangout of the wildest crowd of hustlers, addicts, prostitutes and pushers I'd ever seen. They called the area

Needle Park. I loved it. I sat at the counter and wrote down everything I heard: a journal of Needle Park, an exercise in construction and sound. I was lucky enough to find the Caffe Cino; I wrote several one act plays for that very small theater, the stage at the Cino was about eight feet square. They seated maybe twenty-five people. Almost all the plays I wrote for that space had two or three characters. There wasn't room for more. The play I was compiling (more than writing) at the coffee shop was my rebellion against the confines of the Cino. It had fifty-six characters in the first draft. It was written in the cafe and in my room above the cafe. Almost everything the character Fick says was said as he ran alongside me in the pouring rain from the seventy-second street subway stop to the downstairs door of the building where we lived on seventy-sixth. I just said, I'll see you around, went upstairs, sat down, wet, and copied it out.

This play was my first collaboration with Marshall W. Mason. We met at the Cino. Joe Cino wanted us to do *Balm in Gilead* there. I don't think he was ever convinced that it wouldn't fit. Michael Powell and I had moved from the upper west side to the Broadway Central Hotel in the village where I finished the second draft of *Balm* (only thirty-eight characters). One night when I couldn't sleep and Marshall Mason couldn't sleep, we met at some coffee shop in the Village. He came to the hotel and read the script (I was probably hovering around, we had two bedrooms, no living room, no kitchen, no bath). Marshall said, "This is going to require a very good director." And left. I assumed he hated it. Later, when Michael Powell had discovered that by "a very good director," Marshall had been talking about himself, we sat down to discuss a production. He talked, I listened. About four hours. He thought it was cool that the play was written in a series of circles, I thought it was invisible. He liked the fact that it was essentially a play about economics. The first line I wrote in the cafe was, This could be Wall Street. I'll cut this short. He knew everything there was to know about the play including things I had hidden, for no one to know but me. We both had near-photographic memories back then, he remembered sections verbatim a month after reading the play. When you find someone like that, you've found your director. Or rather, you have if he can direct. Marshall can.

Balm in Gilead was the first original full-length play done Off-Off-Broadway. Ellen Stewart sat outside the door of her LaMama ETC. (Experimental Theater Club) to keep people from entering during the performance. The place was packed every night, a line formed downstairs, people had to be turned away. Ellen was worried the crowd would draw the cops. The last night of the run she let everybody in and sat outside the door to ward off the Fire Marshal if he made a surprise visit. I don't know if she ever saw the play.

PRODUCTION

Balm in Gilead was first presented by Ellen Stewart at the Cafe La Mama Experimental Theatre Club, New York City, on January 26, 1965. It was directed by Marshall W. Mason, with the following cast:

John	Marvin Alexander
Ernesto	Thomas Ambrosio
Carlo	Howard Benson
Babe	Savannah Bentley
Rust	Claris Erickson
Bonnie	Linda Eskenas
Fick	Neil Flanagan
Franny	Frank Geraci
David	Gary Gusick
Tig	Paul Kilb
Rake	John Kramer
Martin	Matthew Lewis
Bob	Harry McCormick
Frank, Al	Jerry Newman
Darlene	Avra Petrides
Dopey	Michael Warren Powell
Kay	Barbara Randolph
Joe	Gregory Rozakis
Terry	Lucy Silvay
Ann	Mary Tahmin
Xavier	Dennis Tate
Stranger	Robert Thirkield
Tim	Ronald Willoughby
Judy	Phoebe Wray

Lighting by Dennis Parichy, assistant director Roderick Nash, stage manager Lola Richardson, assistant to the producer Zita Litvanas.

Balm in Gilead was presented by the Circle Repertory Company and the Steppenwolf Theater Ensemble at the Circle Repertory in New York City on May 15, 1984. It was directed by John Malkovich, with the following cast:

John	Paul Butler
Ernesto	Giancarlo Esposito
Carlo	Lazaro Perez
Babe	Debra Engle
Rust	Billie Neal
Bonnie	Tanya Berezin
Fick	Terry Kinney
Franny	Jeff Perry

David..Brian Tarantina
Tig ....James McDaniel
Rake..James Picken, Jr.
Martin ....Jonathan Hogan
Bob ....Bruce McCarty
Frank ....Zane Lasky
Al...Burke Pearson
Darlene ....Laurie Metcalf
Dopey ....Gary Sinise
Kay..Betsy Aidem
Joe ....Danton Stone
Terry..Karen Sederholm
Ann ....Glenne Headly
Xavier..Tom Zanarini
Stranger...Tom Irwin
Tim..Mick Weber
Judy ....Charlotte Maier
Children..Adam Davidson, Eben Davidson,
Erinnisse Heuer, and Samantha Kostmayer

Set and lighting by Kevin Rigdon. The production then transferred to the Minetta Lane Theatre, where it opened on September 6, 1984.

CHARACTERS

A number of "hoods" (A general term that could cover almost everyone in the play, but defines more specifically the petty thieves, bargainers, hagglers, pimps. They will sell anything including themselves to any man or woman with the money, although they could not be described as homosexuals. Their activities in this area are few and not often mentioned.):

Bob
Xavier
Tig, a male prostitute (hustler)
Martin, a heroin addict
Rake, a hustler
Dopey, a hustler-addict
Ernesto, a hustler—Colombian

Some are junkies as well, as noted, some are hustlers; definitions overlap. Dopey is a heroin addict as well as a sometimes-not-too-good hustler. What they are now is not what they will be a month from now. A number of the men have no special classification; they might have part-time jobs at times; they might do a number of things, but are not involved in any specific activity:

Tim
Carlo, a Colombian
John, the waiter-grill man

A number of the girls are lesbians; some have boys' nicknames; they might be prostitutes as well:
Terry
Rust
Judy

Other characters include:
Fick, a heroin addict who sometimes provides a background to the rest of the action
Babe, a heroin addict who sits stony silent at the counter through the first half of the play (When the set is moved, she walks beside it.)
Kay, the waitress
Franny, an almost transvestite boy—very beautiful, very feminine
David, much like Franny, not so "lovely"
Bonnie, a prostitute
Ann, a prostitute
Stranger, about thirty-five
Frank, about fifty-five
Al, a bum, about fifty

The production should concentrate on the movement of the whole, slowly focusing on Joe and Darlene:

Joe, a New Yorker, typical middle-class metropolitan background. He is twenty-four, good-looking, of average height and build. He has dark hair. He has a guarded reaction to everything and everyone. He speaks clearly.
Darlene, an attractive girl, twenty to twenty-three; recently arrived from Chicago; she speaks with a candid, Midwestern voice that sets her apart from the sound of the rest of the play. She is honest, romantic to a fault, and not at all bright. The actress playing Darlene should be aware that she is supposed to be stupid, and not the sweet, girl-next-door, common-sense-saves-the-day type of ingenue.
Four black entertainers
Four children

Most of the characters are about twenty-three to thirty years old.
The play covers a week or two just before Halloween. The pace of the play, except in a few scenes, should be breakneck fast. There is one intermission.

SCENE

An all-night coffee shop and the street corner outside. Upper Broadway, New York City.

The café is represented, or suggested, in the center of a wide, high stage. There are a counter and stools (one unit) and across a wide aisle, a row of booths (one unit). They should be constructed so the actors can raise and move them easily. There is also some indication of an area behind the counter; and a skeletal indication of a front door and large front window.

Actors wander onto the set from both sides and back; they gather in the café and outside, where the street corner would be (downstage left). There is a generally congested feeling inside the café—when it is crowded there are always a few people standing in the aisle. The stage should look open; a general feeling of looseness should be conveyed in the design of the set and the random wandering of people. The confining factor is their number.

Much of the play consists of several simultaneous conversations in various groups with dialogue either overlapping or interlocking. These sections should flow as a whole, without specific focus; they rise and subside and scenes develop from them.

Everything seems to move in a circle. Within the general large pattern the people who spend their nights at the café have separate goals and separate characters but together they constitute a whole, revolving around some common center. They are the riffraff, the bums, the petty thieves, the scum, the lost, the desperate, the dispossessed, the cool; depending on one's attitude there are a hundred names that could describe them. They live within as rigid a frame, with its own definitions, as any other stratum. Their language, their actions, their reading of morality is individual but strict.

BALM IN GILEAD

ACT ONE

A noise from a crowd begins and reaches a peak as the curtain rises. From the wings come four black entertainers who sing a rock'n'roll song with much clapping, dancing, etc. They are accompanied by a typical clangy, catchy instrumentation. From far out on the apron they sing to the audience—very animated. As the song fades out, and they begin to move (still singing) back off the stage, the noise from the group rises again.

FICK *(Outside the café, to one of the four singers as the song ends. Fick will talk to anything that moves.)* Hey, fellow, buddy; you got a cigarette? Baby? Hey, fellow—could you—hey friend?
(They are moving off.)

FICK Screw it. *(To someone else.)* Hey buddy? *(He wanders to the street corner group of Dopey, Ernesto, Joe, and Rake.)*

BOB *(As one of the singers runs by him he reaches out and grabs his behind. The crowd in the café notices this and laughs. Bob whirls around to them.)* I never seen a singer yet that was goosey!
(Crowd laughs.)

ERNESTO Yeah, you watch your mouth! *(He laughs.)*

TIG *(From the café.)* You just watch that, Terry-boy.

JUDY All right! Come on. If we're going to get goin' in here, get goin', get that table out of the way, come on; line them up a little.
(A few people straighten the booths into rows.)

TIG *(Overlapping.)* What are you, some kind of housewife, Judy?

JUDY *(To David.)* You're the housewife, aren't you sweetheart?

DAVID You're the fishwife, Judy. Fishwife, Fish. Pheew!

FICK *(On the corner, to Joe.)* Hey, Joe; Joe.

JOE I'm going in.

DAVID *(To Judy.)* A better housewife I'd make, sweetheart, than you ever will.

BONNY *(To Franny and David.)* You ought to be chased out of the neighborhood. You clog up the air with a lot of fairy dust. Fairy dust.

FRANNY *(Overlapping.)* Who you calling a name, you truck driver?

FICK *(To Joe, overlapping.)* Me too, in a minute; you in with Chuckles like they say? I heard you're going to be tying in with him. If I wasn't, hey, such a junk, you think he'd take me?

BONNY Who you queers think you are?

DAVID Who you callin' queer, George!

BOB Shut up, over there!

JOE *(To Fick.)* He might, you work on it, okay, Fick?

DOPEY Get lost, Fick.

FICK *(To Joe.)* You know why I will? You know why I'll work on that? Because, hey, one thing Chuckles will give you is a good protection, you know? They hear you're tied in with Chuckles they'll leave you alone, baby.

TERRY *(Over Fick's speech; she is very drunk!)* All you queens.

JOE *(Cutting into Fick's speech.)* Okay, Fick, that's enough.

TIG *(At the counter to pay—someone has bumped him.)* Come on, God.

FRANNY *(To Terry.)* Why don't you shut up before I beat you over your head with your dildo?

TERRY You trying to say something?

FICK *(To Joe.)* I didn't mean anything by it.

JOE You just talk too much, baby, you know it?

FICK *(Joking.)* You wouldn't get Chuckles after me, would you? Look at me, man, I'm, hell, I'm weak as a kitten.

FRANNY *(Over, to Terry.)* Ah, your mother's a whore—

TERRY You trying to say something?

TIG *(To Frank, counting his change.)* What the hell are you talking about—

FRANK Why don't you stop coming in here, you don't—

TIG What the hell, you're trying to screw—

FRANK *(Cutting in.)* Get on out now.

TIG You trying to cheat me outta four bucks, baby, you can't pull—

FRANK I never cheat you outta nothing.

TERRY *(Over, to David and Franny who are watching Tig and Frank.)* You queers just sit down, take it easy.

TIG I gave you a five, a five, you son of—

FRANK You get on out of here.

TIG You want to step outside? You want to step out from behind that counter, baby? You watch it, Frank.

JOHN *(Cutting in.)* Come on, Tig, give up, go on out.

FRANK Get out of this place.

TIG *(To John.)* Ah, come on, I gave him a five, man, you know what he's trying.

JOHN Come on, go on, Tig.

TIG *(Leaving café for street corner.)* You wait, Frank; you'll get yours, buddy.

FRANK *(After Tig has gone.)* Get on out of here, bum!

TIG *(Yelling back heatedly now.)* All right, now, goddammit I'm out, you just shut your mouth, Frank. You stupid bastard.

FRANK You get on, bum!

TIG Buddy, you're really gonna get it one day, Frank, and I want to be there to watch it. You're gonna get your head split open, dumb bastard.

FICK *(This exchange should begin during the exchange above, cued by Frank's "You get on out of here.")* You wouldn't do something like that, would you, Joe?

JOE Just don't talk so much. What makes you think I even know Chuckles?

FICK You're not going to turn him down are you? Something like that?

JOE We'll see, won't we?

FICK 'Cause, man, I wouldn't do that, I know that. Course you're a strong guy, I'm weak as a kitten. That's too much of a hassle for me. I'd take some of Chuckles' protection, man; he—
(Joe pushes him away slightly and walks to the café.)

FICK Yeah, well, nice seeing you, buddy; you come around any time. Any time, we'll talk again, babe, okay?
(Joe enters the café.)
(Note that in production, each group, and there are several of them, must maintain a kind of life of its own. The group on the street corner, for instance, usually Rake, Dopey, Tig, and Ernesto, loiter with nothing much to say. Improvised, unheard conversations may be used. Characters may wander along the street and back, improvise private jokes, or stand perfectly still, waiting. The same goes for groups in the café, such as Terry, Rust, and Judy. Their lines should come from scenes developed within the situation. Aside from this, it should be mentioned that everyone in the café [with the exception of Babe and Fick] looks up the moment someone enters the café: a kind of reflex "once-over" to evaluate any new opportunity or threat.)

TIM *(At the counter, to Frank.)* Hey, Frank, could I have a hot tea, okay?

FRANK Shut up. All you hoodlums.

TIM What the hell did I say? *(To himself.)* I'm kinna drunk.

FRANK Just shut up that. Hoodlums. This is a decent place; you guys ruin it for everybody!

DAVID Why the hell you yelling at him; he hasn't done nothing.

TERRY Shut up, Frank.

TIM *(Over.)* I didn't say anything.

RUST *(Running into café.)* Hey, they got Jerry Joe in the can!

BOB Jerry the fairy?

DAVID Watch who you're calling names.

RUST He tried to put the make on a cop.

BOB They gonna book him?

JOHN *(To himself.)* Dumb fag.

RUST Whatta you mean? He tried to put the make on a cop. Hell, yes, they'll book him. He had eight bombinos on him! Man, are they hot for that stuff.

(General crowd reaction.)

FRANK Come on, knock it off.

KAY Fry two, John.

FRANK I'm going now, Johnnie; you take over.

RUST I wish I'd seen his face!

FRANK *(As Dopey tries to enter the café.)* Now keep out. Come on, you know you don't get served, come on get out. Junkies and dopes and whores—

FRANNY Who's a whore?

FRANK —What kind of a neighborhood is this? I'll go, Johnnie.

BOB *(To Frank.)* Swinging.

FRANK I'll swing you, right out of here. *(Exits.)*

JOHN Come on, now, keep it down.

TIM May I have a tea, please?

BONNIE *(At a booth, reading a check.)* What the hell is this, fifty cents for one Coke, you think this is the Ritz?

JOHN There's a sign right there, fifty cents minimum at booths; if you don't have it, don't sit there.

BONNIE Screw it, I'm payin' no fifty cents for one Coke.

KAY *(To John.)* Toast with that.

BOB Fifty cents you can get a good high.

BONNIE Gimme a cheese sandwich; hell, if I'm going to spend a fortune. One goddamned Coke.

KAY And a jack.

DAVID *(Cutting in—to Bob.)* Come on up to my room, it won't kill you.

BOB Knock it off. *(To Ann.)* How much you make tonight, Ann?

ANN Huh?

DAVID *(Joking more than anything.)* Come on up with me, it won't kill you.

BOB How much scratch? Jack? Tonight?

ANN None of your damn business. Ask Sammy, you want to know.

TIG *(Has wandered back in; he is standing near Ann.)* You still keepin' that bum? What's he do with all that dough?

ANN He banks it. Or at least he'd better be banking it.

BOB Yeah, he banks it with Cameron or Chuckles.

ANN He don't truck with that junk. He'd better not; I'd crack him over the head.

TIG Feed him bennies you'll keep him limp—he won't go messing around.

KAY *(To Bonnie.)* Whatta you want on the cheese?

ANN I don't need him limp; limp for five minutes he can limp out in the ever-loving street.

BONNIE I don't care—Christ.

BOB Who's name does he bank it in?

TIG Come on, how much you clear last night?

ANN Clear? It's all clear; what do you think I do make out an income-tax report?

DAVID *(To Bob.)* You comin' up?

BONNIE Hey, Kay, make that a cheeseburger.

JOE *(To Ann.)* He keeps at it—I like his drive.

ANN I like sex drive.

KAY Make up your mind!

JOE That's all you ever think about. I'm working now, I tell you.

ANN You think I don't work? I'll show you my bunions.

JOHN *(To Terry.)* Whatta you want for a quarter?
    (Suddenly lights dim into full blink for a second only. Dim on all of café; spot on Joe. Held for a second only, with no reaction anywhere else.)

KAY Onions on that?

BOB *(To Ann.)* I got something you could use.

KAY You want onions on that?

DAVID Well, are you?

BOB No, I'm not coming up! Look, I don't dig boys; fags. Understand? Not unless you got a roll on you.

DAVID Don't knock it till you've tried it.

BOB I happen to like tits. You got tits?
    (General laughter.)

BONNIE And another Coke. Put some ice in it this time, okay?

ANN Come on up, Joe. I won't bite you. Sammy's out.

JOE I told you I'm a working boy, now.

ANN Yeah, I'll bet. You pushing your box? Hustling it down to Forty-second?

JOE Who, me? Not on your life.

KAY *(Calling to John.)* All the way.

BONNIE *(To Kay.)* Grilled onions, why not.

JOHN *(To David who is leaving.)* You pay?

ANN You are; I'll bet.

DAVID Yes, I paid; I paid half an hour ago.

BOB You get tits, you come back and let me know.

DAVID You go to hell. Who needs you?
  (David leaves café as Martin enters, bumping into him.)

DAVID Watch out, for Christ's sake. *(Exits.)*
  (Martin spots Joe from across the café.)

ANN Come on up, Joe.

MARTIN Joe, hey!

ANN Hey, John; give me another coffee. You're getting worse than Frank.

JOHN Watch your language.

ANN What'd I say?

MARTIN Hey, Joe, you got any?

JOHN You said Frank.
  (Ann laughs.)

JOE Any what?

MARTIN You know. Come on.

TIG *(Ordering.)* Plain Pepsi.

JOE What you want with me? I got nothing you want.

ANN *(To Joe.)* You got something I want.

TIG No ice.

MARTIN Joe, no kiddin', I gotta. Man, you don't know! Don't play games with me, baby.

JOE I'm not playing games, Martin.
  (The quartette have entered café and are standing in back. They harmonize in an off-key improvisation a rock'n'roll song, with someone using a table for a drum.)

BOB Hey, Tig.

MARTIN Just one, Joe. I gotta, man. You don't know.

TIG *(To Bob.)* Yeah, what's in it for me, huh?

JOHN *(To Ann.)* You wanted coffee. Cream?

TIM I think I'm gonna be sick.

JUDY *(To Tim.)* You okay?

MARTIN Come on, baby.

JOE Go where you usually go.

JUDY You want a tomato juice or something?

TIM God, no.

JOHN Cream, Ann?

TIM Okay.

ANN Black.

JOE Go where you usually go.

TIM No I don't, either.

ANN You got the lousiest service.

MARTIN I go to Jerry Joe.

BOB *(Overhears, turns around, then back.)* Jerry the fairy?

MARTIN Yeah, well, Jerry the fairy's in the can. In the box, man. Come on, Joe. I heard you could.

JOE You go to Jerry Joe? That's a sad turn of events.

TIM I'm all right.

MARTIN Don't play with me, baby. What's the matter with you guys, you think as soon as you get a pinch to push you can play games and play big shot with everyone.

JOE I'm not playing games, Martin. I'm your friend. I don't follow what you're talking about is all. You're not making sense.

MARTIN Come on, Jerry Joe's in the can.
     (Phone rings—John goes to answer.)

JOE Look, Martin. If I was just starting out—I couldn't take on the whole neighborhood, now, could I?

MARTIN Why not, man; corner the market.

JOHN *(On the phone.)* What?

JOE Yeah, and get cornered.

FRANNY *(To Tig.)* Have you seen Lilly?

JOHN *(Holding the phone.)* Anybody here named Carol?

FRANNY If that's my husband, tell him I dropped dead. *(Exits.)*

ANN If that's Sammy, tell him I'm turning a trick.
     (All laugh.)

ANN Under the table. *(Laughs.)*

BONNIE You could do it too.

ANN If anybody could, honey.
     (John hangs up the phone.)

TIM Could I have another tea, John.

JOHN Sure.
     (Tig gets up to leave.)

JOE Why don't you go somewhere else, come on.

MARTIN 'Cause I come to you. What the hell's wrong? Come on, buddy.

TIG *(Yelling to John.)* Hey, what time you get off?

JOHN Seven in the morning.

TIG Whatta you work, seven to seven?

JOHN Yeah. Swingin' hours, huh?

TIG Christ! *(Leaves café for street corner.)*

MARTIN What's wrong, huh? I come to you.

ERNESTO *(Enters the café from the street corner.)* Coffee. Lottsa cream. No, black. Black. And a chocolate cupcake. How much is a cake?

JOHN Twenty-five. Big one's thirty.

ERNESTO Just the coffee's okay. Black. Black.

ANN Black.

JOHN Black.

JOE Look!

(Fick enters over Joe's line and begins his long wandering dialogue.)

JOE Look! Martin, baby.

(Sudden dim again. Spot on Joe and Martin. Everyone holds their positions. Stop-motion. Fick's dialogue and movement continue over the pause as though nothing else were happening.)

JOE Look…You come back about ten o'clock. And I'll see. Okay?

(Spot dims on Joe and Martin and then natural lighting resumes.)

JOHN *(Fakes a blow to Ernesto's side.)* Come on, I'll show you. Take that. Pow!

ERNESTO *(Fake reaction. Sudden violence here, though it is only a kind of horsing around.)* Not in the liver—I'll get you for that one…

TIG *(On the corner. Slaps someone on the back.)* You're a pal.

ERNESTO *(To John.)* You're a pal!

(Bob leaves café for street corner.)

ANN *(Very rapid exchange here. To Ernesto.)* You're a pal.

MARTIN You're a pal, Joe! You're great! *(Hesitantly.)* You're sure? *(Starts to go.)* Sure?

JOE Ten o'clock. I'll see you. Don't go talking to anyone, okay?

MARTIN You know me, I'm your friend.

JOHN *(To Martin.)* Did you pay?

MARTIN You don't know how cheap you make a fellow look. Asking did he pay. You make people look cheap talking like that. You make people feel cheap talking like that. *(Exits.)*

FICK *(This dialogue begins in the background of the previous scene at Joe's first "Look!" Very softly.)* Man, it's getting cold out there, isn't it? Hey, John, fix me up with a coffee, could you? Warm up a little bit, you know what I mean? That's no good, walking around out there dressed like I am in this weather, I mean it isn't cold yet, but it's getting there and I'm not going to be dressed any warmer in another month when it comes. Kid like me. That's no good for you—you know, with alcohol you're not so bad because it's in your blood stream, you know, but with horse like I take you got to watch out 'cause you don't notice the cold and the first thing you know you're sick as a bitch, man, and about all I need is to go into the hospital or something like that and let them start looking me over, you know? That's about like all I need, man. What is it, about October?

About the middle of October, huh? Damn it'll be getting really cold before long. You know what I mean?

BOB Hey, Tig, I got something you'd like I bet. Hey Dopey.

TIG What?

RUST *(To Kay.)* Miss, could I have a soup?

ANN *(To Joe.)* What are you into now?

TERRY *(To Kay.)* Two, okay? What is it?

DOPEY Yeah, what?

BOB I'll bet.

KAY *(To Terry.)* Bean—lima.

JOE What do you mean?

ANN What are you into now?

RUST Christ. Well, okay.

JOE Come on, keep it down.

ANN *(Standing up.)* Well, I gotta go, if you aren't coming up. You just watch yourself, Joey buddy. *(She pays her bill.)*

KAY Two soup, Johnnie.

JOE Dammit, don't worry about me. I know what I'm doing.

FRANNY *(Re-enters the café.)* Has anybody seen Red tonight? *(Ann exits.)*

JOE *(To Franny, making up for being irritated by Ann.)* Not since last night, baby.

FRANNY *(Flat.)* Jerry Joe's in the can. Had about a dozen bombinos on him.

JOE *(To Franny, irritated suddenly.)* Go get laid, why don't you?

DOPEY *(On the corner; to Rake.)* I tell you I kicked it.

FRANNY *(To Joe over.)* Who's tickling your ass? Be like that, I don't need you. You're working for Chuckles now?

JOE Mind your own, sweetheart; you live longer.

RAKE Sure.

JUDY *(To Terry.)* I'll be back. *(She goes to Tim.)*

DOPEY No, I did. Yes, I did.

RAKE Hell you did.

DOPEY I will, you wait.

TIM I'm sick. I knew I was.

KAY *(With soup, to Rust and Terry.)* It's hot.

JUDY You okay?

FRANNY Chuckles can kiss it, honey; my second husband was a pusher. I don't owe him nothing; he's not my type.

JOE *(Getting up.)* Why don't...

TERRY *(From the back of the café, regarding Judy.)* Now she thinks she's some kind of wet nurse.

RUST *(To Terry.)* One's just like the other.

(Bob and Tig enter café from corner. Al enters café from offstage.)

JUDY Hey, Rake. Over here.

(Rake leaves the corner, enters the café, looks around.)

JOHN *(To Rake.)* Come on, come on, Rake. We can't serve you. Run out on checks—go on, back out in the street, Rake. You know that.

RAKE *(To John.)* Screw you. *(Exits to corner.)*

CARLO *(Enters. To Tim.)* Hello.

TIM *(Sick.)* Not now, Carlo.

CARLO Ernesto, ¿cómo está?

AL Give me a coffee, okay? Noisy, ain't it?

KAY Coffee, okay.

TIM *(Gets up, Judy follows him, trying to take him home.)* Damn, I think I'm sick. None of you are worth a good—

ERNESTO Carlo

JUDY Come on you're drunk as a judge. Come on, let's get you home or somewhere, okay?

ERNESTO *(To Carlo.)* ¿Qué pasa, Chico?

TIM Carlo can hardly speak English even. *(To Judy.)* Take your hands. Not worth a damn. *(Staggers forward.)* Take your—dike, you go with girls. Mess around with your own kind.

TERRY *(Over.)* I don't care where she sleeps or who she sleeps with!

JUDY Come on.

TIM Take your hands off me, you go with girls. You're a whatsit. *(Aside to the audience.)* She's a whatsit, without a gizmo.

JUDY Come on, you're drunk.

TIM At least I'm drunk on drunk, not on junk like everyone...

JUDY Come on, Tim, you're drunk. You're sick, Timmy.

TIM I'm sick?

JUDY Come on, go on home, Tim.

TIM *(To audience.)* Listen! *(Aside, to himself.)* Oh, damn; I'll bet I've been drinking again. *(To audience.)* Now you listen! Dammit, this is important! *(Judy turns him around and they move toward the door.)*

TIM *(Over his shoulder to the audience.)* Now you watch this. Here.

FICK Terry, you got a cigarette, huh?

AL *(To Tig.)* She's gonna take him!

TERRY *(To Fick.)* Come on, get lost.

KAY *(To Judy.)* What'd you have?

JUDY I'll be back!

(Judy and Tim exit as Darlene enters.)

TERRY She can sleep in the damn hall for all I care!

RUST *(To Terry.)* I don't get it.

AL It happens every time. Did you see that?

BOB *(Looks up as Darlene enters the café.)* Well, dig that.
    (Darlene sits at counter, John comes to wait on her.)

AL You get hurt, see? Every time. And then finally you learn not to pay any attention to anything.

TIG Yeah, I know. Well, don't let it bother you.

BOB *(To Darlene.)* Can I buy you a cup coffee? Can I just buy you maybe? Look, I got thirty cents somewhere.

AL And then you just don't let anything bother you at all.

DARLENE *(To John.)* Coffee, please.

AL And you still get hurt.

JOHN *(To Darlene.)* Right.

KAY *(Yelling to John from back.)* Draw one!

BOB You belong here? You new?

KAY *(Yelling to John.)* Two!

TIG *(Interested in Darlene now.)* She's not the talkative type.

DARLENE *(Quietly slips off the stool. To John.)* Never mind.
    (She turns to go but there is a crowd at the door. Bob stands in front of her.)

TIG Well, don't run off, sweetheart.

FICK *(From the back.)* It's cold—it gets cold.

DARLENE Come on.

BOB I'm sorry if I'm in your way, but I can't move. Look.

DARLENE Come on, I'm leaving.

TERRY She can sleep in the alley for all I care!

TIG Oh, am I in your way?

DARLENE Oh, screw it. Go away. *(Turns to the counter and sits again.)*

JOHN *(To Darlene.)* You order coffee?

TIG You're new. You know anyone around here?

BOB Well, be a little sociable anyway.
    (Franny in exiting bumps against Bob, Bob against Darlene.)

BOB Hey, I'm sorry. *(Turns around, to Franny.)* Watch where you're going!

FRANNY Oh, suck it; if you were sober maybe you could stand up. *(Exits.)*

TIG What are you, mad at the world?

RUST And she better stay gone.

BOB *(To Tig.)* Screw it, forget her. Let's go.
    (Dopey enters café, takes a seat.)

JOHN Come on, Dopey, you're going to fall asleep.

TIG Don't bother to speak. *(Goes to the back of café.)*

BOB Screw it.

DOPEY What do you mean, I'm awake. Look! I want a cup of coffee.

JOHN I know, but I'll give it to you and you'll be asleep on the damn table. You do it every time, Dopey.

(John turns to get him coffee.)

KAY *(To Bob who has stopped in the doorway.)* Come on, you're holdin' the door open!

TERRY *(Much louder.)* I don't give a good goddamn if she sleeps with Margaret Truman!

(Bob exits.)

DOPEY *(To prove he's awake.)* Kay? Could you hand me the cream, please?

(At the back of the café Terry falls against a booth. Much commotion. She has spilled coffee on Bonnie. They sit her down again.)

RUST, BONNIE, TERRY *(Variously.)* Come on.

God, look at that all over me!

Where the hell.

For Christ's sake, where the hell are you going?

Watch it, fellow.

Sit down, take it easy.

All over me. Goddamn.

Do you have a rag?

Miss? Now just take it easy.

Why don't you sober up?

(Lights dim for only a second, during the above exchange, with a spot on Darlene.)

AL *(To John.)* They every one of them steal. They all steal, you know?

TIG *(To Ernesto.)* Spices and things, you know.

(Ann re-enters.)

JOHN Yeah. Well.

(Darlene and Joe exchange several glances.)

AL Every girl you see; they all steal. You take them up to your room and they'll steal something every time. You fall asleep and they'll sneak out and steal something.

TERRY *(Over, from the back.)* I'm sorry. I'm sorry. I am.

(Dopey is falling asleep on the table.)

AL And then they tell you they left the door open.

JOHN I know. No, I don't, but I know.

AL They all steal.

(Momentary lull. The quartette begins a soft blues from the back.)

JOHN When it gets quiet in here you almost think something's gonna happen.

KAY Quiet all of a sudden, ain't it?

ANN *(To John.)* You want somebody should scream or something?

JOHN Oh, go back out on the street!

ANN It's dirty out there. I think I'm going to write to the Department of Sanitation. I made sixty tonight.

JOHN Sixty scores or sixty bills?

ANN Four scores—ha!—and thirty-eight cents. I always end up with odd change; never can figure out where the hell it came from.

JOHN You're so rich, so buy me a drink, teacher.

ANN Sammy would slug me, I spend his money on you.

TERRY She can just kiss it.

JOHN Why do you keep him anyway?

ANN God, you'd better go back to school.

RUST Miss, could we have another coffee? Two more.

(Darlene moves her cup now to the seat by Joe. Takes the seat next to him.)

DARLENE Do you mind?

JOE How should I mind?

DARLENE Well, look, if you're thinking or waiting for someone…

JOE No, I'm not waiting for someone.

DARLENE I saw you looking at the clock.

JOE I'm waiting for ten o'clock. *(He drinks.)*

(Darlene takes a cigarette out, he lights hers and his own.)

DARLENE Thanks.

TIG *(To Ernesto.)* You know in Egypt they had salves and things that could cure anything.

DARLENE That's better than those other two creeps were acting. Did you see them?

JOE They're just high. They're OK usually.

TIG Cancer even! It says so.

ERNESTO Show me where, you can't.

TIG It does.

DARLENE Why are you waiting for ten o'clock?

TIG Hey, John; you ever read the Bible?

JOE I'm meeting someone.

JOHN What?

TIG The Bible, stupid.

JOE Like a business deal. A transaction.

JOHN Sure. When I was about twelve.

ERNESTO Yeah?

JOHN I didn't understand it.

TIG Hell, you wouldn't anyway. You know they had embalming fluid back then?

ANN What'd they do, drink it?

ERNESTO Show me where.

TIG Go away.

DARLENE What were they high on?

JOE Huh? How should I know?

(Ernesto pays check and exits to corner.)

DARLENE On dope, or just drinking?

JOE You don't get high on ginger. Bombinos, speed; you don't scream it out—you know, you don't yell it out like that.

DARLENE Do you like that?

JOE Are you kidding?

DARLENE Me either—eye-ther.

JOE Not on your life. Once is enough.

DARLENE Oh. What was it like?

JOE Are you kidding? Like getting sick as a bitch. Depends on what you're taking though. New, are you?

DARLENE Well, have you seen me before?

JOE No.

DARLENE Are you sure?

JOE Yeah.

DARLENE How do you know?

JOE I'd know.

DARLENE *(Complimented.)* Thanks.

JOE I remember faces. You see me standing around, you'd think I was just as stupid as the next guy, but I look—and I watch people, you know? And I study them when they don't know. You learn a lot. Where you from?

DARLENE I'm from Chicago.

TIG *(Comes from the booth to John at the cash register.)* Could I have change for cigarettes?

DARLENE *(Pausing.)* My sister used to come around here, though. She's living off somewhere right now.

JOE Who's your sister?

DARLENE Oh, you wouldn't know her. It must have been four years ago. She used to write me.

TIG *(Hits the machine.)* This damn thing!

DARLENE Sometimes.

JOE What'd she do?

DARLENE Oh, I don't know. *(Affected.)* We used to exchange letters. She'd write and I'd think, God—New York! *(Pause.)* She was...like her. *(Nods to Ann.)* Of course, she was very pretty, you know.

JOE Ann? A hooker. She sold it?

DARLENE Well, you needn't be high and mighty about it.

JOE Who is?

DARLENE She used to make—sometimes a hundred dollars a night...twice that sometimes.

JOE So does Ann, but she loves it. *(Yelling out.)* Don't you Ann?

ANN Don't I what?

JOE Just say yes.

ANN No. Hell, no; it's a lie if he's saying it. *(Turns away.)*

JOE She goes for free as much as she charges.

DARLENE She didn't come here for that, of course. She came here to do something else. I forget what; you know. But you look and you don't get anything and you—resort, you know? To something else.

RUST *(To Terry.)* I wouldn't worry about it.

JOE Naw, Ann didn't either. Ann's a schoolteacher. Was going to be; came here to do something like that. When she got here they tell her she can work part-time or something.

TERRY It doesn't affect me.

JOE She told 'em to kiss it. She got a raw deal.

DARLENE Yeah. You know what I'd make as a waitress? Maybe sixty dollars a week. Less maybe. Tips included.

JOE You been here long?

DARLENE A month.

JOE Month? You must have saved up.

DARLENE Are you kidding? I came here with about seven dollars.

JOE You get a room around here yet?

DARLENE I'm across the street, in the Towers. And probably I'll get...

JOE And one upstairs? Everybody does.

DARLENE My sister had a room; this same place. I didn't ask you what your ten-o'clock business deal was.

JOE Yeah, you did.

DARLENE Well, I didn't care. *(Pause.)* It's a filthy place upstairs. Have you see it up there? I looked around this afternoon already. I've never seen cockroaches like that. I mean they should get a bravery medal or something. They play games on the floor right in front of you. They don't even run from you.

(Dopey has awakened. He looks at his coffee and gets up to leave.)

KAY *(To Dopey.)* Hey, you pay?

DOPEY I don't have anything.

KAY Coffee.

DOPEY I didn't even touch it. I gotta get outside.

(He leaves café for corner.)

JOE You know I might be able to help you get a room. Save you some dough, maybe. After the first week or two they'll get on to you and kick you out.

They got fellas that hang around to spot girls who take people up. You'll have to get one of the boys around to rent a room in his name and then he'll rent it to you. See? They don't really care, just so long as they look legal. Most of the guys, though, would make you pay through the nose.

DARLENE Why? I mean why should I get a room from someone else?

(Judy enters and goes to cash register.)

JOE It's just the way you have to do it. All these guys in here—a lot of them— they rent a room out for about eight bucks a night. That's not much when you're making a hundred.

KAY *(To Judy.)* You owe for a burger and a Coke.

JUDY I'll get it.

DARLENE It sounds like a lot to me. Eight dollars a day? A room's only twelve a week. No girl's gonna do that.

JOE They got nothing better to do with their money. Most of the girls keep a fellow anyway. Give most of their money to some guy. Then he treats them like shit. Don't ask me. Over half of them. So they can be seen with someone steady, you know.

JUDY *(Regarding Rust and Terry in the back booth.)* Well, isn't that cozy?

DARLENE I wouldn't believe it.

(Joe shrugs.)

DARLENE I mean I believe it, but how can they ever get any money saved up or anything? If they're giving it away? It's pretty sick, isn't it? Everybody living off everybody like that?

JOE You won't get away from that, I don't care where you go. You'll either make a pile of money or go broke. But like I said, most guys would charge eight bucks. I could probably get you a room for maybe only four or five.

DARLENE I don't think so.

JUDY *(To Kay.)* How much do I owe you?

JOE You'll either go broke or make a pile.

KAY Ninety-five and that guy's two teas.

DARLENE I made two hundred dollars one night. That's what I've been living off of. One guy; man, one night.

JUDY Just me; he can come back and pay.

JOE Don't expect it every time.

(Rust comes up to the counter.)

DARLENE And I didn't have to do anything.

RUST Give me a glass of water, Kay.

JOE Much.

KAY Just hold it a minute!

DARLENE Nothing. He felt sorry for me or something. He was a customer—in this café? And the boss fired me. I was right out on the floor and got fired on the spot. And this guy came over to me on the floor and said, let's go have a steak or something to eat, you don't want to work here anyway. Let's go have a steak. He was my first customer at the café. I walked right off the floor and we went to his room and he gave me two hundred dollars.

RUST Could I have a glass of water?

JOE What, did you roll him?

JUDY *(To Rust.)* First things first, honey!

DARLENE No! I told you. He gave it to me. He felt sorry for me or something.
(Dopey has been standing on the corner, talking to Rake. He turns to the audience, walks a little away from the others. The action continues in the café behind him during this speech.)

DOPEY What he's saying—about renting rooms and all—see—well, there's no reason for it but when a girl—or around here anyway most of the girls have a guy that—kinna looks after them. After all, it's a rough neighborhood; but that's not the only way he looks after them, if you follow my meaning. And the girl sorta keeps him. The guys that are lucky. He lives up in the room—sleeps in the day and the girl uses the room at night. Maybe you think they're being exploited—the girls, I mean, because they don't get ahead. Every dime goes to the john—that's the fellow. And he eventually pulls out—runs off with it—after he's stashed it in a savings account somewhere. But these girls aren't getting so much exploited because they need these guys. No one's forcing them. One leaves, then right after they get over it they're out looking for someone else. Only someone *better.* You know? Like Ann is probably half expecting her john—this guy's name's Sam, or Sammy: she's half expecting him to leave. He's been around seven or eight months; that's about par for Ann. *(Pause.)* Well, it's because they want someone around and because after all balling with old men all the time can get to be a drag—of course not all of their scores are old men. They get just as many good-looking guys; young fellows; high school kids and like that, they pay. Well, maybe you don't like to hear that but they do. So it's not that they get sick of the old men all the time. But these guys that they ball, they aren't—around. You know? They aren't *around.* They want probably to know someone probably. See they're—well. And they don't get new things! I mean these girls don't go out and get themselves dresses and jewelry and things. I mean they get things, but not for themselves, see; for the guy who's with them. New clothes and rings and stuff—all kinds of crap and well because it's no kind of a lark crawling in and out of bed all night and in the morning they maybe want someone who won't leave, see. Won't get up and take off. *(Very quick.)* And then they buy these guys things so the guys around can see how they keep their johns in luxury, you know. *(Pause.)* It's natural as anything. They want someone familiar. You know—to know somebody's touch or their manner or like the texture of his skin. Even if the guy's still asleep in the morning. You can picture it. And this usually keeps them from getting much else. That's what he's trying to tell her only she'll know after a while anyway because it's just a natural thing. So she'll find it out anyway but not till she's there herself.

JUDY *(To Kay.)* Don't forget the little bitch's glass of water.

RUST *(To Judy.)* Who're you talking to?

JUDY She's gotta wash out a bad taste in her mouth.

RUST You talking to me, you talk to me.

JUDY You just take it for what it's worth.

RUST You got something to say, say it.

FICK You got a light, Ann?

JUDY Go on back to the peach in the corner.

JOHN *(To Rust.)* Sit back down. I'll bring it to you.

RUST *(Returning to her seat.)* Tell her to shut her filthy mouth.

JUDY You want to know what a filthy mouth is?

JOHN Come on...

JUDY I'll rub your face in the sewer you try to...

JOHN Come on, sit down or get out now.

JUDY *(Sitting immediately.)* Give me coffee!

(Rust sits down at the booth. Dopey walks away from the audience and then comes back, a new thought. A bit irritated.)

DOPEY You know, though, what—I was thinking what she said; before that, about the cockroaches and all upstairs and she's right, it's a crawling bughouse up there; what really gripes me, she mentioned all the roaches playing like games on the floor up there. A roach's *attitude* just gripes the hell out of me. But what burns me, I've been reading up, not recently, but I saw it somewhere where not only was the roach—that same, exact, goddamn roach that we know—not only were they around about two million years before man, you know, before we came along: Anthropologists or whatever, geologists over in Egypt or somewhere, looking for the first city, they dug down through a city, and straight on down through another, you know, they're piled up like a sandwich or in layers like a seven-layer cake. And they cut down, down through one century to the one before it and the one before that, and every one they found more goddamned cockroaches than anything, and they got before man ever existed and like in the basement of the whole works, there those damn bugs still were, so they've been around, like I said for about a million years before we came along. But not only that! They've made tests, and they found out that a roach can stand—if there was going to be a big atom explosion, they can stand something like *fourteen times* as much radio-whatever-it-is, you-know-activity as we can. So after every man, woman, and child is wiped out and gone, like you imagine, those same goddamn cockroaches will be still crawling around happy as you please over the ruins of everything. Now the picture of that really gripes my ass.

(He wanders into the café.)

JOE *(Reaches into his pocket.)* Did you ever see one of these?

DARLENE What? What is it, an hourglass?

JOE Yeah, that lasts about three hours. That's a bombino. That's what Bob had. You asked how he got high.

DARLENE I don't want it!

JOE I'm not about to give it to you. It's worth money.

DOPEY Coffee.

DARLENE How's it work?

JOHN Aw, come on, Dopey. You'll just go asleep.

JOE It works wonders. See?

DOPEY Whatta you mean?

(John ignores him this time.)

JOE That's one jolt in each side. And you break it open, see, and take a tube, a needle and a—

DARLENE A needle? Oh, God. I thought that's what—

(Joe makes a motion injecting it into his arm.)

DARLENE That's terrible! That just makes my knees weak.

JOE I better not let anyone see me doing that; they'll think I'm really shootin' up.

(Darlene laughs.)

JOE That's the easy way. I just got one of these. Mostly it's heroin, and that and some of the others you heat up in a spoon with a match.

DARLENE I don't want to hear it.

JOE It's a lotta trouble.

DARLENE And they pay for it?

JOE Sure. They love it. You gotta sorta coax them along; play with them. They have to get it and they expect it to be tough to get.

BONNIE *(At counter.)* That's highway robbery.

DARLENE They have to have it. That sounds awful.

JOHN *(To Bonnie.)* Everybody makes a living.

JOE That's the idea. It doesn't happen overnight or anything.

BONNIE I'm not complaining.

(Xavier enters.)

DARLENE How much does it cost you?

JUDY *(To Bonnie.)* You get sick of it back there?

JOE Usually about four. I can make maybe thirty bucks on a carton. Sometimes more. The goofballs are worth about twice as much profit. But they're the devil. They're wild. You never know what the hell they're going to do to someone.

JUDY What are they saying?

XAVIER Hey, Joe!

BONNIE I'm not in it; whatever you're thinking.

JOE Hi, there, buddy.

JUDY Well then, just stay out of it then.

XAVIER You goin' down to Forty-second later?

JOE Naw, not tonight. I thought I'd turn in.

XAVIER Nothing's doing down there anyway.

JOE Stick around here. Where you been the last two days, man?

XAVIER Around. Sleeping around.

JOE You still talking about going off? Your old man going to send you some bread?

XAVIER I don't know. I don't think so, though. I think maybe I'd like to go to Paris, it's better there. People come back from there they say it's wonderful. Beautiful girls.

JOE So what's wrong with the girls here?

XAVIER *(Laughing.)* Maybe they all know me.

JOE Maybe. Your friends think Paris is great, huh?

XAVIER If I go and it's wonderful as that, I'd stay.

(Babe coughs. Looks up dreamily and around. Sinks back down. Xavier looks around to her and back.)

XAVIER Maybe girls here aren't so beautiful. *(Laughs.)*

JOE Oh, don't look at Babe. Nobody's like her, man.

DARLENE What's wrong with her?

XAVIER She's very bad off.

DARLENE I've been looking at her.

JOE You're telling me she's bad off.

XAVIER She's—you know—that's no good. She can't go a few hours, I bet. She has to have another. She's on her way right out of it. When they get that bad. On her way off.

DARLENE She's on her way off that stool, anyway.

XAVIER No, no. A junkie never falls off a stool. They lean out and lean out and they get just to the point and they're way out and their seat is way over there and they start slipping off the stool, and they start shifting back, moving back the other way. A drunk will go right off—pow—like that— one jerk and he's on the floor. But a junkie never falls off. You see if I'm wrong.

DARLENE I didn't know that.

XAVIER You see if I'm wrong. Look, I'll see you.

JOE No, come on; stick around.

XAVIER I'll be back in a few minutes. *(Exits.)*

JOE He runs around all the time. He says he'll see you soon and you don't meet him for a month. He's a nice guy. Xavier. *(He gives it a Spanish pronunciation.)*

DARLENE What?

JOE They call him Xavier. He's Colombian. His old man owns a bunch of hardware stores down there. He's up here though—and the old man won't give him a cent.

DARLENE I think he'd be better off back there, then. Is he working?

JOE Huh? I don't know what he does. He's going to Paris or somewhere next summer.

DARLENE Huh. What was his name?

JOE *(In English.)* Xavier.

DARLENE No, the other one.

JOE *Xavier.* The same thing in Spanish. Like Joe and José, you know.

DARLENE Yeah. Oh.

JOE *(Holding the bombino out in his closed hand.)* You want this?

DARLENE Me? No, no. I don't want that.

JOE Not to take, I thought maybe you'd want it for a gift to remember me.

DARLENE I don't think so. Thanks. What if I got caught with it or something. Then where would I be?

JOE It wouldn't be no worse than getting caught taking some guy up to your room. Same thing. Trouble either way you look.

ERNESTO *(From the corner.)* Hey, Joe. Have you seen Bob?

    (Ernesto and Rake enter the café.)

RAKE Yeah, you seen him?

JOE *(Gets up.)* Yeah, he went up to around Eightieth Street.

RAKE What time?

JOE *(Turns.)* What time, Darlene? The fellow in the orange jacket?

DARLENE Oh, just a few minutes ago.

ANN I better be going back out into the dirty street.

JOHN Yeah, make a little dough.

DARLENE About fifteen minutes or so ago, I'd imagine.

ANN Dough's ass; I'm tired.

BONNIE Back trouble, honey? I know what you mean. You seen King?

ANN You seen Sam?

JOHN *(To Ernesto and Rake.)* You gonna order?

BONNIE Not tonight I haven't.

ANN Neither have I, the bastard.

ERNESTO Ain't I a steady paying customer?

JOHN Are you?

ERNESTO I am when I got the bread. You find me a john, I'll buy something. Okay? *(To Joe.)* A few minutes ago? I'll see you around. How late you gonna be here?

JOE Ten, eleven. I'm leaving early.

JOHN Come on, Rake; you guys. You're blocking the door.

ERNESTO I'll see you around. *(To Darlene.)* So long.

RAKE See you.

(They drift back to the corner. Dopey gets up, tired of waiting for service and wanders off.)

DOPEY Shit. Try to get served here.

DARLENE You saw my name on the purse.

JOE Yeah.

DARLENE You said it like we'd been introduced and known each other for years.

JUDY *(At far end of the counter, as Rust leaves the booth again.)* You really cozy back there, are you?

RUST What?

JOE A queer named Jerry Joe got pinched last night. He used to pick up some scores around here. You know? And they caught him with a dozen bombinos on him.

JUDY You cozy back there?

RUST Whatta you mean?

JUDY Whatta you mean, whatta I mean? I got eyes.

DARLENE The pills?

RUST Well, whatta you see?

JUDY I got eyes, goddamnit. I can see.

JOE The other. The pills would have been worse.

RUST Why don't you go back there, you're so worried.

DARLENE You better watch yourself then.

JUDY Go back there! I've had about enough of you.

JOE They didn't pick him up for that. That's what I was saying. You're telling me I'm in a dangerous business.

RUST Nothing's happening you can't see.

JOE They picked him up because the stupid fairy tried to pick up a cop. That could happen just as easy to you, you don't play it careful.

JUDY You sawed-off little bitch, you moving in? You moving into our pad?

DARLENE I guess you take your chances.

RUST It'd serve you right if I did.

JUDY I've had about enough of you.

RUST Go back to your sick friend.

JOE It turned out good for me. One of his guys—Martin—came to me already. I'll probably get a few more. He had his finger in everything, Jerry Joe.

JUDY Get your hot little ass out of here, now.

JOE Push a little; sell a little. Man, I bet he looked funny when that cop flashed his badge. Serves him right for being so stupid.

TERRY *(Standing up, very drunk.)* Just can it now, Judy. Nothing's happening.

FICK *(To John.)* Could I have a coffee? I think. And a bowl of soup? It's getting cold out, huh?

RUST I'm gonna get this bitch out of my hair.

JOHN *(To Rust and Judy.)* Watch it now.
      (Phone rings. John goes to it, answers it.)

RUST *(Flares up now.)* You're not gonna get nothing.

JUDY I'm gonna teach you to break everyone up.

RUST You're gonna get your ass kicked is what you're gonna get!

JUDY You little bitch, you can just get the—
      (She slaps Rust, Rust returns the slap. They scrap a second, break away, Rust has a fork from one of the tables.)

RUST Okay, you jealous cunt, now you mind your own business.

JUDY *(Aware of the spectacle, past anger, hurt now.)* Why don't you mind...you stay away from Terry.

RUST Go slapping people around. I'm not interested in her!

JUDY You stay away, I saw you!

RUST You been asking for it all night!

JUDY *We been together eleven months; you stay away!*

RUST I'm not bothering her.

JUDY Go on...

RUST *(Throws the fork down.)* I'm leaving.

JOHN *(Hangs up phone.)* You people sit down or get out.

RUST I'm leaving, goddammit.

JOHN *(To all three.)* Come on, clear out. We can't have fights in here.

RUST Just mind your own business!

TERRY *(To John.)* Nothing's happening.

RUST *(Storming off.)* She can pay.

TERRY *(Calling to Rust.)* Get your coat.

RUST I don't want it! *(Out to street corner.)*

JOHN Now keep it down. That's all out of you two or outside.

TERRY Bring another coffee over.

JUDY *(Whimpering.)* I can't help it.

(They talk quietly in the booth.)

DARLENE What's wrong with them?

JOE Huh? What?

DARLENE Nothing.

(Phone rings. John answers it.)

JOE *(Trying to regain Darlene's attention.)* In a month or so I'll be making—well, really good money. Some guys like me, they got fellas working for them.

DARLENE Sure. You know how to handle yourself. That's good. You remind me of this guy I knew in Chicago. Cotton. He knew how to handle himself.

RAKE *(On the corner. To Rust.)* Aren't you cold?

RUST No.

RAKE You'll catch cold.

JOHN *(At the phone.)* I'll see. I don't know.

RAKE You're gonna catch pneumonia.

RUST Just mind your own business, okay?

JOE Yeah, well, you learn quick enough. I'll be making really good money. You have to be careful, of course.

DARLENE Well, who doesn't?

JOE You'll be all right.

RAKE *(Rust has said something to him quietly.)* I can't go in there either.

JOHN *(Comes to the side of Joe.)* Telephone. Sounds like one of Chuckles' fellows. Perry, I think.

JOE Yeah? Tell him I'll be back in an hour or so.

JOHN Okay. Don't take calls here—I told you before.

JOE I didn't ask him to call me here. I'm not going to talk to him here. You know that.

JOHN Okay.

JOE *(To John.)* Okay. *(To Darlene.)* Besides, the fellow I'm tying in with— Chuckles. That was a friend of his. You don't cross him. You don't cross Chuckles.

KAY Toast me a muffin.

JOHN Toasted muffin.

JOE You don't say yes today and say no tomorrow.

DARLENE Yeah. I gotta go back over to the hotel.

(She gets up.)

JOE I thought you were working.

DARLENE Working?

JOE You know.

DARLENE I thought I'd get to bed and kinna look around the neighborhood tomorrow and see if there's anything open.

JOE Job?

(He gets up.)

DARLENE Or something. If anything's open. You have to live.

JOE Yeah.

DARLENE Do you want to walk me across the street? I'd like you to.

JOE What are you, a little old lady or something? Sure I will; protection.
(He pays.)

DARLENE I mean if you're not doing anything.

JOE No, that's okay.

DARLENE I won't let you miss your ten-o'clock appointment.

JOE Screw that. Martin would wait all night. *(Exit.)*
(Dim almost out on café interior. Patrons inside walk to the front of the café and stand in a line across stage, back to the audience, forming a "wall." There is a space about four feet wide at the center of the wall, forming a doorway. Joe and Darlene walk down the wall slowly.)

DARLENE I haven't seen the neighborhood at daytime yet.

JOE Neither has anybody else.

DARLENE I'll bet.

KAY *(From the café, distantly.)* Scramble two with bacon, John.

DARLENE It's getting cold.

JOE Yeah.

DARLENE There was snow last night.

JOE Was there?

DARLENE Not much. It didn't stick. Just a little. It's too early for snow.
(She walks inside the doorway and turns. He is outside.)

JOE Yeah, you'd think so.

DARLENE Look, I don't want you to be late for your meeting, if you're meeting someone.

JOE It isn't important. What do you have in mind?

DARLENE I don't know. Do you want to come up? You can. I'd like for you to. You know. If you want to.

JOE Yeah, I'd like that.
(Rake leaves his place in the wall and comes toward the audience.)

JOE I been thinking about just that for the last hour.

DARLENE Me too, really.
(They go through the "door," out of sight behind the "wall" of people.)

JOHN *(From the café.)* You're sure as hell not going to make any money like that!
(The "wall" moves to close the doorway behind them.)

RAKE *(To the audience.)* You travel around. I mean hustlers travel around, after all they follow the sun, staying where the weather's warm. In New York, north, you know, when it's hot here. And in the winter they begin to drift down toward Miami Beach so it's warm. And out to California. All around. You hear a lot about Miami Beach but you don't hear that it's winter quarters for about half the hustlers in the country. I guess they don't advertise that—but the johns know it. A hustler tries to keep where it's warm. I don't know if it's because of warm weather and all or whether they just try to keep up a good tan, you know? What the hell, it's healthy. But you travel around and you start seeing differences in people. In the way people act from one place to another. Like in New York—the main difference between people in Chicago and New York is in New York everyone carries an umbrella. If it's the least bit cloudy you can depend on it, every goddamn plumber or electrician or construction worker or executive in New York carries an umbrella. It's just the way they think. They don't think about it. But see, Chicago, there it's this symbol or something. See in Chicago you're never going to see a construction worker carrying one of those narrow little rolled-up rapier kind of umbrellas. Or any other kind. It's unmasculine, see. They won't have it. In New York, sure; but in Chicago, not on your life. Fairies and old women, some, not many, carry umbrellas when it's really cloudy. But everyone else stays clear of that sort of thing. *(Pause.)* Consequently they get rained on a lot in Chicago.

(The "wall" disperses. People move off and back to the café, in every direction. There has been a bed set up behind the wall. Joe is in undershorts. He sits on the edge of the bed, then lies back, propped up on his elbow. Darlene has just slipped on a half-slip and bra. She stands over the bed for a moment. Then moves away a bit. The scene should be dimly lit. Rake walks off.)

DARLENE *(A little breathless.)* Oh, Lord. I'm all over sweat—perspiration. So are you. Look at you. Do you want a cigarette? How about that?

(Joe remains uninterested in her throughout this scene; quite remote.)

JOE Sure.

DARLENE Jesus. *(She hands him a package of cigarettes and matches.)* Here you are, baby. *(Walking away.)* Let me get a towel. I feel like I'd gone for a swim. I'm wet and all, but I mean, my legs and arms weigh a ton; I just feel like I'd been swimming for hours. I'll get a towel or something, how's that?

(Joe lights a cigarette.)

DARLENE I thought I'd swipe this towel when I move, when I get an apartment of my own. It's got the name of the hotel across it. I thought that'd be funny; hanging in a regular bathroom. *(She dries her neck and arms on the towel.)* Oh, that's more like it. Here, let me. You're perspiring like a maniac.

JOE Throw it over.

DARLENE Here. *(She rubs his belly.)*

JOE Come on!

DARLENE It's not going to hurt you.
   (She starts to dry his chest and face, Joe pulls back.)
JOE Come on, Darlene. For Chris' sake! *(Pushing her gently away.)* For Chris' sake! *(He takes the towel.)*
DARLENE What? You take it then. Where did you put the cigarettes?
JOE Over here.
DARLENE *(Artificially gay, goes to them.)* Oh, swell. Lord. What time are you supposed to see that guy?
JOE What guy?
DARLENE I don't know. The guy that you're supposed to see. I don't know his name.
JOE Oh, for Chris' sake, I told you, Martin hangs around that corner all night long. If I miss him at ten he's around at eleven. It isn't important. He'll be there. He's a junkie.
DARLENE Looks to me like you all hang around there all night.
JOE Well it's an important place around here.
DARLENE You made it sound so mysterious.
JOE I don't have to answer to him. That's for damn sure. *(He puts his shirt and pants on, bragging.)* Look, you want to know something? You want to know something? I knew what I was doing. I keep a sharp lookout for myself, you don't have to worry about that. I watch people and size them up. And this guy Chuckles you heard me mention?
DARLENE Yeah?
JOE The guy who had someone call me back at the café. Now, this guy is probably the most important pusher—he doesn't push himself, but he supplies—and you don't screw around with him. I got in touch with Chuckles a while back and told him I wanted to get cut in. Make some dough around the neighborhood. Hell, he'd been watching me for weeks. Months! And we made this deal. He gave—not give!—Chuckles never gave anyone the time of day. But he loaned—on credit—you know? He loaned me about a hundred dollars' worth of stuff…
DARLENE What kind of…
JOE Dope. Heroin. I told you…
DARLENE What do you do with it? You sell it to that guy?
JOE On credit. See, I sell it now and make twice or more profit. All I give him is his hundred. But see there's this—it's not this once only. If you're in with this guy like I wanted to be, you're in for a while. And chances are, like almost everyone you'll get picked up. A guy just starting runs all the risks. You can be about so clever. But once I sell that stuff—see, I'm in up to my throat. Hell, I'm in already. You don't butt out on Chuckles. You don't just carry it around.

DARLENE You don't sound very pleased about it.

JOE He loaned it to me for twenty-four hours, you know? And they been up a long time now. Day before yesterday. I'm just not thinking straight on it. You don't cross him, though.

DARLENE I guess not, but if you think it's too dangerous...

JOE The sentence for pushing H is about thirty years! Hell, I'm in with Chuckles already.

DARLENE But if you don't want to be, you could talk with...

JOE *(Getting up.)* Christ!

DARLENE No, really. I've always felt if people just talked about their problems they can always work something out...

JOE Yeah, sure. What time is it?

DARLENE I don't know. Let's see.

JOE You want to call down and ask the desk?

DARLENE No. I have a wrist watch, I'm not that poor.

JOE What time is it?

DARLENE Well, I'm trying to read it, it's small! It's one-thirty.

JOE Christ! Oh, Christ!
(The people who have left the stage begin to drift in in the background, occasionally crossing in front.)

FICK Hey, hey, Tig?

TIG Sure, don't even ask. Any time. Christ. *(Takes a cigarette and gives it to Fick.)*

DARLENE Why, do you have to go somewhere?

FICK *(Badly wetting and destroying the end of the cigarette.)* God, look at me slobber all over it. I'm a mess. Jesus.

JOE Jesus. *(He puts on his jacket.)*

DARLENE Do you have to go somewhere?

JOE Yeah. I'll see you tomorrow or if you come back tonight.

FICK I'm such a damn slob. Look at that. I'll get it though. *(Wanders back into café.)*
(Joe goes into the café. Darlene exits. The bed is removed. Lights up on café; very late at night. Ann is considerably more disheveled. As lights go up the first rock'n'roll song blasts out of the juke box. John immediately reaches under the counter and turns it down.)

TIG Hey, that's my song.

JOHN *(Over, to Joe as he enters.)* Martin was looking for you, Joe.

JOE Let him look. When?

JOHN God, I don't know; hours ago. Chuckles called you on the phone.

JOE He did? *(Shrugs.)* Coffee. What did you tell him?

JOHN I told him you left early.

JOE *(With a swagger.)* What does he want with me?

JOHN Yeah, I wonder, huh.

JOE How'd you get it so quiet in here?

JOHN Wait ten minutes. It'll be a madhouse. We had a dishwasher walk out.

JOE I never knew you had one.

ANN *(Entering.)* Coffee, okay, John?

JOHN Coffee for teacher.

ANN Oh, can it. Did you see that john? That last one?

JOHN See who?

ANN That fellow I took up.

JOHN No.

JOE Naw.

ANN God, was he sick.

JOHN You get all kinds, huh?

ANN All kinds and varieties.

JOHN How much was he worth?

ANN Fifteen. What the hell. You seen Sam? He's not been around?

JOHN Your boy friend? No.

ANN God, was he sick. Hey this guy last night—you should have seen him. He had a roll of bills, I've never seen anything like it. He owns some gas stations around—three or four and he'd just made the rounds and collected from them. He must have had six or eight hundred. And I'm feeding him booze and walking the floor trying to figure some way of getting it and he's getting ready to leave. And I keep talking about everything I can think of. Pulling him back. God, I'll bet he thought he'd got hold of an eager demented whore for sure. I nearly went nuts. Kept him in the room for an hour trying to think of some way to get it.

FICK *(To Tig in the back booth.)* You notice how cold it's getting?

JOHN Can't you stick to an honest living?

FICK Bet it snows. Me with no goddamned overcoat.

ANN Ha. He must have had six hundred. *(Pause.)*

FICK Goddamn.

ANN What the hell, who needs it? *(To Joe.)* What are you so quiet about anyway?

JOE Can't I be quiet?

ANN Sit over there like the bird that caught the cat.

JOE Can't I be quiet?

ANN No. Oh, hell. *(Gets up.)*
     (At the back a Stranger, who has entered, gets up to pay his check.)

ANN Oh, hell. Hell, hell, hell, hell, hell. *(Wanders out.)*

STRANGER *(To Joe.)* You Joe Conroy?

JOE Who are you?

STRANGER Are you Conroy?

JOE What are you? Some kind of cop or something?

STRANGER You pretty big around here?

JOE Who, me?

STRANGER You must be thinking you're pretty hot stuff around here.

JOE Hey, John, could I have cream with this, huh?

STRANGER You don't screw around with Chuckles; you don't cross Chuckles, Conroy. You ought to know that.

JOE What's that?

STRANGER You're a little late, and we understand. But business is business. So we'll have to have interest on the little loan.

JOE Like what?

STRANGER Like a hundred a day—every day you're late. Man, that's sad news. You're due to lose money at that rate, you know? *(Exits.)*

JOE I'm not crossing nobody. Beginning when? Hey. *(Pause for a second.)* Hey, John. You know that guy?

JOHN *(From the end of the counter, looks up.)* No. Never saw him, don't think.

JOE I think he's some kind of cop.

BOB *(Entering with Tim.)* Yeah, yeah, yeah; whatta you think, whatta you think? Hey, John, we'll take a booth—coffee and we'll leave, okay?

JOHN Fifty cents a person minimum.

BOB Come on. Whatta you thinking about?

TIG Hey, buddy.

BOB Whatta you thinking?

JOHN Fifty cents.

TIM Since when?

JOHN Since year one. Look, do I own the place or do I work here? I work here.

BOB *(To Tig.)* Spare me a dollar till tomorrow morning, okay? I gotta pay someone before he—

TIG I got no dollar.

(Lights begin to fade on the scene.)

DOPEY *(To Rake and Ernesto on the corner.)* It's here, right? This is it.

RAKE No, God. Not yet.

JOHN Sit somewhere.

BOB Come on, tomorrow morning.

DOPEY It is, go on, man; get it there.

RAKE *(Pushing him back.)* Come on.

FICK Damn, is it getting cold, man? Do you know what happened, Tig? To me? You know why I'm so mussed up? Did I tell you?

BOB Just a minute. We'll take a booth, okay?

FICK I told you, huh.

JOHN Fifty cents a person.

BOB Oh, for Chris' sake.

FICK Do I, Tig? Do I?

TIG Do you what, Fick? I don't know what you're talking about.

RAKE *(Under his breath to Ernesto and Dopey.)* Okay, this is it.
    (The lights are very dim on café. Ernesto, Rake, and Dopey come forward downstage center to audience.)

ERNESTO We got this song here; we do this song.

DOPEY Read it.

RAKE I'll say it first, so you know the words or you couldn't make it out.

DOPEY It's a round.

RAKE It's a round and you can't understand the words if you don't know them.

DOPEY And the name is—see…

ERNESTO It's about us.

RAKE Yeah. The name is—see it's us; this is our song about us.

DOPEY We stand around on the corner all night, see, and don't do nothing.

RAKE You know, with our hands in our pockets like. Come on, Bob; you're in this—Tim, come on.
    (Tim and Bob come to the group.)

BOB What's up?

RAKE *(To Bob.)* Wake up!

ERNESTO *(Over.)* And the name is "Men on the Corner." Fellows on the corner, like that.

RAKE *(Ready to read the words from a piece of paper that he has taken from his pocket.)* Okay.

ERNESTO *(To audience.)* I'm not in it. *(Goes into the café.)*

RAKE It's this round. This is just the words:
    They laugh and jab
    cavort and jump
    and joke and gab
    and grind and bump.

DOPEY *(Quickly.)* See? It's us.

RAKE They flip a knife
    and toss a coin
    and spend their life
    and scratch their groin.
    They pantomime
    a standing screw
    and pass the time
    with nought to do.
    They swing, they sway

this cheerful crew,
with nought to say
and nought to do.

(Dopey begins the round as sound as Rake is finished, followed by Tim and Bob and Rake in that order. The melody is shockingly gentle; rocking; easy; soft; lilting. In the background with a minimum of extraneous movement the people in the café silently lift every stick of furniture, the "set," about three feet off the ground and turn the set—as a turntable would—walk the set in a slow circle until it is facing the opposite direction as at the beginning. They set the furniture down in place and sit. The round ends.)

DOPEY *(As the last line of the round is sung.)* See, the words of this one make some sense anyway. If you read the other one—the rock'n'roll at the beginning of the show—it would sound like this: y-ooo, y-ooo, yackie-yackie do, y-ooo, y-ooo, yackie, yackie…

ERNESTO *(To Dopey.)* Come on.

DOPEY What would I do yackie, yackie do, y-ooo, y-ooo…

ERNESTO Let's go.

DOPEY Isn't that a bitch?

RAKE Come on. Bob, you and Tim go on back.

(Tim and Bob enter café as Dopey and Rake go back to the street corner. To the audience.)

RAKE We'll see you.

(Lights up in the café.)

FICK You didn't see it, Tig; I tell you they had me pinned, man. Down in this hall-thing. Four or five big black cats, they must have been huge…

DARLENE *(Entering the café.)* Hi, Joe.

JOE Hi.

DARLENE Couldn't sleep. I thought you might be here.

JOE Sure.

(All of Fick's dialogue in this scene is over Darlene and Joe's scene, as a background. Very soft at first here. Fick is in the back of the café. To Tig who is not listening. Fick's dialogue is continuous.)

FICK I mean, big, strong fellows; fighters. They pushed me into this doorway. Right into the door, and down this hall and back into this dark place there in the hall there.

DARLENE What's wrong.

JOE Whatta you mean?

DARLENE You look like something was wrong is all.

JOE Do I?

DARLENE What's wrong? You can tell me.

JOE Nothing, goddammit. Come on—you come in here and in three seconds flat you start telling me I'm crazy or something.

DARLENE I didn't say anything like that.

JOE Hell you didn't.

FICK See, they thought I had a bottle on me, and I said I don't drink, and they didn't know I was high, you know. And they're standing over me and they feel around and see I don't have any money on me and I said, shit, man, you think I walk around with money? I mean, look at me now, do I look like I carry money around with me? I don't have any money on me.

DARLENE I just asked. Hell! Look at you!

JOE Don't look at me then.

DARLENE What's bugging you anyway?

JOE Nothing. Dammit. Darlene. *(Nicer.)* What the hell am I going to do with you anyway?

DARLENE *(Nicer.)* I don't know. I swear I don't. You let me know when you come up with something, though, you hear?

JOE Yeah. I'll think of something. *(Pause in their conversation.)*

FICK I get four dollars, I shoot it, man it's all I can afford. About twenty dollars a day, man, most days I don't even know where it came from, cause I'm high, man, and I don't remember, I can't think. And they start roughing me up and I said, man, you got the wrong boy. Why don't you rough up someone your own size?

JOE You want a cup of coffee?

DARLENE Sure. Why not. John? I won't sleep now, anyway. *(Pause.)* Did you get back in time to see that Martin?

JOE Oh, Christ. What the hell difference does it make? I told you I don't owe him nothing.

DARLENE I didn't know. I take it from that you didn't get back in time.

JOE What business is it of yours, anyway?

DARLENE Well, I just wondered. For Christ's sake. If you can't even be civil.

FICK I mean even if I was a big cat, see, I'm small, but even if I was a big cat I wouldn't go roughing up people like that. They fairly gave me hell, and beat the tar out of me. I just balled up in the hall there and didn't move, I mean, if I get up they're going to get at my face and all, and I just balled up and had to take it.

JOE Well, if you have to nose into everybody's business.

DARLENE I don't give a good goddamn if you saw him or not. Or Chuckles even.

JOE Then why the hell did you bother to ask?

DARLENE Forget it. Christ. Excuse me for living.

JOE Just keep your nose in your own business. You have business of your own to worry about. Darlene, for Christ's sake.

FICK 'Cause I couldn't get even one good punch in at them. I couldn't get one good punch at them. I mean, look at me. I'm weak as a kitten. What would you expect, I started shooting H when I was about thirteen. And hell, that's a long time ago now; I mean I wasn't a tough kid or nothing like that, but I could protect myself, you know, I could spar around, but Christ I can't even see anything half the time, I can't follow things around you know and they're kicking me around the hallway there.

(Tig starts to get up, sits back down.)

DARLENE Pardon me for living.

JOE Go get laid. You can't mind your own business. You come in here and...

DARLENE Jesus. Just forget it.

JOE Okay. It's forgotten. *(Pause.)*

FICK No, don't go away now, listen to this, just listen to me now. See these guys were kicking me around and I can't do nothing. But what I'm saying, if I could get a couple of big guys, you know, a few big guys, you know, a few big guys and go up there, go back there.

DARLENE Christ! *(Pause.)*

JOE You want coffee?

DARLENE I don't know.

JOE Suit yourself.

DARLENE Yeah. OK John?

JOHN Got it.

JOE Christ.

DARLENE Are you in trouble? Be serious now.

JOE Yes. Dammit, there. You feel better now?

FICK I couldn't do nothing myself, I mean, I just laid there, man. But if I could get a couple of big guys, a couple of fighters and go back there. No, don't run off, I'm not talking about you, but you're big fellows, you could look big. See I know these mothers; I seen them around here all the time. And they know I don't have any bread, they know that.

(Tig moves to a different seat. Fick continues as if Tig were still there.)

DARLENE Is it serious?

FICK But with a couple of fellows, fighters, they'd run like hell, they wouldn't start nothing, you'd see.

JOE Yes.

FICK They'd run like a couple of scared mothers. I mean we wouldn't have to do nothing or nothing, they'd just turn tail and get the hell out of there.

DARLENE Are you going to work for him?

JOE I don't have much of a choice. One of his friends—one that I'd never seen before—paid me a visit here to inform me I'd owe Chuckles a hundred bucks a day interest till I paid him off. Now are you happy?

FICK See, they'd think I had friends, see, and they'd know not to fuck with me any more, as soon as they saw I had a couple of friends they'd not mess around with me, you know what I mean?

DARLENE You can't get money like that, can you? Can you? What are you going to do, Joe?

JOE I don't know yet! I don't know. What, yet. I gotta think.

(They sit quietly, looking up out toward the street.)

FICK I mean, I was just walking down the street and they came up on me like they was important, and they start pushing me around, you know. And they pushed me into this alley, not an alley, but this hallway and back down the end of that to this dark place at the end of the hallway and they start punching at me, and I just fell into this ball on the floor so they couldn't hurt me or nothing. But if I came down there with a couple of fighters, a couple of guys, like my friends, it wouldn't have to be you or anything, but just a couple or three guys, big guys, like walking down the street, you know. Just so they could see I got these buddies here. See I'm on H, I mean, I'm flying and I gotta talk man, but I'm serious now; just a few guys and they'd leave me be, maybe, because they'd think I had these buddies that looked after me, you know; cause I—you know—they kicked me up, if I wasn't on H, man, they'd be pains all through me—you know—walking down the street by myself—I start looking around and wondering who's out there gonna mess me up, you know. I get scared as hell, man, walking down around here, I mean, I can't protect myself or nothing, man. You know what I mean? You know what I mean? You know what I mean? You know? I mean if I had these couple—of big buddies—fighters—you—you know—if I had a couple of guys—like—big guys—that—you know, there's like nothing—I could—like, if you walked around with these buddies, I mean you could do, man—you could do anything....

(Long pondering pause. He looks to everyone one at a time. No one moves. He turns and looks at Babe. She raises her head as if to speak and very slowly looks back down to the counter. Fick looks to the guys on the corner.)

DOPEY *(On the corner. Turns to audience. Clearly.)* We'll call an intermission here.

CURTAIN

ACT TWO

Early evening. Only Frank, Ann, Judy, and Terry are in the café. Ann is the only person seated at the counter.

DARLENE *(Enters the café. She sits a few stools from Ann.)* Could I have a coffee, please?

FRANK *(In a rather good mood.)* Sure, miss.

DARLENE John isn't on yet, huh? He come on about seven?

FRANK Yeah.

DARLENE And I think maybe—what's the little cupcake? Are those chocolate all through?

FRANK White. Chocolate frosting.

DARLENE Oh. No. Nothing else, I guess. I'm not really hungry.
(She looks toward Ann. Darlene drinks a moment and pours a great deal of milk into the coffee.)

FRANK Watch that milk—all that's not good for you.
(You should have the feeling he's more worried about the price of milk.)

DARLENE It isn't?

FRANK It'll make you fat.
(He walks to the far end of the counter.)

DARLENE Oh, that's one thing I don't worry much about. *(She looks toward Ann who is drinking coffee and smoking a cigarette, looking out the window in a half-dream.)* Isn't your name Ann? *(Pause. No reaction. Ann probably hasn't heard her.)* Ann? I thought, if you're busy or...

ANN *(Turns to her. Does not recognize her at first.)* Yes?

DARLENE I don't know many people around the neighborhood yet. I've seen you around. A friend of mine knows you real well. Joe knows you, I think.
(Frank sits at one of the booths, reading a paper.)

ANN Joe? Conroy? Chuckles' fellow? Or is he?

DARLENE I don't—short—but not too short. Real cute—sexy; dark hair. I don't think he's Chuckles' fellow, but he knows him, I believe.

ANN Conroy. God yes, I know Joe.

DARLENE Isn't that terrible, I forgot his last name. I just blanked out.

ANN Conroy.

DARLENE Yes, I know. I remember it now.

ANN Sure. I've seen you with Joe, I know now.

DARLENE I'm Darlene.

ANN Fine.

DARLENE Joe said you came to New York to be a teacher.

ANN Oh, God.

DARLENE Didn't you?

ANN Who remembers?

DARLENE And you're from Nebraska. I'm from Chicago, so that's not far off.

ANN Minnesota.

DARLENE *(Puzzled for a moment—smiles.)* Illinois.

ANN I'm from Minnesota. You're from Chicago.

DARLENE Oh. Minnesota. I said something else, didn't I? *(Pause.)* I been here about a month, I guess. He—Joe—talked about you a lot.

ANN He must have!

DARLENE Oh, it was all good! *(Realizes it couldn't have been good. Embarrassed hesitation.)* I saw you this afternoon.

ANN Me?

DARLENE I was up early for a change; I had to go down to Port Authority and get some things I'd left there. You were walking down uh—uh—over toward that church; the whichever one—I don't know—there's a market there and a bakeshop.

ANN I don't know.

DARLENE Yes, you do. You were with this guy. Probably your boy friend. Real big fellow.

ANN Boy friend for the next fifteen minutes probably—Oh, no! That was Sam. That is my boy friend. If you can call it that. He dragged me out of bed to look at a TV set some bum friend of his mopped from a PR apartment. Ratty old contraption. He couldn't get either one of us focused.

DARLENE *(Has been listening too intently, too amused.)* Huh?

ANN Some clunk friend of his was trying to fence a bum set for twenty-five bucks. I dragged him down to some store and bought a new one.

DARLENE Really? That's wonderful.

ANN He didn't like it, of course. There wasn't anything that needed to be done on it. Tinkered with. He didn't want to watch it unless he could conquer it first. His room is one solid mass of parts and tubes and coils and wires and various masculine symbols like that. Of course, he is one solid mass of—but that's another conversation altogether. You're from Chicago. I went to Chicago when I was about four, I think.

DARLENE Really? Yeah, I grew up there. It's not like New York at all.

ANN Yeah.

DARLENE I know what you mean about radio parts and nuts and bolts and everything. That's funny, the way you put it. *(Pause.)* Oh, I like New York all right, I guess. It's like a whole different place, you know.

ANN I imagine.

DARLENE I mean back home is like a small town compared to here.

ANN For me, too.

(Martin enters café.)

DARLENE You're from Minnesota?

ANN Ashville, Minnesota.

MARTIN Pardon me. Ann. Right?

ANN Yes?

MARTIN *(Mumbles.)* I thought so; I wondered, there's this guy I've…

ANN Speak up, baby, I can't hear you.

MARTIN I said, there's this guy, I know he comes around here.

ANN Who's that?

MARTIN I don't know, I know I heard he was around here, I've seen him around. Spanish fellow, dark…

ANN I don't think I can help you on that one, there's a *lot* of Spanish guys floating around here. *(She starts to turn away.)*

MARTIN He's a Colombian guy; dresses very smart.

ANN Are you talking about Xavier?

DARLENE That's who I was gonna say, Xavier.

MARTIN Yes, yes, that's him; that's him.

ANN Sure, everybody knows Xavier. *(Spanish pronunciation.)*

MARTIN Have you seen him around today?

ANN I don't think so.

MARTIN *(Overlapping.)* Has he been in here today?

ANN Not that I know of.

MARTIN A Colombian guy, very smart dress—

ANN Yeah, I know who you mean. *(To Darlene.)* Sorry, you were saying it's—

MARTIN Do you know where he'd be; or where he lives or anything?

ANN No, I'm afraid I don't.

DARLENE He's been around this week, though. With Xavier you never know when you're going to see him.

ANN He runs around a lot.

DARLENE He says I'll be right back and you won't see him for a month sometimes.

ANN Sorry. *(Pause.)*

MARTIN Yeah. *(Pause.)*

DARLENE *(To Ann.)* That guy that you were with, the tall—

MARTIN *(Overlapping, conversational level.)* You don't suppose that he'll be in right away?

ANN I tell you what, you could undoubtedly catch him later on this evening; why don't you come back?

MARTIN Yeah. I just wanted to see him about something.

ANN Well, if it's important I could—

MARTIN No, no. It's not important.

ANN If I see him do you want me to tell him to stick around?

MARTIN No. No, that's okay. I'll probably run into him, you know, this evening. Thank you.

ANN Sure.

FRANK You want something?

MARTIN No, no, thanks.

FRANK Coffee or something. It's getting cold out.

MARTIN No, I'll be back, no thanks.

DARLENE What was the fellows name again?

ANN Him? I don't know, I've seen him around.

DARLENE No, the tall guy; you know, that I saw you with?

ANN Sam?

DARLENE Yeah. You're not married to him, are you?

ANN God, no.

DARLENE *(Laughs.)* I know what you mean. That's funny. *(Pause.)* Those two that always sit around in here, you know; the dark headed one and she's got a little baby? Are they married? Or do you know?

ANN I don't know. No one knows. I don't imagine, but they'd probably tell you they were.

DARLENE It's a cute little baby, really. I don't know if I'd bring him here at all hours of the day and night like that if it was mine, though.

ANN Well, some people would give anything to look respectable.

DARLENE *(Pause.)* I know one thing: I sure feel like you do about marriage. I mean, I just don't know. Like you said. I know this guy I used to go with—when I first got a room of my own, up on Armitage Street? Do you know that part of Chicago?

ANN No. But then I was only four.

DARLENE Oh. Well, most of the streets run either east and west or up and down, you know—one or the other. But some of them kinna cut across all the others—Armitage Street does, and some of the other real nice ones. Fullerton Street does.

(I don't know if it's important, but Fullerton Street does not. In other words, Darlene rather prefers the vivid to the accurate.)

DARLENE And they're wider, you know, with big trees and all, and there are all of these big old lovely apartment buildings, very well taken care of, with little lawns out front and flower boxes in the windows and all. You know what I mean? And the rents, compared to what they try to sock you with here. The rents are practically nothing—even in this neighborhood. *(Pause.)* My apartment was two flights up, in the front. It was so cute, you'd have loved it. They had it all done over when I moved in. I had three rooms. And let's see—there was just a lovely big living room that

looked out onto Armitage Street and a real cute little kitchen and then
the bedroom—that looked out onto a garden in the back and on the
other side of the garden was Grant Park—or some park, I never did know
the name it had. But there were kids that I just loved playing out in this
park all the time. And then I had this little bathroom, a private bath. I
had—it was funny—I had a collection—you know practically everybody
collects something...

ANN Yeah, I know what you mean.

DARLENE *(Laughs.)* No, not like that! I collected towels, if you must know.
You know, from all the big hotels—Of course, I didn't get very many of
them myself, but friends of mine, every time they went anywhere always
brought me back a big bath towel or hand towel or face towel with some
new name across it. I'll swear, I never bought one towel in all the time I
lived there! It was funny, too, it looked real great in a regular bathroom
like that; these hotel names. Everyone just loved it. My favorite one was—
from this—oh, this real elegant hotel—what was it's—I don't even
remember the name any more I had so many of them. Anyway, the apartment, in that neighborhood and all, cost me practically nothing compared to what they want for a place not half as good in New York. And I
lived there, and this guy I was going with, you know, that asked me to
marry him? He lived across the hall. He moved into the apartment next to
mine. Really, Ann, you should have seen him. He was slow, everything he
did, and quiet; he hardly ever talked at all. You had to just pump him to
get him to say the time of day. And he had white hair—nearly white; they
used to call him Cotton—he told me—when he was in Alabama. That's
where he's from. He was living in the apartment next to mine and we
were always together, and there just wasn't any difference between his
place and mine. We should have only been paying for one rent. Half of
his stuff was in my place and half vice versa. He used to get so pissed off
when I'd wash things out and hang them up in his bathroom or in the
kitchen and all. You know, over the fire there. But we were always together—and we finally decided to get married—we both did. And all our
friends were buying rice and digging out their old shoes. Cotton—he
worked in a television factory, RCA, I believe, but I couldn't be sure.
That's why I started thinking about him when you said this Sam had elec-
trical parts all over the apartment. Old Cotton had, I'll swear, the funniest temperament I ever saw. If he got mad—*(Almost as though mad.)*—he
wouldn't argue or anything like that, he'd just walk around like nothing
was wrong only never say one word. Sometimes for two or three days.
And that used to get me so mad I couldn't stand it. Have you ever known
anyone who did that?

ANN Yeah, I know what you mean.

DARLENE Just wouldn't talk at all, I mean. Not say one word for days.

ANN It sounds familiar enough.

DARLENE It used to just burn me up. And he knew it did, is what made it so bad. I'd just be so mad I could spit. And I'd say something like; what's wrong, Cotton? And just as easy as you please he'd reach over and light a cigarette and look out the window or something. Turn on the radio. I just wish I had the control to be like that because it is the most maddening thing you can possibly to do someone when they're trying to argue with you. I could do it for about five minutes, then I'd blow my stack. Oh, I used to get so damn mad at him. Agh! *(Pause.)* Course I make it sound worse than it was, cause he didn't act like that very often. Fortunately. But you never knew what was going to provoke him, I swear. It was just that we saw each other every hour of every day—you just couldn't get us apart. And when we decided to get married all our friends were so excited—of course, they'd been expecting it probably. But we were so crazy you'd never know what we were going to do. I know he used to set the TV so it pointed into the mirror, because there wasn't a plug-in by the bed and we'd lay there in bed and look at the mirror that had the TV reflected in it. Only everything was backwards. Writing was backwards. *(She laughs.)* Only, you know, even backwards, it was a better picture, it was clearer, than if you was just looking straight at it.

ANN Yeah. So did you?

DARLENE Get married? Oh, Lord, it was such an or*deal!* We got—now you have to know Cotton for this to be funny to you—but when he went for his blood test I nearly died laughing. He's got these real pale eyes and just no color, you know—a pink color all over him; absolutely the lightest-skinned person I've ever known who wasn't sickly or something. They called him an albino; you know what that is?

ANN Yes.

DARLENE It's a kind of horse. And Cotton's eyes were kinda pink and trying to be blue, so they came out a kind of lavender. You'd have thought he couldn't be a lighter color and be alive. And when the doctor stuck the needle in him, oh, Lord, he faded out like a dollar shirt. I've never seen anyone in my life get that white in three seconds flat. I don't mean he fainted or anything, but you should have seen him. He was so damn scared it was really great of him, because he didn't make a fuss or anything. I said, honey, do you want to sit down or something? And he just said, oh, no. Cotton wasn't weak either—he was tough as they make 'em. He was pale and all like I said, but he was strong as an ox and rough. He was always in some fight, beating the pants off someone or other.

(*Chattier.*) We went to this doctor Lillian—a girl friend of mine—went to when she thought she was pregnant, but she wasn't, thank God. And I think it was the following Saturday, the license office was only open till noon or one o'clock, I remember. And Cotton was supposed to work, but he got off; we went up to City Hall for our license. They're building a new building for City Hall in Chicago, or I think they are. I *hope* they are! They didn't have any air conditioning or anything—naturally, and of course it was in the middle of summer: July eleventh. On a Saturday. Anyway, this old building covers a whole block, right out to the sidewalk and it must be fifty years old. Everything is that old style of heavy old marble and gold spittons everywhere. And you go—going to the marriage license place—you go up these real wide marble stairs about a block wide and sway-backed, you practically break your neck on them they're so worn down in the middle—and there's this hall upstairs somewhere with the door to the bureau at the far end and by the time we got there—and we didn't get there till about eleven—there must have been two hundred people up there waiting in line. Most of them couples waiting to get in for their license. There was this line—you've never seen anything like it. We got up to the top of the stairs and saw all those people in line and Cotton and me both said, Oh, my God! at the same time. And some of the kids who had come with us, I thought they'd just drop. You've never seen anything like it. I wish I could remember some of the things that our friends said about it, too, because they kept us in stitches all morning. (*Pause.*) God, you should have seen the people waiting there in line. It was hot and all. Of course this was Chicago, but I'll bet it'll be the same, or about the same everywhere. There was every size and shape and color a person you've ever seen or could hope to see. God, there was Puerto Ricans and whites and redheads and Negroes and redheaded Negroes; and a lot of people were chattering away in some jibberish language that nobody could understand. And kids you'd think was only about fourteen years of age and old people who must have been—one couple—must have been sixty if they were a day. You see everything. And this is hard to believe probably but you can go down to the New York City Hall and I'll bet it's the same there; I'll swear about twenty of the girls in line waiting for their marriage licenses were pregnant. Honest to God. It looked like the maternity ward in a hospital. And I mean real pregnant—six or seven months along—and I couldn't help thinking if this many are this pregnant this far along, I just wonder how many are three months or two months along and nobody can tell it.

And of course there were some mothers and fathers that had dragged along. If you ever want to see a trapped look in a boy's eyes—I mean, they were smiling, and talking all very seriously with their prospective fathers-in-law, all very man to man, standing beside their fat, ugly—really ugly, some of them—girl friends, but in their eyes they were wondering how the hell they were going to get out of this one. And some of the girls were dressed up. Some of them were in jeans and had their hair in curlers and you'd just want to die looking at them—and then some of them were dressed to the teeth. Knee-length wedding gowns; you know; not expensive, but pretty and veils and the whole bit—a bunch of roses or gardenias or something and after they got their license they went around a kind of mezzanine railing to the Justice's office across the way. The Justice of the Piece's office some of the kids starting calling it. That's the kind of thing they were saying all day. But if I was going to wear a dress like that to get married in, I know one thing: I wouldn't do it in his little office—you could look right across into the room and the carpet was worn all down—it was just a mess of a place. I couldn't even watch—I just bet they felt so foolish all dressed up like that with this noisy line outside and that stupid rug. But they seemed happy enough about it, I guess. You couldn't help wondering if the boys who were marrying the pregnant girls were really the fathers of the kids or not. And if the boys weren't wondering the same thing. I just hope that all the kids turned out for the mothers' sake to look exactly the spittin' image of their fathers.

And if this hot, messy, stupid crowd wasn't enough, with everyone crowding all over this hall: there was this guy, all fat and toothless, or nearly, and bald, who kept trotting down the line saying, "Stay up against the wall, now, give the boys room to get in. They got you up against the wall now; now you let them in!" And pretending what he'd said didn't have any dirty meaning at all. And laughing. Some of the fellows and the men—the fathers and all—laughed and carried on with him. I can't remember exactly what he said but it was like: "The quicker you get in the quicker you get it in." I mean he just wasn't funny at all. I thought Cotton was gonna bust him one. He just *served* to make everyone a little more nervous and jumpy than they were anyway. Everyone got so tired and just kept looking and everyone was so down. Naturally the girls who were pregnant were mostly just looking down at the hall floor, and they'd look up like nothing was wrong. I guess everyone just wanted to get the hell out of that building. I know I thought, *Christ, aren't we even moving? You know?* With, let's see, with Cotton and me there was two friends of his that I didn't know too well, and a girl friend of mine, so we weren't as bad off as the kids that had come down there alone. Not at first. We were talking and cutting up and all. And after a while you get so tired and exhausted you just stand there. And everyone was more stupid and ugly than you can imagine and Cotton got in one of his moods. You know: quiet as a stone statue or something and I tried to get him out of it. It was like he blamed *me* for all the waiting and all. And then when we finally got in, after creeping along all afternoon, there was three tables and after we got inside the room the line split into three lines and we went to one of the tables—and the guy who asked the questions—real crazy questions too, but I can't remember any of them now. I should, too, because they were such crazy questions. This guy was friendly and nice and Cotton became hisself again, which was about time. Anyway that guy was nice and friendly, considering he'd been doing the same thing all morning with one couple after another. And all the guys joked kinna dirty, but friendly and we finally got the license and they had the certificate from the blood test and all; and we went back out to the kids that waited for us. They were sitting down on the steps, just about to die it looked like. I don't know how they did it. But a lot of the couples were worse off than we were—there seemed like thousands of them still hanging around up there when we left. Elizabeth—that was the girl friend of mine who came along, stood out on the front steps there with the license and read it out—every word. Outloud. And everyone was laughing and carrying on. Christ, they were a fun gang. They were about the most fun kids I've ever been with in my life. And let's see; we went for a drive, trying to cool off, I remember. And anyway, to make a long story short, we probably went to a drive-in movie, out somewhere. We were always doing that because Harold had his car. And when we got home I put the license on the dresser, stood it up so we could look at it. Cotton said if we'd all been getting two dollars an hour the thing was worth about thirty dollars, I'll bet. *(Pause.)* When had we decided to get *married?* I think at first we were going to do it the next day—Sunday, but we'd been out all night that night and by the time we got up that Sunday it must have been seven or eight o'clock in the evening. And then we were going to do it the next week. And, I don't know—something came up—one thing or another. Cotton was out a lot, but he still came over and all, and he still wanted to and so did I. I really did. I wanted to more than anything because he was about the greatest guy I'd ever met. And I don't know. I know one time when I was trying to straighten up the place—trying to get a little order out of my room, I put it in one of the dresser drawers and it finally got buried under a pile of stuff. I've got it though, I ran across it again when I was packing things together to come here. Hell, old Cotton had cut out months before that. He kept coming over for a long time, but I might not be able to tell when a guy isn't really interested in me at first—I mean if they just say they are, I believe them—I mean what else can you do? But I can sure as hell tell when they start losing interest. Not that you can do anything about it. Old Cotton would give me a kiss and squeeze me once and slap me three or four times quick on the rump. And say, "Okay!" like I was dismissed or something. Like he had better things to run and do at that particular moment. "Okay! Hop up!" Hop up. Good Lord.

But he hadn't chicken out of it—getting married—he just never got around to it. I've sometimes wished we just had gone out of town, out to Glen Ellyn or somewhere at a Justice of the Peace, somewhere. You know. It just got to be such a mess we never even talked about it after a while, and the license got shuffled up with a lot of other things, and got a bend across it, all bent up. He was a nice guy, too. He moved on back South somewhere. Georgia, I think. Not Alabama, I know. And he'd had a lot of great friends, too. I liked them a lot. God, did we ever have some *times* together. The whole...gang of us. God. We used...to really have some... times together.

(The quartette is together at the back of the stage. They harmonize in a rock-'n'roll wordless "Boo, bop, boo, bah, day, dolie, olie day" kind of rambling that gets louder and eventually takes over the scene. Frank has left; John is in the café now. Joe and Dopey and Rake have gone to the corner. David and Franny enter the café.)

DAVID Hi, John; you got any coffee?

JOHN Sure.

FRANNY Two.

ANN I'll get it.

DARLENE No, that's okay.

ANN It's okay. Sam couldn't possibly miss a quarter.

FRANNY Do you have a menu in this place? For Chris' sake.

(Xavier and Babe enter. Babe is not high but is so far gone that you couldn't tell. She speaks very thickly and to the floor and it should be just barely possible to understand her. Their scene should be played on the street, some distance from the corner, very slowly. Joe enters from the other side.)

JOHN *(To Franny.)* Hold it a minute. *(To Ann.)* Thanks.

(Ann and Darlene remain in the café for a moment.)

XAVIER *(To Joe.)* Hey, friend.

JOE *Xavier!* What are you doing?

XAVIER Where was you yesterday?

JOE Oh, I was busy. Where you going?

XAVIER You want to come up?

JOE *(Looks at Babe, nods. Babe stares blankly at him.)* Where you going?

BABE Come on, Xavier.

XAVIER We're going up on the roof a minute.

RAKE *(From the other side, singing to himself.)* They laugh and jab, cavort, and jump!—

DOPEY Shut up. For Chris' sake.

RAKE What's wrong.

JOE No, I been up there. What for?

DOPEY You get on my nerves.

BABE *(To Xavier.)* Haven't you got one? A something?

XAVIER We've got to go on up.

(Ernesto joins Dopey and Rake.)

BABE Come on. You have to have something. You used to have a cord or something, didn't you?

XAVIER Yeah, someone borrowed it, didn't give it back.

BABE *(Looks at Joe's belt.)* Uh, do you think I, would you...

(Joe slips off his belt, rolls it up, and hands it to Xavier.)

ANN I just wonder where the fuck Sam's run off to.

BABE Good, great. That's thin, that's fine.

JOE I'll see you when you come down. Don't lose that!

XAVIER *(Rather shyly.)* Come on up.

JOE No, I'll see you when you come down. Don't lose that.

XAVIER I'll bring it right back. We'll see you.

JOE Yeah, look; I'm not staying around here long, I might be inside when you come down, okay?

XAVIER Sure, man. We'll be right back. You should come along.

JOE You go on.

(Xavier and Babe exit.)

JOE Jesus, Xavier.

(The quartette sings the first four or five lines of "There Is a Balm in Gilead" in the back, a jazzed-up version.)

DARLENE *(Comes out of the café. Sees Joe and goes to him. Their scene is played on the street corner.)* Hi.

JOE Hi. You been calling over to your room for me?

DARLENE No, you said not to. Why, has the phone been ringing?

JOE Yeah. It's probably Chuckles. I don't imagine it took him much to discover who I was with the last few nights. You being new and all.

DARLENE Almost everyone I've seen all day asked me where you was.

JOE Yeah? What'd you say?

DARLENE *(Smiles.)* I told them I thought you went to a movie.

JOE Really? That's pretty good. That's funny. Say, you know Xavier?

DARLENE Sure. Someone was looking for him.

JOE I saw him. Pushing now. I'll bet he has been all along. He was with Babe.

DARLENE Babe? Really? *(She has no idea what to say.)*

JOE I'm not going to.

DARLENE Not what?

JOE I'm not going to. I decided not.

DARLENE Really? Oh, God, I'm glad, Joe. Oh, I really am. How are you gonna do it?

JOE I gotta think of some way to get these back to Perry or Chuckles. I'll just give him what he gave me and tell him I've changed my mind.
    (Franny enters.)

DARLENE Oh, I'm glad. I really am. You'll do something else all right.

FRANNY *(On the street opposite the corner.)* Hello, Ernesto.
    (The quartette begins a very low, highly harmonized version of the hymn "Balm in Gilead" that follows the tempo of Joe and Darlene's slow, rather dreamy scene.)

DARLENE Did you sleep till six?

ERNESTO *(With deep insinuation, grabby Franny around waist.)* You like it?

FRANNY I'm not really interested, no.
    (As Tig joins Dopey, Franny, Rake, and Ernesto.)

FRANNY Hi, Tig.

JOE About six. I didn't get to bed till late.

DARLENE I know.

TIG *(With hand on crotch.)* You like it, Franny? You think you could use something?

FRANNY I'll bet you think you're a man. Don't you know—

DARLENE When are you going to see him?

FRANNY —men don't dig boys? They sure don't dig fairies.

TIG Depends on what it's worth to you.

JOE I don't know. Soon as I can. I got to call him or something.

DARLENE When did you decide?

FRANNY You really think you're hot stuff, don't you?

TIG How much is it worth to you?

JOE Just a minute ago.

DARLENE What'll you do?

JOE Hell, there's a thousand things to do.

ANN *(Exiting the café.)* Franny, you're stealing all my business.
    (Group laughs.)

DARLENE Sure.

FRANNY *(To Tig.)* You really think you're good enough to charge?

TIG Five bucks an inch'll get me fifty, Franny.

FRANNY Who from? Not me.

JOE When did you wake up?

FRANNY I'll charge you double.

DARLENE Since about ten…

TIG How much can you take?

FRANNY As much as I need and want.

TIG Put your money where your mouth is, sweetheart.
  (Group laughs. Tig is very close to Franny.)

DARLENE I went down to the bus station. I had some clothes still in a locker there; I thought I'd never get them.

FRANNY More than you got, sweetheart.

TIG How do you know?

DOPEY Watch it, Tig. *(His back is to the audience, hands in pockets.)*

ANN *(Turns and goes back inside.)* Watch it, Franny; he'll take you up.

FRANNY Come on, back off a little bit. I'm only human.

KAY *(Entering café.)* Hi, John; I'm a little late.

JOHN Hi, Kay; that's all right.
  (Fick enters.)

DARLENE *(Over some of the above.)* The neighborhood isn't bad at all in the daytime. It's perfectly respectable.

JOE Is it?

DARLENE Well. Nearly.

RAKE He can take care of himself.

FRANNY I'll bet I could take care of him better.

TIG You think you could take about half of that?

FRANNY Half of what? I don't *see* anything.

RAKE Watch that one, though, Tig.
  (Group reaction.)

ERNESTO No lie, Tig.

DARLENE The people look like anyone else. Almost.

JOE Almost. That's funny.

TIG You think you can take about ten bucks' worth, real quick-life?

FICK *(Inside the café.)* Hey, John? Am I frostbitten? Look at my ears.

JOHN What?

DOPEY Why don't you take us all on, huh?

RAKE Game for that?

FICK Hey, Ann?

DARLENE You want a cup of coffee or something?

JOE In a minute.

FRANNY No, it's not my game.

DARLENE I talked to Ann all afternoon.

FRANNY Sorry, Rake.

JOE She's a wild kid.

DARLENE Kid, hell.

FICK Hell.

ANN Hell no, you aren't frostbit. It's not even cold out.

FICK You sure?

FRANNY It won't be real quick, I can tell you that right now.

FICK 'Cause I can't tell.

TIG I'll let you savor it a hour maybe.

KAY How's business been?

JOHN Not good, not bad. Coffee, Ann?

FRANNY Or three. I could give you a ride you won't forget.

ANN Why not.

TIG You think so, huh?

JOE She's nice, I like her.

DARLENE So do I, really.

DOPEY *(Turning his head around. To audience.)* Are you getting any of this?

FICK Could I have a coffee?

JOHN *(To Fick.)* Are you awake?

FRANNY How long do you have to hang around your friends here?

FICK Awake?

TIG What friends?

RAKE I don't believe it!

FRANNY Believe anything, baby.

TIG What can I tell you?

FICK What is it, November?

DARLENE I like her. I talked her leg off.

  (Joe laughs.)

FRANNY Come on up, you springy son-of-a-bitch.

TIG You better be all you claim.

ERNESTO Want a party?

FRANNY I'm not dressed for it. *(To Tig.)* I'll just bet you got action like a jack rabbit.

TIG How much is it worth to find out?

FRANNY *(As he and Tig start to leave.)* Well, we'll talk about it. Okay?

JOE You want to go in?

DARLENE Might as well. I've been in all day, though.

  (Joe and Darlene enter the café.)

RAKE *(To Tig and Franny.)* Hey, you're gonna lose it, baby.

FRANNY I never had it.

  (The next four speeches are delivered rapidly over the above.)

ERNESTO You'll get split open, Franny!

RAKE Rip him apart.

DOPEY Give it to her.

ERNESTO Make him cry for mercy, Tig.

TIG I'll have him beggin' in five minutes.

FRANNY Quit bragging and get to work. I'll see you guys later.

(Group laughs. The group moves back a few feet. Tig and Franny exit. The Stranger should be standing where the last line of Franny's is spoken.)

DOPEY *(To audience.)* Wheeh! Jesus.

ANN *(Leaving the café and joining the group.)* Did he do it? The son-of-a-bitch! Damn Franny.

RAKE You got Sammy.

ANN Damn Sam. I been trying to make Tig for a month.

ERNESTO Don't tell Sammy.

ANN Screw Sammy.

DOPEY Franny'll end up like old Howie yet.

ANN Poor old Howie.

(Darlene and Joe sit in a booth.)

DOPEY Poor old Howie.

(Group laughs.)

RAKE Son-of-a-bitch!

(Group laughs.)

RAKE Wire…*(Laughs.)*

ANN God, that's funny. It really is.

(During Ann's following speech the café is filled by the same people as in the beginning scene of the play. Black and orange crêpe-paper streamers are lowered very slowly in a typical crisscross Halloween decoration. A dime-store skeleton and a pumpkin should lower straight from the ceiling. The quartette is rehearsing the opening song in the back.)

ANN *(To audience.)* There's this joke: I can't tell it. Not a joke joke, but like a private joke on this guy Howie from around here.

RAKE *(Over, in background.)* Poor old Howie.

ANN Like the devil gets his due, you understand. See, he's always around for three or four dollars, I don't know how much, I never bothered to ask, but the guys around here could always pick up a few bucks from Howie. He's not an old guy either, I mean not all that old, but they'd step into a doorway or some dark place along the street or some rest-room, you follow me, and the guys would make about four or five bucks—a symbiotic kind of relationship—you know, the guys get the money and Howie gets, or derives, his benefit from it too: This is sounding vulgar as hell and I thought I could tell it clean. Well, anyway—Fuck. Howie gives them a quickie blow job in a subway john or somewhere—Christ, we're all adults and know about that, I'd hope, by now, anyway. And this is very important to him. Like a junkie needs his shot in the arm. Well, poor Howie, God love him, never hurt anybody, was down in the Village and just out to see the sights, not approaching anyone or anything, at least no more than he could help; just walking around and some guys jump him. Figure him for a good rolling, and maybe they got a few dollars off the guy and left him pretty beaten up but that wouldn't be so bad for Howie, you know—and he made it to the hospital. Over to Saint Vincent's, see, and they gave him X rays and he's got his face knocked in and his teeth loosened; nothing really bad or serious or permanent, you understand. He'll be back in shape in about a month; but in the meantime he's got this broken jaw…

RAKE Hey, Ann; come on.

ANN So they wired his mouth shut!

(Group reaction. Ann laughs at her own joke.)

DOPEY Poor bastard, Howie.

RAKE Poor Howie.

(Group laughs. Fick exits café. Ann re-enters.)

FICK *(As he passes Ann.)* Hey, Ann, you got—hey you…

(She goes back into the cafe.)

JUDY All right! Come on, come on. If we're going to get goin', get goin'; get that table out of the way, come on, line them up a little.

(They straighten the booths into rows. Blocking on these repeat scenes should be as the first time through exactly.)

TIG *(Overlapping.)* What are you? Some kind of housewife, Judy?

JUDY *(To David.)* You're the housewife, aren't you, sweetheart?

DAVID You're the fishwife, Judy. Fishwife! Fish! Pheew!

FICK Hey, Dopey, you got a cigarette, huh?

DOPEY Somewhere.

BONNIE *(To David.)* You ought to be chased out of the neighborhood. Dirty up the neighborhood with a lot of fairy dust.

DAVID *(Not Franny, this time.)* Who you calling names, you truck driver?

BONNIE Who you queers think you are?

DAVID Who you callin' queer? George!

BOB Shut up, over there!

JOHN *(Not Tig.)* Come on, God.

TERRY All you queens.

DAVID *(To Terry.)* Why don't you shut up before I beat you over your head with your dildo?

TERRY You trying to say something?

DAVID Ah, your mother's a whore—

TERRY You trying to say something?

(Four Children, three boys and a girl, enter the scene. They are dressed in regular clothes; they all have on Halloween masks. The boys wear comical masks; the girl a woman's mask. They carry big paper bags and go about saying "trick

or treat." No one in the café pays the slightest attention to them. The scene is repeated as though they weren't there. All new material is ignored by the others.)

JOHN Come on, now; keep it down.

TIM May I have a cup of tea, please?

  (Carlo enters.)

TIM Hi, Carlo. Over here.

CARLO *(Trying English.)* Hello. Correct? Yes, hello. Correct?

TIM *(With Spanish accent.)* Correct. Near enough.

  (The next few lines will be over the repeat below, beginning with Bonnie's speech; but they should be loud and excited.)

TIM Try the numbers, though. That's what you're working on.

CARLO Numbers. No. *(Quickly counts to ten—as a joke—in Spanish.)*

TIM No. No. No. In English. In English. How you ever gonna learn anything?

ANN He'll never get it anyway.

CARLO Yes!

TIM Yes, he will. You wait.

BONNIE What the hell is this, fifty cents for one Coke; you think this is the Ritz?

JOHN There's a sign right there, fifty cents minimum at booths; if you don't have it, don't sit there.

FICK *(On the corner, to Dopey.)* Hey, ain't we seen this once?

DOPEY It's important.

A CHILD Trick or treat!?

FICK They're new!

DOPEY Shut up, for Chris' sake.

BONNIE Screw it; I'm paying no fifty cents for one Coke.

KAY *(To John.)* Toast with that.

BOB Fifty cents you can get a good high.

BONNIE Gimme a grilled cheese, hell, if I'm going to spend a fortune. One goddamned Coke.

KAY And a jack.

BONNIE Christ, you'd think this place was the Ritz!

DAVID *(To Bob.)* Come on up to my room. It won't kill you.

ANN It won't kill you, Bob.

STRANGER *(Enters and comes to Joe.)* Hi again.

JOE I don't know you.

BOB Knock it off.

DAVID Come on up with me, it won't hurt you.

BOB *(To Ann.)* How much scratch? Jack? Tonight?

ANN None of your damn business. Ask Sammy, you want to know.

JOHN You still keepin' that bum? What's he do with all that dough?

ANN He banks it. Or at least he'd better be banking it.

BOB Yeah, he banks it with Cameron or Chuckles.

ANN He don't truck with that junk. He'd better not; I'd crack him over the head.

(Dopey has turned to the audience as the Stranger first spoke. Dopey's speech is over the scene in the café. He speaks to the audience, quite casually.)

DOPEY See, what happened, the whole thing—Joe's a nice guy; he really is, but you bum around and you bum around and you start to wonder just how the hell you're going to ever get out of it; and you think if you could get in a good position—if you could get in with Chuckles. See, there's a lot of dough being made around. And he figured he'd have some of it. But see, he really didn't like the idea, the risk, of pushing, so he wasn't tough enough for it. And it's as simple as that. And Chuckles is big. These guys are big, some of them. Those boys are about as powerful as anyone in the country, I guess, and you don't cross them is the thing. It isn't done. Everything would have been okay, but, see Joe didn't know till a few days ago that he didn't want to go in with Chuckles. And Chuckles just naturally thought that Joe was holding out on him. Now for once he was patient. He sent a fellow to tell Joe to shape up. You saw that all right. And he tried to protect his investment. But even for once is a rare thing with Chuckles and Joe just didn't let him *know*. Now Chuckles is a big guy around here. He bleeds these guys around here. He can't have them see him made a fool of. And he gave Joe time. *(This last is almost screamed over the scene in the back.)*

FICK *(To Dopey.)* He did, that's true. That's true as can be. He wouldn't do that for me.

DOPEY *(Still to audience.)* So now they're gonna kill him.

FICK Joe?

DOPEY Yeah.

FICK We ain't seen this, have we?

(Dopey shakes his head, quietly; mouths, "No." They turn toward the stage to watch.)

STRANGER *(This follows Ann's last line before Dopey's speech to the audience: some of it will be covered by the end of Dopey's speech. He takes a cattle syringe from his pocket.)* You ever see one of these?

JOE What?

STRANGER One of these?

JOE A syringe? Christ, look at the size of it. What is it, a works for elephants? *(He laughs.)*

STRANGER For livestock. For cattle and pigs.

JOE You don't use something like that. That's too fancy. You use a works. An eye dropper, a piece of dollar. A needle.

TIM *(To Carlo.)* One, two, three, four, five.

STRANGER You do, huh?

CARLO No. No.

TIM Show then. One. Come on. One.

A CHILD Trick or treat.

JOHN Get out of here, you kids, go on.

STRANGER You do?

JOE They do. Why do you show me that?

ANN *(To Tim.)* He'll never get it.

CARLO One!

TIM *(Not too loudly.)* Bravo.

JOE *(Over.)* I've got no use for it.

DARLENE *(To Joe.)* What's wrong?

TIM Two. Come on.

JOE *(To Darlene.)* Nothing.

STRANGER Chuckles wanted you to know what hit you. Understand? That's a four-inch reach. You don't screw Chuckles. Understand?

JOE *(Stands. To Stranger.)* I got something to tell him.

DARLENE What? What is it?

JOE No! Come on.

JOHN *(To the Children.)* Go on, scram. Get out of here. Scram out of here. Go on!
    (Dim on the café. Spot on Joe and Stranger. Stranger reaches back and stabs Joe underhanded in the heart.)

BOB God!

TERRY Jesus!

DARLENE *(Over.)* No!
    (Simultaneously, the Children run out with the paper sacks flapping over their heads. They are screaming and yelling joyously. They split and two go one way, two another. They circle around the café and enter from the back and run through again. Lights up on café. The scene is repeated.)

JOHN Go on, scram. Get out of here. Scram out of here. Go on!
    (Dim on café. Spot on Joe and Stranger. The Stranger stabs Joe as before.)

BOB God!

TERRY Jesus!

DARLENE *(Over.)* No!
    (The children run out and circle the café as before. Lights up on café. The scene is repeated.)

JOHN Go on, scram. Get out of here. Scram out of here. Go on!
    (Dim on café. Spot on Joe and Stranger. The Stranger stabs Joe.)

BOB God!

TERRY Jesus!

(The children run through the café.)

JOE *(Pulls a number of white packets from his pocket and spills them all over the floor in front of him.)* I don't want them. I don't want it! Take them! Take them back! I don't want them!

(The children split in twos and run off screaming.)

DARLENE *(Over screaming.)* No, no, no, no!

(The Stranger runs off. Joe falls among Bob, Terry, Ann, Carlo, and Tim. Joe is taken behind the counter, away, out of sight of the audience. Not hidden, but removed from audience's sight. There is a time lapse. No one mentions the stabbing. Darlene sits through this scene without comment or without looking up.)

TIG *(Instantly, as soon as Joe falls. Frank is behind the counter now.)* What the hell are you talking about...

FRANK Why don't you stop coming in here, you don't—

TIG What the hell, you're trying to screw—

FRANK *(Cutting in.)* Get on out now.

TIG You trying to cheat me outta four bucks, baby, you can't pull—

FRANK I never cheat you outta nothing.

TERRY *(Over, to David.)* You queers just sit down, take it easy.

TIG I gave you a five, a five, you son of—

FRANK You get on out of here.

TIG You want to step outside? You want to step out from behind that counter, baby? You watch it, Frank.

JOHN *(Cutting in.)* Come on, Tig, give up, go on out.

FRANK Get out of this place.

TIM Try again.

ANN He's not gonna git it, I know.

CARLO Yes.

TIG Ah, come on, I gave him a five, man, you know what he's trying.

JOHN Come on, go on, Tig.

CARLO One.

JOHN Come on, go on, Tig.

TIG *(Leaving.)* You wait, Frank; you'll get yours, buddy.

FRANK *(After Tig has gone.)* Get on out of here, bum!

TIG *(Yelling back heatedly.)* Alright, now, goddammit I'm out, you just shut your mouth, Frank; you stupid bastard. Buddy, you're really gonna get it one day, Frank, and I want to be there to watch it. You're gonna get your head split open, dumb bastard.

FICK *(Very clearly during the fray, to Dopey, who ignores the question)* Hey, where's Joe?

RUST *(Running in to café.)* Hey, they got Jerry Joe in the can!

BOB Jerry the fairy?

DAVID You watch who you're calling names.

RUST He tried to put the make on a cop.

BOB They gonna book him?

RUST Whatta you mean? He tried to put the make on a cop. Hell, yes, they'll book him. He had eight bombinos on him! Man, are they hot for that stuff. *(General crowd reaction.)*

TIM She's right, you'll never learn.

CARLO *Sí*—no, yes! I will.

TIM Say, "Yes, I will."

CARLO Yes, I will.

(General crowd murmur to themselves during this.)

TIM You're getting the wrong damn accent. Just repeat it. Take it slow. You'll learn.

ANN Not a chance, Timmy. He's never learned anything.

TIM He will. One.

CARLO *(Repeating rapidly.)* One.

TIM Two.

CARLO Two.

TIM Three.

CARLO Three.

TIM Four.

CARLO Four.

TIM Five.

CARLO Fife.

TIM Five, Carlo; five, five!

CARLO *(Overlapping.)* Yes, I know. Five.

TIM Good, six.

CARLO Six.

(On "six" the quartette enters with a downbeat as at the beginning, singing the first five bars of the rock'n'roll song.)

TIM Come on!

ANN *(Loudly breaking it up.)* No. Stop it! No, stop it. You can't do it that way. It isn't right.

(They stop, wander off for a retake.)

ANN *(Apologetically.)* It's just not it, you know—not right.

(During Ann's speech Tim and Carlo have begun counting again. They reach "seven" and the quartette returns as before with as much of the song. Ann and John shout them down. Everyone is wandering about aimlessly.)

ANN *(To quartette.)* No, come on. Stop it.

TERRY *(To quartette.)* Knock it off—come on.

ANN *(To John.)* It's just not the way to end it.

(Quartette exits as before.)

JOHN I *know.* Try to tell them something. God.
   (Tim and Carlo have started over again. Dopey, Rake, and Bob have run up to stop the quartette.)

TIM Four.

CARLO Four.

TIM Five.

CARLO Five.

TIM Good, six.

CARLO Six.

TIM Seven.

CARLO Seven.

TIM Eight.

CARLO Eight.

TIM Nine.

CARLO Nine.

TIM Ten.

CARLO Ten.

TIM Good!
   (At "ten" Dopey, Rake and Bob begin their round, downstage center. This time not as a round, but all singing softly and liltingly.)

DOPEY, RAKE, and BOB
   They laugh and jab
   cavort and jump
   and joke and gab
   and grind and bump.

   They flip a knife
   and toss a coin
   and spend their life
   and scratch their groin

   They pantomime
   a standing screw
   and pass the time
   with nought to do.

   They swing, they sway
   this cheerful crew,
   with nought to say
   and nought to do.
   (The cast hums the tune very softly. During the song the crêpe-paper and

Halloween decorations ascend slowly. Everyone in the café picks up the "set" as before and slowly walks the set back toward its original position. Babe walks, as before, beside the others, not carrying the set. The lights dim slowly at the beginning of Dopey, Rake, and Bob's song.)

FICK *(Over the singing, cued by Tim's "Good!" He is wandering about the stage as at the beginning.)* Hey, buddy, hey, fellow...hey, you got a cigarette on you? Hey...Hey, Ann? Uh, cold, huh? Uh, Dopey, you got...Hey... Hey...

(The song has finished. Several continue to hum. Everyone sets the "set" back in its original place and takes a position similar to the beginning, only Fick is sitting at a table and Darlene and Ann are at the counter, backs to audience. The lights hold at about half.)

RAKE *(To no one, looking at no one.)* You travel around, I mean a hustler travels around...

DOPEY *(To no one, to himself.)* And they cut down, through one century to the one before that, and the one before that....

FICK *(At the booth, to himself.)* You know what I mean? You know what I mean?...You know what I mean?...I mean...

DARLENE *(To Ann, very slow, tired, after a kind of sigh.)* And, I don't know. Everyone was so tired and so down, and I thought, Christ, aren't we even moving? You know?

(The lights have faded out. Curtain.)

END OF PLAY

The Sand Castle

or

There is a Tavern in the Town

or

Harry Can Dance

For LoVerne and Tony

INTRODUCTION

I went to San Diego to go to college at San Diego State. I would live with my father and stepmother, my two paternal brothers and two girls, wards of the state, they had taken in. I lasted about six months in the house. (See *Lemon Sky*) After I was kicked out I moved in with other students at State. Not the people in this play. This is just where I spent every hour I could, drawn by the incredible poet LoVerne Brown and her children and their friends. I've kept myself out of this one. Well, actually I've kept us all out. The story is absurd, a foolish plot to display a wonderful extended family.

All my friends were writers. I took a class called Directed Writing to share one class with Owen, who was a year older than I. The class was really Undirected Writing. Owen said he was going to write a story. I said I would too. I might never have started writing without that class. Sasha was in the class. So was Jill, I think. We all passed our work around, being mildly critical, feeling like writers. When I moved to Chicago I continued to send stories back to Sasha, whose actual name was Tanya, for criticism. When I wrote that first play (Since, I pray, destroyed) I sent a copy to her and one to LoVerne. LoVerne said it didn't matter if it was any good, she was proud of me for having finished it. Love that woman. Sasha/Tanya was a little more critical but equally encouraging. I told her if I ever had anything published it would be dedicated to her as she had become my only sounding-board. At school we had a writing club. We sat on the floor in a big circle, maybe fifteen of us, passed around a gallon of wine and read our stories aloud. At Circle Rep, starting years ago, and now at The Lab, we do essentially the same thing, saving the wine for the day's end. It may be that nobody else needs a cheering section, encouragement, feedback, but it was very important to me. Still is.

When I left San Diego, not to return for twenty-seven years, the whole crowd came downtown to the bus station to see me off. We said we'd keep in touch forever.

PRODUCTION

The Sand Castle was first presented at La Mama Experimental Theater Club, in New York City, in August, 1965. It was directed and designed by Marshall W. Mason; and the lighting was by Dennis B. Parichy. The assistant to the director was Charles Golden. The cast, in order of appearance, was as follows:

Kenny ....Walter Harris
Sasha ....Joyce Aaron
Owen ....Michael Griswold

Joan ....Claris Erickson
Calvin ....John Kramer
Irene ....Angela Wood
Clint ....Beeson Carroll

CHARACTERS

Irene, a thin, quiet woman of considerable bearing, 40
Owen, her son, 22
Joan, her daughter, 20
Kenny, her son, 12
Sasha, a friend of the family, 20
Clint, Irene's boyfriend
Calvin, a friend of the family, 26

SCENE

The living room and front porch of a house, the last on the street, on Ocean Beach, San Diego, California.

On the back wall of the living room is the door to Irene's bedroom (right) and an alcove with doors to Owen's bedroom and Joan's bedroom (left). On the wall left, is a door to the kitchen which would be at the back of the house. The room is furnished with necessities: the sofa is a kind of iron cot with bolsters, there is a large old dining table and four unmatched chairs around it near the kitchen door. Several bookcases are against the walls. They hold a symbiotic combination of old, old novels and heavy college textbooks. The bookcase, a desk, everything is covered with papers. Papers and books are stacked in several corners. There is an overstuffed chair with a floor lamp behind it near the door to Irene's bedroom.

The floor of the house is covered with a light dusting of sand. It would be impossible to keep out.

The high, hard beach rises behind the house and obscures the ocean which is heard distantly throughout the play. The house should seem almost to be growing up from the beach rather than being half-covered by it. The front porch is covered with sand. It piles up from the yard against the steps, almost making a ramp. The yard is surrounded by a low adobe wall, there are a few scrubby plants in the sandy yard.

It is still quite light outside when the play begins, half an hour or so after sunset.

Summer.

THE SAND CASTLE

Irene is seated, quite proper, rather tired, at the chair, reading, Owen is play-
ing solitaire at the dining table, Sasha, also at the table, her chair a little out
from the table, is looking indifferently through an old school annual, Joan is
sprawled on the sofa looking through several books. Kenny comes forward,
Joan hums the first few notes of a tune, Irene says softly "shhhh," without look-
ing up. Joan looks to her brother, who hasn't noticed, so intent on his announce-
ment of the play, and smiles tolerantly as Kenny speaks to the audience.

KENNY *(Brightly.)* I get to begin the play now, and I get to close it later on with
little narrations—little scenes or speeches. And I sing in one of the songs
too, later on. *(Clears his throat.)* I'm Kenny, the younger son, and there's a
sister named Joan—my sister—and my brother named Owen and our
mother is—we call Reen, her name is Irene. Our last name, the family
name, is Renolds, after our father who was killed in the war, but you don't
have to worry about that because it doesn't have anything to do with the
play.
(Owen says "Thank God," without looking up. Joan laughs at this, quickly
covered up. Kenny continues without hearing them.)
KENNY And there's a neighbor, a girl who comes over all the time, she spends
all her time here and she's just like one of…
SASHA *(Looking up from the book, quite casually to Joan.)* Who'd you have in
psych? Last term? Didn't you get…*(Realizes Kenny is announcing the play.*
Shuts up quickly with a grimace, sinks into her chair shyly and goes back to
the book.)
KENNY *(After a brief tolerant pause.)* Her name is Sasha. She's a friend of my sister's.
(Joan mouths "Professor Morton" behind Kenny. Sasha mouths "Who?" Joan
repeats the name, Sasha still not understanding, repeats "Who?" then shrugs
and goes back to the book. Kenny continues without pause.)

KENNY She's over all the time, they're all juniors and seniors up at State. And there's another friend of the family called Calvin. He's digging around in the bedroom right now but he comes on in a minute. He's got a boat and he's married. He studies, I think, either at State or at the Scripps Institute of…

OWEN *(Interrupting.)* Oh, for Christ's sakes, Kenny, would you shut up and get on with it?

KENNY *(Quickly.)* Okay. *(Momentarily stopped, not knowing if he should shut up or go on, questioningly half-turns.)* Well, which do you…

OWEN Go on with it. God.

KENNY *(Rapidly now.)* And there's a boy friend of Reen's—that's our mother, remember—his name is Clint. He drives a bus past here and stops in. You'll see them all anyway—you see them now, and they'll—the others—will be easy enough to—you know—to—you know—to figure out. *(Pulls more erect, quite unconsciously.)*
(Everyone seems to tighten, straighten, become more aware of themselves as Kenny announces rather formally.)

KENNY The Sand Castle. Or There is a Tavern in the Town. Or Harry Can Dance. *(A tight little bow of the head in spite of himself. He turns and goes into Owen's bedroom.)*

JOAN *(Immediately to Sasha.)* Professor Morton.

SASHA Oh, god. He's a creep.
(Irene simultaneously clears her throat gently.)

KENNY *(Simultaneously, as he enters Owen's bedroom.)* Okay, Calvin.

OWEN *(Beat. Playing solitaire, directing an orchestra broadly with both hands waving in the air, sings loudly to himself.)* There is! A tavern in the town!

EVERYONE *(Including Clint, Calvin and Kenny off stage. Those on stage turn directly to the audience. Singing very loudly. Not Owen.)* IN THE TOWN!

OWEN *(Surprised.)* Come on, shut up for Christ's sake; can't you hear I'm trying to concentrate? I'm nearly winning.
(Everyone is still. Owen takes three cards, looks at them, plays one. Studies a moment. Singing to himself in a high sincere falsetto.)

OWEN In the town.

CALVIN *(Enters from Owen's bedroom. He has an armload of very old comic books.)* Hey, look what I found. I didn't know you had all these, Owen. *(Dumps them on the floor.)*

JOAN *(Over.)* Oh, god.

CALVIN Lord, remember comics?

JOAN Don't drag those things out here, Cal, they'll be here for a month.

IRENE Owen and Kenny must have a thousand of them.

OWEN *(Has noticed but not said anything. Quietly to the cards.)* Put them back when you're finished, too.

SASHA (*Walking over to Calvin who has sat on the floor.*) What? Good Lord, Batman.

CALVIN There must be hundreds. There's a Wonder Woman in here somewhere. God, she was almost my foster mother. (*To Irene.*) This was when I was about eight, of course.

OWEN (*Without looking up.*) Shhhhhhh.

IRENE Owen's almost winning.

OWEN Don't tear those up, either.

KENNY (*From the bedroom.*) Hey, Joan?

OWEN (*Pause. Singing quietly.*) And there my true love sits her down.

KENNY (*Off.*) Joan? (*Pause.*)

OWEN (*Pause. Singing quietly.*) ...Sits her dow-wn and...

KENNY (*Off.*) Joan?

JOAN Well, what? For Christ's sake, Kenny, I'm not deaf—

KENNY (*Off.*) I can't find my shoes in here.

JOAN —Honestly, you'd sit in there for an hour if nobody answered you without ever saying what, just screaming *Joan* over and over. (*Back to her book.*)

KENNY (*Off.*) Joan? (*Slight pause.*)

JOAN Oh, god. Well, what? Jesus.

KENNY (*Off.*) I can't find my shoes, I told you and I know I took them off here because I remember last night when you said why was I wearing my shoes I had them on and when I went to bed I kicked them off at the foot of the bed by that little table there.

JOAN (*An aside, disgruntled look at the audience, then back to the door. Portentously.*) Why are you telling me all this? I haven't seen them, Kenny.

KENNY (*Off.*) Owen?

OWEN (*Without looking up.*) Go to hell.

SASHA (*To audience.*) They're this typical American family, see.

KENNY (*Off.*) Have you seen them?

JOAN (*Reading.*) What do you want with them?

KENNY (*Entering.*) I want to wear them. (*To audience.*) Hi, again. That was me yelling. Wouldn't that be a great entrance if you hadn't seen me before?

IRENE (*Just a word over.*) Do you need them, Kenny?

KENNY I don't especially need them, but a fella likes to know where his shoes...

OWEN Kenny, I'm trying to concentrate.

CALVIN (*Reading.*) God, was she great.

SASHA He's cheating anyway.

OWEN Who's cheating?

SASHA (*Back to a comic.*) I thought you were concentrating.

OWEN *(Singing loudly.)* Fare thee well, for I must leave you, do not let the parting grieve you…

CALVIN and SASHA *(To audience. Pizzicato.)* And re-mem-ber that the best of friends must part. *(Sasha says "Some-times part.")*

CALVIN Take it!

SASHA *(Instant vamp. Mock-torch singer, moving from Calvin to Owen. Much hips, breasts and sex.)* Fare thee well, for I must leave you, do-oo-oo not let! The parting! Grieve you!

KENNY *(Over the above.)* I'm going out. I don't need my shoes. I guess they're just gone!

OWEN Come on, I'm losing. Be a little quiet.

(Kenny swings out the screen door, off the porch and off.)

CALVIN We can't. We must bid farewell to your fair-weather brother. *(Waving off.)* Fare well, fair-weather brother. Fare thee well. Adieu.

JOAN and SASHA *(Calvin has a speech at the door over this charade. Both Joan and Sasha are up. At "Adieu" they begin to perform a kind of soft—high-stepping sister act for the audience. Obviously semi-choreographed, they dance and sing as Calvin waves off to Kenny.)* Adieu! Adieu, kind friends, adieu. *(Sasha: Adieu, adieu.)* I can. No longer stay with you. *(Joan: Stay with you-oo.)* I must hang my head from a weeping willow tree—*(Sasha: [a spoken aside] What the hell are the words?)* AND MAY. The world go well with thee! With thee!

CALVIN *(Over the above. Narratively. Waving off.)* There he goes. Sinking into the sunset. That's the way, Kenny. Rape all the women and ravage the lands. Kill a dragon or two. Tote that barge, rape those women, lift that skirt! Look at him. There he goes across the beach—all the way to New York City, U.S.A. *You'll make it, Porgy!*

OWEN *(Who has been trying to ignore them.)* SHUT UP!

(Calvin, Joan and Sasha break into a full, loud song and dance, creating a general havoc. Very bawdy, all over the stage. Also a semi-choreographed dance with kicks, etc. Owen is trying to get them out of the house. He throws a comic book at Joan. They march around his table—he tries to save his card game; destroys the game himself by tossing all the cards into the air. During this they sing loudly.)

CALVIN, JOAN and SASHA There is a tavern in the town. In the town.

And there my true love sits him down. Sits him down.

And drinks his gin, by a weeping willow tree.

And never, never thinks of me. Of me.

(During the song Sasha comes straight to the audience—kicks her legs Can-Can fashion two or three times and says in a wildly wicked flirt: "Hi there!")

"Oceanside three—four seven four nine." and goes back to the group. As Owen continues to push them out the front door.)

CALVIN, JOAN and SASHA Fare thee well for I must leave you!

OWEN Leave already. Leave. Part!

CALVIN, JOAN and SASHA Do not let the parting grieve you!

OWEN Like hell it grieves me, go on—outside.

CALVIN, JOAN and SASHA And remember that the best of friends must sometimes part.

(As Owen continues to chase them and straighten the chairs up after them, etc. Calvin opens the front screen and they all march out.)

CALVIN, JOAN and SASHA Fare thee well for I must leave thee—do not let the parting grieve thee—And remember that the best of friends must part.

(Owen throws a pillow that hits the front screen as Calvin quickly closes it behind them.)

OWEN Friends, hell. Part! If I had a front door I could really shut them out. I'd lock them out on the porch.

(Irene through the dance, began by sitting, amused. Toward the end she stands—looking just a bit worried, apprehensive. Now she is smiling again.)

KENNY *(As Calvin, Joan and Sasha burst out onto the porch, Kenny enters with Clint, who is carrying his jacket, two six-packs of beer, his change gadget from the bus and his hat.)* Clint was parking his bus.

JOAN Hi, Clint.

CLINT *(Handing Joan the beer.)* Take this. You got any ice? They can't stay cold for long.

CALVIN Ice! Ice!

OWEN *(Inside. Over the above—begins to pick up the cards and return them to the table.)* Damn them, I'm certain I could have won that hand, too.

IRENE *(Also over the above.)* I think I heard Clint's bus.

CALVIN Ice! *(Enters living room and crosses to kitchen.)* Do you have anything perishable in the icebox? I didn't think so. I want to borrow your ice. I'll bring it right back. *(Exits to kitchen.)*

IRENE Sure, you're welcome to it, I suppose.

OWEN Now, don't start tracking through here again. Just—

SASHA *(Re-enters. Crosses to her book, picks it up and goes back out front.)* I forgot my book. We're having a picnic on the grass. Joan and I are going to strip and Kenny and Cal will play the mandolin.

IRENE *(Laughing.)* What grass?

CALVIN *(Entering from the kitchen with a small block of ice on tongs.)* We're improvising grass, actually. You should do something about your lawn.

OWEN Perhaps we could do something about our lawn if we could get everyone off it for a minute.

CALVIN *(To Irene. Over the last of Owen's speech.)* Clint brought us a half-case of beer.

CLINT *(Out front.)* It's a stupid day to drive anyway. At least it's cooled off some from what it was.

JOAN *(Out front.)* No business probably on a Saturday.

OWEN *(Over above. To Calvin.)* You're dripping.

CALVIN *(Not moving.)* That's great of him, huh?

(*Sasha opens a beer out front that spews up in the air.*)

IRENE Calvin, you're not going to have time to get any work done if you don't get at it before...

CALVIN Just one beer and I'll get right at it. God, what a school teacher.

IRENE You asked me to prod you; I'm prodding.

OWEN You're dripping all over—

CALVIN *(Leaving the living room.)* Your floor's sandy.

KENNY *(Enters and crosses to the kitchen as Calvin goes out.)* Clint's here, Reen.

CLINT *(Simultaneously—to Calvin.)* Great, great. Hey, Irene?

OWEN *(Who has followed Calvin to the door.)* Well, you'd be sandy too if you lived on a beach with a hundred maniacs running through—*(The screen door slams in his face.)*—the house and all over the beach and back and forth. Wouldn't you?

JOAN *(To Calvin about the ice.)* That'll do fine.

CLINT *(Looking up to Owen.)* Hi, Owen.

OWEN Hi, Clint. God—

CLINT *(Coming in now. To Irene.)* I left the bus running out front.

OWEN *(Turning from the door.)* —damn.

CLINT You want a beer? I'll bring you one in.

IRENE Hi, Clint.

(*He pecks her on the cheek.*)

CLINT I'll get you one. Hey, Calvin? Another one, okay? Buddy? Pitch it in.

OWEN Pitch it in, oh, god.

CLINT *(Catches it.)* It's not too cold, I'm afraid. God, a day like this, huh? *(Opens it. It spews over the table, over Owen's cards.)* Damn, look at that!

OWEN Awh, come on, Clint. Damn.

CLINT What's wrong? Too warm, huh?

OWEN Your can of beer spewed up when you opened it and went all over the playing cards.

CLINT *(Lightly tosses him a towel from the back of the chair Sasha was sitting in.)* Sorry. Here. *(Lays his jacket across the chair, sits the change gadget on the table.)* I just got a minute. I left the bus running. How come you got that ice, your fridge not working?

IRENE No, it went out yesterday. I mentioned it.

CLINT You just got the icebox? Hey—Calvin. Bring that ice back in here. Stupid. You can put the beer on top of it in the box. I ask him if there's ice and he brings it out.

CALVIN *(From out front.)* Yeah? Okay.

SASHA Don't shake them up.

OWEN Soaking wet. They smell like brewery passes.

CLINT So how's your day?

IRENE Warm, but okay. How's yours?

CLINT Ah, bad. No problems but it's a stupid day for a bus. I'm sorry I couldn't get off. They didn't need busses today. I stopped off at the Surf and talked to the guys awhile, I'm still ahead of schedule.

IRENE Everyone's on vacation. The beach was packed.

CLINT It's too hot for out there.

OWEN *(To himself.)* What we need around here is a scout leader.
(Calvin, Joan and Sasha come trailing across the room with ice and beer. Sasha and Calvin go into the kitchen. Joan carries nothing, stands near the kitchen door.)

CLINT *(To Irene.)* Maybe tomorrow we could take a ride—us two, okay? Up into the mountains or somewhere.

IRENE *(Very pleased.)* Wonderful. That would be fine.

CLINT Everyone's up in the mountains anyway.

JOAN God, we're all so stupid; I don't know why we didn't think of bringing the beer in instead of the ice out.

KENNY *(Comes out of the kitchen, with a peanut butter sandwich, leans against the doorway.)* Yeah, you are.

CLINT Sure, the milk'll spoil.

KENNY *(Over the sandwich.)* There isn't any.

CLINT Well, whatever.

OWEN There's a little piece of butter and an empty instant coffee jar.

CLINT Wouldn't that be fun? I'd like that.

IRENE I'd love to. I'll pack us something to eat, if you'd like.

CLINT Good then.

IRENE I haven't been up in the mountains for years.

CLINT Well, we'll remedy that. Just us.

JOAN What?

CALVIN *(Re-entering with Sasha.)* All set.

SASHA We put them right on top.

JOAN *(To Clint.)* What?

CLINT Just never mind, nosey.

JOAN Well, what?

OWEN He said never mind, nosey.

CLINT *(To Irene.)* You don't have classes on Sunday do you? When's that thing over?

CALVIN *(Picks up several books from the desk.)* I've got to get something done.

OWEN I don't know why, you've wasted the whole day.

IRENE Next week. Too bad, too. It's been fun.

SASHA *(To Irene.)* Sure it has.

KENNY *(To audience.)* It's always like this. Sometimes worse.

CALVIN *(To Sasha who is collecting Owen's cards.)* Do you want to help me with this?

CLINT *(To Irene.)* College kids, huh?

SASHA *(To Calvin.)* No, thanks. What'd you want me to read to you?

IRENE Most of them, not all.

KENNY *(Over the sandwich. To the audience.)* See, Reen's a teacher out at this summer conference for writers. They have lectures and like that for two weeks every summer—like a convention. And Reen's one of the main poetry speakers. She used to be a poet—a real one, and she was published in all the little magazines and in a lot of the big ones and books and so she's this big name out there. I mean it's been twenty years probably, but she's still a great teacher. And she instructs the college graduates and all that want to be writers.

IRENE *(Quickly.)* They're not all graduates, Kenny.

CLINT *(Finishing his beer.)* Look, I gotta run. I have to put the bus in the barn and then I'm through.

IRENE Swell.

CLINT I've been on another twelve hours; we aren't supposed to do that. Everyone's on vacation.

JOAN I'll bet it's good money, though. *(Joan straightens Clint's coat on the back of the chair.)*

CLINT I suppose.

IRENE Did you leave the bus running?

KENNY Is Jill coming over today, Calvin?

CLINT Yeah, I'll spend all the tax-payer's money. I thought I'd just be a minute. I always stay longer. Wonder why? *(He takes the jacket.)*

CALVIN *(To Kenny.)* I don't imagine, why should she? No, I don't imagine.

OWEN She can't run all over, Kenny, my god.

JOAN *(To Owen.)* Why not?

IRENE I'm glad you do stay, Clint.

OWEN Well, she shouldn't.

SASHA Why don't you still write, Reen?

IRENE *(Softly. Quickly.)* I will.

CLINT What time you want to get started in the morning?

SASHA Of course, how could she around here?

CALVIN *(Having trouble trying to read.)* That's what I was going to say. I can't even read.

CLINT What time you want to start in the morning, Irene?

IRENE What? Oh, whatever you think. Early?

OWEN What's wrong with around here?

SASHA *(To audience.)* Isn't he great? A real jewel, huh?

CLINT I think early, yeah. You sure you have time to fix up some food for tomorrow?

IRENE I'm sure.

JOAN *(Pleasantly.)* What about tomorrow?

OWEN *(To Joan.)* Mind your own business.

CLINT *(To Sasha who is finishing her beer.)* You drink all that beer and I'll whack you one, you hear?

SASHA *(Provocatively.)* Clint! Please, I'm an innocent girl.

CLINT You see her dancing around when I came up?

JOAN Sometimes we just feel like dancing.

CLINT Just don't drink all the beer up.

SASHA Admit it, you weak, groveling male; you're under my spell.

CLINT *(He and Irene are moving toward the front door.)* Yeah, You just leave four cans of beer for us for tomorrow or you'll be under something.

SASHA You can only go so far with me, Clint. If you know what I mean.
(Clint and Irene laugh.)

IRENE *(Gently.)* What are we going to do with her? I don't know.

CLINT She'll find out.

SASHA *(A parting shot.)* You want me for my body!

CALVIN Come on, I'm trying to read.

JOAN Honestly, Sasha.

CLINT The bus will probably be hot as a bastard.

SASHA *(Calling.)* There's a full moon tonight.

CLINT *(As he and Irene go out onto the front porch.)* I'll full-moon you. *(To Irene.)* The bus'll probably be steaming hot.

JOAN You'd say anything, God.

OWEN As a matter of fact, there's no moon at all tonight if you're interested.

SASHA *(Starting to lay out the cards for a game of solitaire.)* Damn. Well, no wonder nothing's working for me.

JOAN You make such an ass of yourself.

CALVIN Come on, I'm trying to read.

IRENE *(To Clint.)* It's beginning to cool off some.

CLINT Muggy night.

SASHA What can I tell you, I'm a sucker for bus drivers; you should excuse the expression.

IRENE It is.

SASHA I like to joke with Clint. It doesn't budge him.

CALVIN You should excuse the—

SASHA —Just get back to your plankton and never mind.

IRENE That'll be wonderful tomorrow; I used to love to drive up into the mountains.

CLINT We have to get an early start though.

IRENE Anytime you want.

CLINT If I stayed over we could start anytime; that's not a bad idea.

IRENE *(She sits on the porch railing.)* What's not a bad idea?

CLINT You heard me. Of course we might not get started at all.

IRENE Yes. I don't think it's such a good idea.

CLINT Well, then, why don't you marry me and we could go up into the mountains every weekend. Have a place up there, maybe.

IRENE Wonderful. With a room for Owen, and a room for Joan and one for Sasha and one…

CLINT Sasha isn't even family. You don't have to take any of them along. Hell, they can take care of themselves by now or they never will.

IRENE You'd think.

CLINT Or we could move up to Fresno if that's what you want. How serious are you when you talk about moving back up there?

IRENE Owen is dead serious, I suppose. And Joan—they can't stand it down here. Kenny it doesn't matter. He doesn't know Fresno at all, he was born down here.

CLINT You might really go back there sometime then?

IRENE I don't know. I don't much—I don't believe I want to, but Owen, that's the only thing he knows, and Joan's…

CLINT Well, hell, then—that's what I thought. Why don't we get married and send them to Fresno. I don't want to go to Fresno. What the hell's in Fresno?

IRENE I don't know.

CLINT So why don't you marry me?

IRENE Oh, god, Clint. *(Smiles at him a moment.)* Look at you. I must be the most ordinary woman in the world. I feel as if I were being hooked by some vast advertising campaign.

CLINT What do you mean, you didn't answer my question.

IRENE To be attracted to you. Look at you.

CLINT What?

IRENE Well, you're Marlboro Country and the Camel Man and Randolph Scott, it's just ridiculous. All the things that we're supposed to believe are masculine and red-blooded in the pulp fiction sense. Your dreadful speech and your laughable—almost self-conscious clumsiness and your honest sincerity and middle-class, proletarian sensibility and even your total lack of good looks.

CLINT Really?

IRENE Really what, Clint?

CLINT You don't think I've got any looks but you're attracted to me anyway, huh?

IRENE *(As though studying him.)* Women would consider you not classically attractive but chock full of sex appeal, I think. And I find that attractive. All-American female snob that I am, and I say to myself, Irene, that's the most obvious thing you've ever done in your life.

CLINT You really think I'm sexy, huh?

IRENE Well, if any of the girls in my class ever came up with a character like you—accurately described, of course—I'd wash her mouth out with soap.

CLINT So why don't you marry me? And we'll go to Fresno or wherever, I don't care. Family or none.

IRENE You watch it, Clint. I just might.

CLINT *(A rather neat dodge.)* I'm not going to give you another chance until tomorrow. In the meantime, just to prove what you say, I think I should stay here tonight.

IRENE *(Just the slightest pause.)* What would they say about that?

CLINT Yeah, you're just trying to get out of it. I thought you said I was sexy.

IRENE Of course you are.

CLINT Sure.

IRENE All American. Bus driver, my god, bowler, baseball fan, beer drinker, you even wear a tenement T-shirt. Those are symbols of virility in this country, didn't you know that?

CLINT What's a tenement T-shirt?

IRENE *(Tucks a finger under the strap of his undershirt.)* That.

CLINT Those are sexy?

IRENE Oh, Clint, you don't know! It's absolutely the knitted materialization of American masculinity in the woman's eye.

CLINT Cheap too, I'm even practical.

IRENE See, you're all-over coarse hair, which is basic. You're basic which is basic and you've got nearly-but-not-quite-crossed eyes. That rather resemble a dumb animal's.

CLINT Dumb, huh?

IRENE Forget that—it's the animal that's important. And you're big.

CLINT Oh, hell yes.

IRENE That seems to be the key to the whole criterion right now. The suave gentleman is definitely out just now.

CLINT Six foot two, two hundred pounds.

IRENE Well, do you realize that a few hundred years ago people never even got that big? You're right off the assembly line. And you've got hands that could cover a dinner plate—and my own daughter came home the other day to inform me flatly that the size of a man's hands definitely pre-disclosed his genital endowment.

CLINT *(Laughing.)* Joan did?

IRENE *(Also nearly laughing now.)* I've been meaning to say something to her about that but I haven't thought of anything yet. I just feel she's totally outrun all knowledge a girl her age is reasonably—at least in a healthy state of mind…

CLINT Well, maybe she's right—

IRENE Oh, I have no doubt about it at all. I just feel I should at least inquire if this knowledge was passed on by some teenage sexual sage or gained first-hand through endless experiment.

(Clint laughs.)

IRENE I mean, when I think of the trial and error even the simplest hypothesis has to be subjected to…

CLINT Come on—you always get off the question at hand, Irene. You're good at that.

IRENE What? Was there a question at hand?

CLINT Are you going to marry me?

IRENE Ask me tomorrow night.

CLINT Okay. Only a dozen times.

IRENE I'll say yes one day and we'll see how fast you run.

CLINT Not a chance, Irene, and you know it.

IRENE We'll see.

CLINT You just tell me and you'll see how high I can jump.

IRENE I bet.

CLINT You're a damn good catch yourself, Reen. I can't go on about it like you do and joke around, but you know it.

IRENE Let's face it, we're the match of the century.

CLINT You're a bright woman, Irene. You know what I mean.

IRENE And you're bright. Bright like a bonfire. Bright-smart, too; in a pseudo-stupid sort of way.

CLINT Now see? You say a dozen good things and you end up calling me stupid. I knew it. You've got to insult me before you send me home. Every night.

IRENE It just wouldn't work, Clint; what can I tell you? What time are you coming around tomorrow morning?

CLINT How about seven?

IRENE Seven? Well, okay.

CLINT It'll be ten before we get anywhere.

IRENE I know, I know. I said that's fine. I'll see you at seven.

CLINT Okay? Good night then.

IRENE *(As he begins to back off.)* Good night, Clint; I'll see you tomorrow.

JOAN *(Looking up from her book. Calling.)* Good night, Clint.

SASHA *(Seductively.)* Good night, Clint.

JOAN *(Over some.)* Oh, god, Sasha.

CLINT *(Calling over some.)* Good night. *(To Irene.)* Seven in the morning, okay then? I'll see you.

IRENE *(Turning toward the door.)* Good. Get some sleep.

(Joan puts down her book and goes to the door.)

CLINT Good night.

IRENE *(Laughing. Waves him away.)* Go on! *(She comes inside, turns to look off.)* *(Joan has joined her at the door.)*

JOAN Clint strikes me as the comfortable type that sits around the living room and watches television. The stay-at-home ilk.

IRENE You think? Probably he would be. I wouldn't mind that, though.

JOAN Would be? I mean by himself. Can't you just see him eating out at some coffee shop or sitting down to a whole string of Westerns with a frozen TV dinner in the oven?

OWEN I can't see him as anything.

JOAN The one-room, kitchenette type; sleeps on the sofa.

IRENE Probably.

SASHA You think?

JOAN In his socks.

SASHA I wouldn't think he'd be happy without a garage and woodsaws and an assortment of graduated wrenches.

IRENE You're probably very nearly right.

SASHA They come all rolled up in a blanket affair—the littlest one no bigger than a pin.

OWEN Ahhhh.

SASHA What?

OWEN *(Sweetly.)* The littlest wrench.

SASHA Shut up.

OWEN It sounds like a story by Oscar Wilde.

SASHA Shut up.

JOAN *(With an edge of superiority.)* No, not at all. Clint's too tranquil to be pothering around with wrenches.

IRENE He's quiet all right.

OWEN Nerveless.

SASHA *(Flatly.)* He's sexy.

IRENE Exactly. The teddy-bear type.

SASHA Right.

IRENE All very faithful and dedicated.

SASHA Faithful and dedicated—god, I love it.

JOAN *(With an irritated edge.)* You're going up in the mountains tomorrow?

IRENE We thought we would.

> *(Calvin, who has been trying to read, with difficulty, now begins to gather up his books.)*

OWEN Hey, great.

IRENE *(To Calvin.)* We're distracting you, aren't we? How much more have you got?

CALVIN Only about a chapter. Are you going to have time to read the paper on—

IRENE Yes, yes, of course. You don't have to ask.

SASHA What?

IRENE I'm his personal secretary this semester.

CALVIN Can I help it if I can't spell?

SASHA I'll bet she writes them for you. How much do you pay her?

CALVIN This one's on mollusk. Shellfish. Mollusca, as Barnes would say; snails, whelks, oysters, that lot.

SASHA Is there a lot of that lot?

IRENE *(Distastefully.)* Oh, lord, Calvin. I loathe shellfish. Clams?

CALVIN Yeah, and worse.

IRENE Oh, dear; oh, well.

CALVIN It'll be hard enough anyway because what I know about cuttlefish you could boil in a thimble, so I mostly just rambled around with a lot of double-talk. *(He takes the books and goes to Irene's bedroom.)*

OWEN *(To Irene.)* You're really driving up in the mountains?

IRENE *(As Calvin goes in.)* Shut the door, Calvin; it's all right.

CALVIN Swell.

OWEN That's great.

SASHA Tomorrow's the day the teddy-bears have their picnic.

JOAN It's a lot of trouble is all.

IRENE Not so...I have to pick up something for lunch.

JOAN I just despise picnics. Really, Reen, what a proletarian idea for Sunday afternoon. You know how long it's going to take you to get there? With traffic? It was probably a wonderful idea a hundred years ago.

SASHA Don't be silly.

JOAN Well, it's just absurd.

IRENE *(Good-naturedly.)* I don't think so.

JOAN *(Irritated.)* Well, Clint will just despise it.

SASHA He knows how to drive.

OWEN She just wants to come along and gum things up.

JOAN Oh, be quiet, Owen; you're not even funny. You're such an ass. *(She turns to look out the door again.)*

OWEN Don't call your own brother an ass; what does that make you? The sister of an ass.

SASHA *(Stacking up the cards from her solitaire game.)* Well, that's it.

IRENE What? Did you win?

OWEN Did you win?

SASHA Well, of course.

OWEN Let's see.

SASHA Too late.

OWEN Good god. With my cards, too. Give them back; I haven't won once in two years.

SASHA Of course not, you cheat. *(Picks up a comic book.)* What's that one.

OWEN Superman meets Plastic Man. Remember Plastic Man?

IRENE Sounds like a pretty uneven match.

OWEN They aren't enemies. Plastic Man makes his body into a shield to protect Superman from a hunk of Krypton.

JOAN *(Imitating Owen.)* Remember Krypton.

OWEN You aren't funny.

SASHA I don't know. I guess I'm getting old. I used to just love Plastic Man and any more all I can think of is all the vulgar things he could do.

OWEN You'd destroy anything.

JOAN *(Turning from the door.)* I think I'll go over and see Jill. You want to come, Sasha?

SASHA Jill? God, no. Not right this minute.

OWEN I will.

JOAN No. She doesn't want to see you. *(Disgusted—which is what she was after anyway.)* You'd drive her nuts.

OWEN What do you mean, I'd drive her nuts? Who sits around moaning all day, just *thinking* of morbid things to say. I honestly believe she just sits around thinking of ghastly tales to tell her. You should hear the things she comes out with. *I'd* drive her nuts; that's ridiculous.

JOAN I don't want to go anyway. Forget I mentioned it.

OWEN You say the stupidest things to her! *(Instant change to a fog of love.)* Oh, Jill!

JOAN Oh, god. You make me sick; you really do.

OWEN You don't even know what I'm talking about. I happen to be in love with Jill…

JOAN Come on, Calvin will hear you…

IRENE *(Over, Quietly.)* Owen.

OWEN I happen to feel it's a very beautiful experience to be able to love someone; I'm not ashamed of it. He knows it.

SASHA Everyone in San Diego County knows it; it's all you ever talk about. Jill and Thomas Wolfe.

OWEN It is not. You can just clam up, too.

SASHA Well, I can understand being mad about her after she gets married, but when she's going to have a baby, I'd think it would turn you off a little.

OWEN *(Adrift.)* Oh, no, no. You should see her. She's so fragile looking, so glowing—I love pregnant girls anyway.

JOAN God.

IRENE Owen, Calvin is trying to read. I don't imagine he can concentrate with us discussing his wife.

OWEN You should see her though.

SASHA You should have been born in the Eleventh Century.

OWEN No, she's so lovely. Isn't she, Reen?

IRENE She looks fat to me. Don't ask me.

OWEN No, she isn't. Women gain extra weight for the baby when they're pregnant.

SASHA It's called baby fat.

(Kenny comes running up the front steps. He trots into the house.)

OWEN You people don't know anything.

KENNY About what? Hey, guess what happened?

OWEN —She's probably home, too. Alone, of course. I don't know how he can do that. I should probably go over there.

IRENE *(To Joan.)* See what you started?

KENNY Reen? Guess what.

SASHA *(To Joan.)* Who did you have second year psych, you remember?

JOAN Morton. I had him all three years.

OWEN He's a creep.

KENNY Where's Calvin?

SASHA He is. What a creep.

KENNY Who? Calvin? How come?

SASHA Professor Morton.

KENNY Who's he?

JOAN A professor of psychology up at State. Jesus.

IRENE What happened, Kenny?

KENNY *(To the audience.)* Is it like this all the time or just when I come in?

IRENE Calvin's in the bedroom.

JOAN He gave the whole class a B minus.

KENNY What on earth for?

SASHA He's reading.

JOAN About cuttlefish.

KENNY Hey, Calvin!

IRENE He's working, Kenny.

CALVIN *(Off.)* Yeah?

IRENE That's okay, Calvin.

CALVIN *(Off.)* No, I'm just finishing, Reen. *(Entering.)* God, this is tough.

KENNY Did he give you a B minus?

IRENE Are you sure you're finished?

CALVIN Near enough. What, Kenny?

SASHA *(Very quickly now, as Kenny starts to speak up.)* How's the cuttlefish?

CALVIN That's the paper, this is water.

JOAN Tides, that sort of thing?

KENNY *(Lost.)* Wait.

CALVIN Density, salinity; that sort of thing.

OWEN *(To Sasha.)* Are you going home tonight?

SASHA *(Fliply.)* Home? Certainly not, I'm going out dancing.

OWEN *(This is a game.)* Oh? Where are you going?

JOAN God, that *is* hard.

CALVIN You're telling me.

KENNY Wait. *(Aside to Sasha.)* I had a line in there somewhere.

OWEN *(Over.)* I never could get that stuff.

SASHA Well, speak up.

KENNY Uhh…

OWEN Where you going dancing?

SASHA Well, to the El Morocco, of course. With Sue and Harry.

OWEN Sue and Harry. Oh, Sue's a great dancer.

CALVIN You'll love Sue.

SASHA Well, Harry's no mean stepper himself.

OWEN I didn't know Harry could dance.

KENNY *(Over.)* Come on…

IRENE *(Over.)* Speak up, Kenny. Step in.

SASHA You didn't know?

JOAN If you think Sue can dance.

CALVIN Well, of course Sue can dance.

OWEN I didn't think Harry could dance.

SASHA *(Brushing it aside.)* Yeah, well let me tell you, Harry can dance, like, I mean Harry can dance.

KENNY *(Rushing in to pick up the lost line. They have been ad libbing.)* Guess what happened!

OWEN About time, Jesus.
 (Simultaneously.)

JOAN Thank god, good grief, Kenny.

CALVIN Way to go, Kenny.

(Owen picks up a comic book, opens it.)

KENNY Guess what happened?

OWEN Well, what? God!

KENNY I'll bet it's the most important thing that's ever...

JOAN Kenny, just tell it or forget it.

KENNY *(Fading off.)* In my life...

IRENE What's that, Kenny?

KENNY You know Sunset Cliffs?

JOAN *(After a beat. Everyone is looking at Kenny.)* Yes, we know Sunset Cliffs. You're impossible.

KENNY Well, they caved in.

IRENE *(Not calm, not excited.)* Really, when?

KENNY Well—I don't know. *(He had expected a different reaction.)* This afternoon sometime.

JOAN How much?

CALVIN That's wild, how much?

KENNY *(Defensively.)* How do you mean?

CALVIN How much land?

KENNY Oh, about—I don't know. Maybe a third of the way to the road nearly.

CALVIN *(Flatly.)* I'll be damned.

IRENE The last time, when was it—

KENNY What?

IRENE The cliffs do that every year or two; they're weak.

CALVIN They're just sandstone.

KENNY Really? What does that mean?

OWEN Well, it means they're weak for one thing.

SASHA Every couple of years they do that. Another chunk falls off.

KENNY I didn't know that. It's spooky, isn't it? They've got—

IRENE I hope you didn't get too close.

KENNY You can't—let me tell you—they've got patrol cars along the road and they have those board fences across the way, and no one is allowed out onto the area there because they think it might do it again.

IRENE Was anyone hurt?

KENNY I don't think so.

SASHA The last time—the middle of the night, there were about four cars parked up there. I think it killed all but one.

KENNY Really? They just went over? Car and all?

JOAN Well, of course car and all; what do you think; it's going to take the people and leave the car?

KENNY Golly.

CALVIN Something like that I always remember—wasn't it Edgar Cayce who proph—

OWEN Yeah, if you want something spooky, Kenny. That's something for you.

KENNY What?

CALVIN I think he's the one—he predicted the beginning and end of some war and whatever the name of the volcano in Japan that erupted and killed so many people...

KENNY Really?

CALVIN And the island that blew up a few years back; he predicted that. And one of the prophecies of his was that during a violent earthquake the whole state of California would slide off into the Pacific ocean. The whole state—part of Oregon.

(Kenny holds his breath.)

SASHA What? Are you sure?

CALVIN Sure. Sometime around now. Within ten years, it's supposed to be.

IRENE Closer than that, I think. It makes you wonder.

JOAN I didn't know that.

(All rather overlapping and chatty here.)

CALVIN It's true, that's one of his predictions.

IRENE I'm not sure it was Cayce, but someone just as accredited as Cayce.

SASHA The whole state? Good god. I don't think I'm glad you told me. Did you know that?

JOAN No, I didn't know that. *(To audience.)* Did you know that?

OWEN I wouldn't worry much.

SASHA Well, I *believe* in that sort of thing.

IRENE That's what he said—

KENNY *(We should see it coming a mile off.)* WOW! This is incredible! When?

JOAN Well, don't be so happy about it.

KENNY The whole state?

JOAN Don't be so damned ecstatic, Kenny-baby, you live in California, don't forget.

KENNY Well, I can swim.

JOAN All the way to Arizona?

KENNY Well, why not?

CALVIN I don't think so.

KENNY Well, that just makes Sunset Cliffs just look like nothing.

IRENE How did it go with the reading?

CALVIN God knows. Salinity—shmalinity, I can't see how fish can live in it. Do you want to look at the paper?

IRENE *(Picking up the paper.)* I can't correct the information, but I'm sure it's right.

CALVIN Well, it's close.

KENNY Is there a book about him?

CALVIN Who, Cayce?

KENNY Yeah.

CALVIN Sure.

KENNY *(To Irene.)* Do we have it?

IRENE No. *(To Calvin.)* Good lord, it's enormous.

KENNY I want to get it.

CALVIN *(To Irene.)* That's good. I'm hoping he'll grade it by the pound.

SASHA Who would have thought you had to work that hard on Oceanography? I thought it was mostly just sailing around.

IRENE You have to work that hard for a Masters in anything.

SASHA I suppose. It's a damn shame, isn't it?

(Joan stays close to the front door during this scene.)

IRENE I'll take it into the room; it won't be long, I don't imagine.

CALVIN Have you ever seen Reen read? It's disheartening; I worked three months once writing a term paper that she read in under five minutes.

SASHA I have, I know.

OWEN She went through *Ulysses* in about three hours. It's just her way of showing off. Are you through with these? *(Referring to the comics.)*

CALVIN Huh? Sure.

OWEN *(Not aggressively irritated.)* You could at least have put them back like I told you.

KENNY *(To Calvin.)* Did we tell you about the fireworks?

CALVIN Why, do you have some fireworks?

KENNY We didn't even tell you?

IRENE He's still trying to compete with your story about Edgar Cayce.

KENNY No, we really do. Tell him. We really do. I'll bet you can see them from across the bay. *(To audience.)* Calvin and Jill live across the bay.

OWEN *(Picking up comics.)* It's weird.

KENNY *(Back to audience.)* On Point Loma.

SASHA *(To audience.)* It's very nice.

KENNY We didn't tell Clint, I'll bet, either.

JOAN He's…I thought we did.

SASHA Did you find out who did it?

KENNY Yes. Last night we could tell; it's this first house, up on the hill. *(To the audience.)* We got these rich neighbors or something up on the hill that shoot off these great skyrockets every night for no reason at all.

SASHA People do that, though.

IRENE They probably like them, it's very nice. *(She goes into her room, shuts the door.)*

SASHA *(To audience.)* You know? They really do.

OWEN Is that all the comics you dragged out?

KENNY Aren't they great, Owen?

OWEN They are. They've shot off two every night for weeks now.

KENNY Just two. Real big ones, though.

SASHA It's probably a short-circuit in their television.

OWEN Don't be silly. They're great. Stay and see them.

JOAN They probably have a lot of rich kids to entertain.

CALVIN Sure. Like they won't go to bed without their fireworks. *(Opens the door to Irene's room.)* If you don't know about something, just call me.

IRENE *(Off.)* Okay, I think I'll be all right, though.

OWEN *(To Sasha.)* I should go over and visit Jill. I haven't seen her in nearly a week.

SASHA You'd only get frustrated. I don't know why you torture yourself with seeing her. She's married. You're not going to get at her for ten years anyway.

OWEN That's not the point.

KENNY *(Heading for the door.)* I'm going.

IRENE *(Off.)* Kenny?

KENNY Yes?

IRENE *(Off.)* Where are you going?

(Calvin remains in the doorway to Irene's bedroom. Owen and Sasha are by the table. Joan is near the door. Kenny walks back to Irene's door, by Calvin.)

KENNY Just down to the beach.

(By now the exterior lighting should be quite dim.)

IRENE *(Off.)* Well, don't go around Sunset Cliffs.

KENNY *(Pause. Flatly.)* Why not?

IRENE *(Off.)* Because it's dangerous. Okay?

OWEN *(Quietly to Sasha.)* It's wonderful just to be around her. Just to talk to her or listen to her.

KENNY No, it isn't. There's policemen.

SASHA God. You're such a masochist, Owen.

IRENE *(Off.)* Well, they're not immortal themselves, you know.

OWEN *(To Sasha.)* You don't seem to understand a thing. You don't know anything.

KENNY *(Over.)* Okay.

IRENE *(Off.)* Okay what?

JOAN *(Turns to Owen.)* Well, you are! Aside from everything else.

KENNY Okay, I'll just go down to the beach and not over to the cliffs.

OWEN *(To Joan.)* You be quiet, too!

CALVIN *(Closing Irene's door.)* What?

(Kenny goes trotting off.)

OWEN Nothing.

JOAN Sasha said Owen was a masochist and I agreed, because he wanted to—,

OWEN Just never mind! You just goddamn well never mind.

CALVIN Well maybe he is.

OWEN Oh, hell, yes. Maybe we all are.

CALVIN *(Looking at the top comic on the stack.)* Have you had these since they were new? Here's a 1946.

OWEN Yes.

JOAN He can't throw anything away.

OWEN I assume that's supposed to have some profound meaning.

CALVIN I'll bet they're worth something by now, you know?

OWEN I wouldn't be at all surprised.

CALVIN How come you haven't sold them?

OWEN I don't want to sell them.

SASHA Why not? I'll bet they're worth something.

OWEN Because I don't like to throw things away.

JOAN *(To herself.)* For Christ's sake.

OWEN What's that supposed to mean?

CALVIN I didn't say throw them away, I said sell them.

OWEN I'm not through with them.

JOAN He's never through with anything.

CALVIN I don't know where you'll put them in there. He's got more junk in— *(To Joan.)* Have you seen his room?

JOAN No. I don't look in anymore. I don't think I want to know.

CALVIN Well, you should see it. It's something else. Did you know you can only get the door open about a foot and a half in there?

OWEN Well, that's my stuff. I know what's in there.

CALVIN What?

OWEN Well, a *lot* of things.

CALVIN You're telling me. You know what you're like? Sasha, did you ever read about those brothers in New York who had the house packed floor to ceiling with newspapers? That's exactly what Owen's going to be like.

JOAN All hermits are like that.

OWEN Who the hell's a hermit?

CALVIN Just incredible. There's a tunnel through the junk to Kenny's bed and about enough room on the bed for him to curl up on the side to sleep. I'm not kidding—it really is. You couldn't exaggerate it.

OWEN Well, there's nothing wrong with that.

SASHA *(To audience.)* He just likes a lot of junk.

CALVIN And Owen must sleep on top of all that trash. You can't find place on his dirty old bed to even sit down. Stuff is piled up to the ceiling.

OWEN Well, what were you doing in there anyway—digging around for comics. It's not so bad. *(To audience.)* It's not so bad.

CALVIN Not so bad? It's jammed. You can't even open the door. It's piled to the ceiling!

OWEN Well, it's a low ceiling!

JOAN I'll bet he hasn't cleaned his room once since we've been here.

SASHA God, Owen.

CALVIN How long is that?

JOAN Since Kenny was born—twelve, thirteen years.

CALVIN God.

JOAN He's got a typewriter in there somewhere.

CALVIN Really? You should look for it. My god, the way you print everything.

OWEN It'll turn up.

JOAN See?

CALVIN No, really—you could use it—all of us could use it.

OWEN Well, why should I worry about looking through all that stuff for it, anyway? It'll turn up one of these days, it's *in* there.

SASHA Good Lord.

OWEN Why are you all three deliberately provoking me? Or trying to.

CALVIN We're not provoking you...

JOAN God, paranoid...

OWEN You are so. First I'm a masochist, now I'm paranoid. I've got to put these away. *(Picks up the stack of comics and carries them toward his door.)*

SASHA How do you know where they belong?

(Calvin picks up his book again.)

OWEN *(Entering his room with the comics.)* I know where they belong—just don't worry. *(In about three tries, with the stuff piled near the door from the inside, he kicks the door shut on them.)*

CALVIN *(Looks up from his book to Sasha.)* Do you know anything about this stuff?

SASHA No. And I don't want to.

CALVIN I've forgotten everything I learned first year.

SASHA That's what you get for going back, they find out how stupid you are, they'll revoke your Bachelor's.

CALVIN You know anything about this, Joan?

JOAN *(Distractedly.)* No, you're the oceanographer. *(She finally wanders out the screen door to the porch.)*

(The porch should be fairly well lightened, but the outside is quite dark by now.)

CALVIN *(Closes the book.)* Well, I don't either. *(Looks up to Sasha.)* You haven't been over.

SASHA *(Lightning fast exchange. Vampingly.)* You *missed* me!

CALVIN *(Sudden wolf—mock rape—reaching for her.)* Yes, you fool!

SASHA *(Comic, violent retreat, screaming.)* Ahhhhhhhhhh!

CALVIN *(Laughs, relaxes.)* So why haven't you been over?

SASHA Well, I didn't know you cared.

CALVIN Jill said if I ran into you to ask you over. She never sees you up at State.

SASHA Jill? What an excuse. You want me for my big chest. It's all over town you've got a mammary fixation.

CALVIN Well…as a matter of fact…

JOAN *(On the porch, moves away from the door. Toward the yard. Quietly.)* Hi, Clint.

CLINT *(Enters from the dark now.)* Oh. Hello, Joan.

JOAN I didn't know you were coming back tonight. I thought you might, but I didn't know.

CLINT I didn't either.

SASHA *(If she and Calvin hear voices, they can't tell who Joan is talking to.)* We used to have about half of our classes together until she switched to Botany.

(Calvin has opened his book again, but isn't reading.)

JOAN I heard you leaving.

CLINT You did. When?

CALVIN I know—you three used to be quite a team.

JOAN The other night—when you wanted to stay overnight with Reen.

CLINT You did. Well, your mom and I joke like that.

SASHA I think they separated us intentionally—the three of us—We nearly blew up the campus a year ago.

CALVIN I heard. In elementary chemistry.

SASHA Elementary hell!

JOAN If it was me I'd have sneaked you in the back door. I'll bet you came back for your keys.

CLINT Did you find them? I couldn't imagine…

JOAN …Because you never lose things—and as a matter of fact you didn't.

SASHA There wasn't anything elementary the way we handled it. I think we were trying to perfect the cobalt bomb.

CALVIN And nearly succeeded, I heard.

CLINT How did you know?

JOAN Because I saw them in your jacket pocket and took them.

CLINT You what? I had to walk all the way back from the barn.

JOAN You're strong.

SASHA It was great. Biology was best. We drove poor Smith out of his mind, though.

CLINT I ought to take you over…

JOAN You better not, I might like it.

CLINT *(Flatly.)* What?

CALVIN Poor old Professor Smith.

CLINT I'm getting all kinds of messages that I'm sure you don't mean…

JOAN I only said if I had the opportunity I'd sneak you in the back door.

SASHA He was a wreck.

CLINT *(Flatly.)* You would.

SASHA We nearly drove him—I think that was only last year…

JOAN Or maybe a walk along the beach.

CLINT It's probably pretty chilly along the beach this evening.

JOAN I suppose, if you're by yourself.

CALVIN *(Hearing the voices out front now.)* Hey, Joan? When were you in Biology with Smith? *(He goes toward the door.)* Who are you talking…Oh, hi, Clint.

SASHA *(Also moves toward the door.)* Hi, Clint. *(To Joan.)* That was last year, wasn't it? With the dog?

CLINT *(Quickly to Joan.)* You going to give me my keys?

JOAN *(Quickly.)* I probably will. *(To Sasha. She does not overreact, but is quite calm.)* What?

SASHA *(She and Calvin coming out onto the porch.)* Professor Smith.

JOAN No, that was last year.

SASHA I thought so. That poor man.

JOAN *(Happily.)* Yes, did we ever run him ragged.

SASHA He didn't know what to do with us. I thought you'd gone, Clint.

JOAN *(Very naturally.)* He's been down at the cliffs, apparently it's not too bad, but they've stopped cars from going by.

CALVIN Did much go?

CLINT *(Making it up.)* No, not much.

JOAN He said he didn't see much.

CLINT *(Naturally now.)* No, it didn't seem like so much to me—of course it's dark, down there.

CALVIN Can you imagine Jill and Joan and Sasha in one biology class? I don't know whatever possessed them.

SASHA It was pretty impossible. We had a ball in biology. Smith retired with an ulcer.

(She, Joan and Calvin laugh.)

SASHA Everyone was working on frogs and salamanders and the three of us…*(Laughs.)*

JOAN Clint said he'd walk me down to the cliffs, I think I'll see what's happened to them.

CALVIN It can't be much.

JOAN I know, but when they're our only natural phenomenon closer than the Grand Canyon…

SASHA It's too dark to see much.

CALVIN They probably have search lights.

CLINT *(Easily.)* Oh, yeah, you can see pretty well…

JOAN I'll give you a report…

(She and Clint walk off into the dark.)

SASHA *(Continuing.)* Anyway, everyone was working on frogs and so naturally the three of us decided to dissect a dog. *(She is laughing, remembering.)* …it was absurd.

CALVIN Yuck. You would.

SASHA Well, there were three of us. *(Laughing.)* What a mess…

CALVIN …come on…

SASHA *(Laughing.)* Oh, you don't know…really—

CALVIN You'll make me sick…

SASHA *(Laughing.)* No, come on—we started out on this very complex system and I forget what we were going to do, but we…*(Laughing through this.)* …decided to follow the nerves from the testicles and see where they went—

CALVIN You would—you three…

SASHA *(Laughing.)* But we didn't have any idea what we were doing…

CALVIN *(Waits a moment as she laughs, smiling at her.)* Well, what?

SASHA *(Still laughing.)* We got all hung up looking for the nerves—honestly— you—won't…*(She breaks down laughing.)*

CALVIN *(Patiently, still smiling.)* Come on…

SASHA *(Laughing, almost unable to catch her breath.)* No…for three…days… we…

CALVIN Well, did you find where it went at least?

SASHA *(Squeaking.)* It was a girl dog! *(Continues laughing.)*

CALVIN *(Sits on the porch railing while she laughs.)* Come on.

SASHA *(Laughing.)* It was funny.

CALVIN I'll bet.

SASHA It…was…a…girl dog.

CALVIN *(Smiling.)* Yes.

SASHA *(Calming.)* Oh, God. I'll—it was so funny. I'll come over. I really will. I'd like to see Silly Jill again. I never see her at school.

CALVIN *(Still looking at her with the same smile.)* You'd better.

SASHA I will. I've been tied up in Spanish.

CALVIN What are you taking, anyway?

SASHA I don't know. Everything.

CALVIN *(Still smiling at her.)* I see you running to the Education Building at three.

SASHA *(Calmed but pleasantly merry.)* Elementary education. They're too young for anything; I'm practice-teaching a pack of terrors. Eight-year-olds.

CALVIN *(Moving a little closer.)* What are you going to be, a school teacher?

SASHA I hope not!

CALVIN *(Closer.)* An old maid teacher, huh?

SASHA I hope to hell not. Not if I can help it. *(Just a touch nervously.)* How is Jill, anyway? I never see her.

CALVIN She's all right—better than most I suppose. Tell me about your pack of eight-year-olds. The terrors.

SASHA I make it sound worse than it is—they're only eight of them; one boy and seven girls. It's a small class but they have the strength of lions. Lionesses, as it were. I call them my pride and joy. They don't have any idea what I'm talking about.

CALVIN *(Fingering her skirt material. Feigning great interest in her story.)* My…

SASHA *(Wickedly.)* My, my, yes—what-the-hell-are-you-*do*ing?

CALVIN My, what big eyes you have, teacher.

SASHA *(Moving away slightly.)* Yes, well, the better to see you with, my dear; and you better believe it.

CALVIN What a large mouth you have.

SASHA Yes, well, the better to—good god.

CALVIN I never see you with many boys, you know?

SASHA Oh, I don't know; how many?

CALVIN Don't back off—come on over…

SASHA Over where? Hey! That sounds like a great war song—*(Singing.)* Over where! Over where!…Calvin! *(She opens the screen door.)*

CALVIN *(Crowding against her.)* What's wrong?

SASHA Come on.

CALVIN What's wrong?

SASHA Come on, Calvin… *(She is trying to go inside, he is trying to make her stay out. Speaking very fast.)* You're a married man—you're pregnant—er—your *wife* is married—or to—Come on, Calvin—you're—good grief… *(Squeezing inside the screen door.)* You're going to be a *father,* for Christ's sake. Good God!

CALVIN *(Entering the living room.)* What's wrong?

SASHA Nothing. I just don't fancy myself hitting the sack with someone's father.

CALVIN I'm not a father yet.

SASHA Well, you're going to be. God.

CALVIN Come on, you know I've always been interested in you, anyway.

SASHA Yeah, well—me too, but you got married.

CALVIN Yeah. And?

SASHA Well, I just don't feel like an extra-curricular activity this evening. I may act like a terrible flirt, but I am a very *puritanical young person.*

CALVIN Bull.

SASHA I belong to the Protestant Youth Group, for Christ's sake.

CALVIN Yeah, sure.

SASHA I assume it's for Christ's sake.

CALVIN Well, what does your little youth group do when they get someone worked up into a hot panting lather? Advise a cold shower, huh?

SASHA Don't tell me you're really irritated.

CALVIN A little, yeah. Yes, dammit, I am a little.

SASHA Come on, stay back.

CALVIN You didn't answer my question, what does your group do after they have someone panting hot down their collar?

SASHA Collar hell.

CALVIN Pants then?

SASHA Well, we're working on it!

OWEN *(Enters from his room. Looks up at both of them, then down.)* Oh.

SASHA We'll think of something! *(She turns to face Owen.)*

OWEN What's up?

    (Sasha looks at him blankly for a full count before she breaks into uproarious laughter and falls rolling on the floor.)

OWEN What's so darn funny?

SASHA *(Still laughing.)* Calvin.

OWEN *(To Calvin.)* You're what?

CALVIN Never mind. *(To Sasha.)* Very, very funny.

SASHA *(Quieting.)* Well, it was.

CALVIN It wasn't really very—I didn't think.

OWEN What?

CALVIN Nothing. Mind your own business.

OWEN Well, I only asked.

CALVIN Well don't.

OWEN How's Jill?

CALVIN What do you mean, how's Jill?

OWEN Well, how's Jill?

SASHA We were just talking about her.

CALVIN Pregnant.

OWEN How is she?

CALVIN Jill is fine, Owen. *(Acidly.)* Why?

OWEN *(Beat.)* What do you mean, why? Why do I ask? Well, because she's pregnant, and very often…

CALVIN I probably would have brought it up, Owen, if anything were seriously wrong with my wife today.

SASHA Oh, god. *(She sits at the table.)* Where did Kenny run off to, I wonder? I thought he was going to watch for the sky rockets or whatever they were.

CALVIN *(Repeating derisively.)* "How's Jill?"

OWEN Well, you didn't say anything all day…

CALVIN Someday you'll check the compulsion to ask after her.

OWEN Well, why should I? Jill's been my friend since Fresno. Before school even—

CALVIN I'd just like to see you be able to bridle it once. It's just dragged out too goddamn long, you know?

OWEN No, I don't know. I thought you came over here to tell us how Jill was getting along. I merely asked.

CALVIN *(Over some, calling.)* Reen? Are you nearly finished with that thing? *(Opens the door.)* Are you nearly finished?

IRENE *(Off.)* Oh. Yes, nearly, I am.

CALVIN I have to get back before long.

OWEN Well, she never comes over anymore or anything…

CALVIN *(Turning from the door.)* Owen, get off my back, will you.

IRENE *(Entering.)* It's very good, Calvin. I haven't finished. I feel like I've spent the afternoon in a bathysphere.

SASHA What's it on?

IRENE A report—one of their—I guess you can't call it a field trip—ocean trips. How is fishing, anyway?

CALVIN I haven't been much.

IRENE I always remember you and Kenny chasing around over the beach after the grunion.

CALVIN It's crabs now; we're collecting for some firm—it should be starfish; if someone could think of a use for starfish they'd make a fortune overnight.

IRENE Kenny's been thinking about abalone all week. You'll have to take him out again if it isn't too dangerous.

CALVIN It isn't too. Kenny's a good diver.

IRENE He still talks about the—what was it?

CALVIN I don't remember. Some kind of jellyfish probably…

IRENE *(To Sasha.)* Calvin took him out on the boat on one of his afternoons—he's still talking about it.

CALVIN There's no money in collecting—there's no money in fishing at all, as a matter of fact. I took a couple of tourists out last week. Ten bucks each. I made fifty dollars, so we're eating this week. That's more than I made all last month trying to fish.

OWEN Well, I'd hope.

CALVIN What?

OWEN Well, that you're eating well. I mean it's rather important.

CALVIN Yeah, well, don't lose any sleep.

OWEN I do think about it as a matter—

CALVIN *(Sharply.)* Well, don't. *(To Irene, breezily.)* Hey, one of the tourists—a woman—you'd have loved her. I don't think the lady's principal interest was in the ocean. At least her attention was strongly divided.

IRENE Really?

CALVIN I probably would have, too—

SASHA With people there?

CALVIN No, she went out by herself. I thought something was funny when she asked. Of course, with people there is okay, too, but it's a different thing altogether. Anyway, I would have except you can't handle my boat and her at the same time. So I may have stumbled onto a whole new money-making proposition.

IRENE Well, if it buys the bread…

CALVIN So, Kenny can come out with me, only where he held the nets and the traps, now he can hold the helm. He'd like that, wouldn't he?

IRENE Oh, he'd love it. Of course, it's not like fishing.

OWEN *(To himself.)* Christ.

CALVIN Well, not exactly—but it pays pretty well, from what I hear. I could probably afford to give him a small wage. Or maybe on special occasions—like once a week—Sundays, maybe—*I'd* take the helm and let him earn a few bucks. See? We'll find a new way to make money out of that wreck of a boat yet.

SASHA I love it. *(Singing lightly.)* I love it. Sailing, sailing; over the bounding waves.

OWEN *(Over some.)* I dislike discouraging you, but there's nothing new about male prostitution. *(With defensive irritation.)* You don't have to go to all the trouble of going out on the ocean in a boat.

CALVIN But that's the beauty of it…

OWEN You can go down to the square and stand in front of Bradley's.

CALVIN But, Owen, the beautiful thing is I'd have this great gimmick.

OWEN It's as old as—

SASHA Owen, you're so impossibly Victorian.

CALVIN *He's* Victorian?

IRENE I think it sounds like a very sound idea, Calvin; you'll have to try it out.

OWEN It isn't funny.

CALVIN Sure. And Kenny could sing—Rock a bye my baby. Or maybe like a gondolier. How about that?

IRENE I don't think Kenny has much of a singing voice—

OWEN I don't think it's funny at all.

CALVIN Well, I work hard on my little boat. I'm just trying to think of something easier.

IRENE On *that* boat I'm not sure that's easier.

OWEN That's just disgusting.

CALVIN *(An edge coming into his voice now.)* Why disgusting?

OWEN Just because your wife happens to be pregnant you think you can joke around...

CALVIN *(Cutting in.)* Owen, that doesn't even enter into—

OWEN Don't tell me it doesn't.

CALVIN *(Quickly, to audience.)* What do you do? You take so much and then you slug him one, right?

SASHA *(Overlapping some.)* Really, Owen, you have to look at the practical side of it.

CALVIN Reen, haven't you told him about the birds and the bees?

OWEN I know what you're talking about. It's your attitude about everything.

CALVIN Owen, you don't know anything.

OWEN I know you think your wife's pregnant and you think it's perfectly all right to go around with other women until she's available again and I think that's disgusting...!

CALVIN I'm not serious, for Christ's sake, Owen.

OWEN You feel you can turn to any old whore in town—you probably spend every night down at some whore house on the—

CALVIN *(Irritated now. Taking the air altogether away from him. A leap up in volume.)* Look—you better read up, Owen; my wife is four and a half months pregnant and though I know there is no way for you to know about those things. And you'll never know about those things, you'll just float around in an amorous fog being vaguely, idealistically romantic, I can and I intend to sleep with Jill until six weeks before the baby's born and Jill intends for me to, so we really—

OWEN *(Shocked.)* You can not! You can not...

CALVIN *(Cutting in.)* Your stupidity is embarrassing, Owen. I can't stay, I'm sorry, Reen.

OWEN You can't do that to Jill; I'm not going to let you—

CALVIN *(Has picked up his books and started to leave. He turns.)* You must discuss it with Jill if you happen to see her again.

OWEN *(Rushing at him as he goes through the door.)* You're a disgusting, maniacal, perverted—

(Calvin has stepped off the porch, he turns as Owen reaches him. He meets Owen and pushes him just backwards—almost gently—so Owen takes a hard awkward sitdown on the top step of the porch. Sasha has sat down inside at the table, trying to look invisible. Irene has come to the door, holding the

screen open. The push cuts off Owen's line. Brief pause. Calvin speaks almost off-handedly, evenly.)

CALVIN Owen, I've been meaning to tell you. You make my wife nervous coming around the house and I can't have her upset just now. Usually, because you're Reen's son I overlook a lot, but I just don't want you around our house until well after our child is born, Owen. Goodnight, Reen. *(Exits.)*
(Owen has sat in stunned silence. He has difficulty getting up, which makes him madder. Screaming into the darkness after Calvin, across the beach.)

OWEN You get the hell out of here and we don't ever want to see you around here ever—with—we don't want—with your filth and dirt—we— *(Looking as if for something to throw.)* You cocksucker! You bastard! You pervert! You just get the hell away from—

IRENE *(Coming from the doorway to him.)* Owen—what on earth do you. Try—

OWEN *(Turning on her as she reaches him. She is on the top step. Owen on the bottom step. He strikes out in rage—not very effectively.)* Get away! You get away from here—get away from me—you're just as bad as he is. You—

IRENE *(Grabbing his wrists and holding him firmly, for all her frailty. All lines are continuous.)* Stop it! Now just stop it! Owen!

OWEN Why do you have him here? Why do you allow him here?

IRENE —You're the only person in the family who doesn't like Cal—

OWEN He's a monster to Jill. He's killing her—

IRENE Why are you so jealous of him?

OWEN *(Falls down in the sand on the steps.)* He said I couldn't see her again. He said I couldn't see her.

IRENE Why are you jealous of Calvin, Owen? I've never seen anything like it—

OWEN *(Overlapping.)* I can't see her—I love her! I love her!

IRENE Owen, Jill has always been our friend and now she's married to Calvin and I firmly believe there isn't a soul in the world who would be better for her than Calvin is—

OWEN *(Cutting in. Violent, long wail.)* Meeeeeeeeee! Me! Me! Me! What are you *say*ing.

IRENE I mean it!

OWEN He's ruining her life. He's making her callous and weary—he's ruined her—

IRENE Owen, Jill's happy with Calvin—

OWEN She isn't! I know she isn't! Can't you *see* that? She couldn't be!

IRENE Calvin has a boat. He works like an idiot for her. He's a top graduate student at Scripps. He's a beautiful, fine young man, Owen.
(Joan enters, followed by Kenny in a moment, during the next speech. They stand away some.)

OWEN *(Getting up.)* You don't understand a goddamn thing. I know that. You don't know Jill and neither does he. He should be over with her—instead he's God knows where and she's off at school and she's working until six after school and he's off on his boat and she's cleaning the house and he's playing pool and she's cooking and he's coming in at eight or nine and she's going off to concerts at night and he lets her when she should be resting and he's dragging her all over town to show off her pregnancy and not coming home till all hours—you don't know her. He doesn't love her—he doesn't worship her or her baby or her *woman-ness* or mother-ness—*(Breaking down some now.)* Jill's the most beautiful thing in the world and she's carrying *life* in her and she's holding in her *body* all—the—*wonder* and *mystery*—*(Turns, running through the house.)* You don't know her. None of you know her at all! You don't know her at all! *(He runs through the house into the kitchen.)*

JOAN What the hell's wrong with him? He's talking about Jill?

IRENE *(Looks at Joan for a moment. With control.)* He had a run-in with Calvin.

JOAN *(Very detached.)* Why doesn't he leave Calvin alone? He can't stay off that—

IRENE Joan, he's in love with Jill. Go on in, Kenny.

JOAN I don't believe that anymore—

IRENE *(Tired, almost flatly.)* You may not understand it, but…

JOAN No, I think he believes he does. She's not a love, she's a religion for him.

IRENE Yes, well, we know that.

JOAN So was it bad, anyway? Or is he just puffed-up?

IRENE Calvin told him he's not to see Jill again until after the baby's born.

JOAN *(Bored.)* Oh, God.

KENNY How come?

IRENE Kenny, go on in, please.

KENNY Well, how come?

IRENE I'm sure he didn't mean it—go on in, please.

(Kenny comes up on the porch but not inside.)

JOAN Well, I'm glad.

IRENE Joan, I don't need you now—

JOAN —No, I really am. He's just been driving poor Jill out of her everloving mind.

(Sasha comes to the door.)

IRENE I'm sure he has been, but that's nothing new to her.

JOAN He can't expect Calvin to stand for that.

IRENE Well, he isn't standing for it. I don't want to talk to you, Joan.

JOAN He takes one look at her and his eyes get so large—*(Joan's line is continuous.)*

SASHA —Come on, lay off him, poor Owen.

JOAN I mean physically dilated, pupils and all, that you just think you're going to drown in them.

KENNY *(At "And all.")* Really?

JOAN I honestly think he thinks it's his baby—

SASHA Oh, come on; he knows it isn't, that—

JOAN I mean inside him.

IRENE You're being ridiculous—please go inside.

JOAN No, now, I'm very good at snap analysis.

IRENE I really don't need you, Joan. Kenny, go on now.

JOAN Well, maybe not that exactly, but—

SASHA *(Cutting in.)* How as Sunset Cliffs?

JOAN *(Briefest pause.)* What?

SASHA How was your walk?

KENNY She wasn't down at—

IRENE Kenny. Kenny, did you go to the cliffs?

KENNY Uh. *(Pause.)* Uh. Do you think I'd do that?

IRENE I'll find out.

KENNY Are you going to check the clay on my boots?

IRENE *(Tired.)* Go on inside.

KENNY Where's Owen?

SASHA He's inside—in the kitchen.

> *(Kenny enters the house and walks toward the kitchen. Sasha, Joan and Irene stay in the same position.)*

KENNY *(Rather quietly.)* Hey, Owen?

> *(Owen comes to the door of the kitchen, holding one of the cans of beer.)*

OWEN What?

KENNY What did Cal say to you?

OWEN Nothing. *(He goes back into the kitchen.)*

> *(Kenny sits at the table.)*

JOAN Irene? I have—

IRENE Joan, go on in to bed, I don't want to talk to you right now.

SASHA I have to go anyway; I have to get my things together. *(She goes in and picks up a book, stays around the table.)*

JOAN *(Very mother-to-daughter.)* No, Irene, I want to tell you something—

IRENE Good god, Joan; you haven't called me Irene in ten years. I don't want to talk just now.

JOAN I want to tell you—

IRENE I don't know why you want me to know. Why is it? What compulsion is it? Anyway, you don't need to bother.

JOAN Bother what?

IRENE You needn't bother. I don't feel like going through it now, Joan.

JOAN What? *(Calling.)* Sasha, what did you—

SASHA What?

IRENE Sasha didn't say anything. My god, my window's open, you—there— *(With a weak gesture to her window.)* You weren't especially quiet. It wasn't anything all that clandestine, really.

JOAN *(Near panic, but quietly.)* W-what? What? I thought—

IRENE Don't be so damn dumb, Joan. Go in!

JOAN I want to tell you! I know it's terrible, I know—

IRENE TELL ME WHAT? That you finally managed to seduce my boyfriend after what? Two years of trying? I should be interested in knowing the language you'd use to tell me that but I'm not for some reason.

JOAN I didn't want to lie—about—I've never once—

IRENE Yes, I know; well, if you want to tell me something you tell me now. Tell me what he said to you; tell me what did he murmur in your ear; tell me how he smells when he's worked into a sweat over my nymph daughter. Did you scream his name out, tell me, or were you transported—

JOAN —No, don't—Irene—

IRENE —And was he? Did you manage to contrive a climax together or did you work on it slowly; tell me about his movement. What is it like to have intercourse with the man your mother is in love with? Did you want to tell me that? You tell me now.

JOAN I only wanted not to lie. I'm ashamed, oh, don't—I wanted to—*(Looking inside.)* Sasha, did you—!

IRENE I'm not interested; I heard as much as I—

JOAN No, now, don't—Sasha, go home! Stay out here, mother, I thought I was in love with—I want you to know what—

IRENE *(With control.)* Go on inside and go to bed, Joan.

JOAN I don't want Clint. I don't want him now, and for years I've—

IRENE Go inside to bed.

SASHA *(Inside. Softly to Owen who is in the kitchen.)* Good night, Owen.

JOAN *(Fiercely.)* Sasha, don't you come out here! *(Looking at her mother. Panicky.)* I'm going to leave, anyway.

IRENE No you're not; you know you aren't.

JOAN I want to leave, I can go up to—

IRENE No, you don't even want to. If you wanted to you would.

JOAN You don't want me to stay home, and I wouldn't either. I don't want…

IRENE *(Only tired.)* I'm not asking you to leave.

JOAN Clint won't be back. I'm sure he won't.

IRENE I didn't imagine he would.

JOAN *(Pause.)* I'm going in to bed. *(She pushes inside the door.)*

SASHA *(With her books.)* I'm going.

JOAN What did you say to her? What did you tell her?

SASHA Nothing.

JOAN You did too.

KENNY What?

OWEN *(From the kitchen.)* Kenny, come here.

KENNY *(Entering the kitchen.)* What?

JOAN What did you know?

SASHA Nothing. Until I started thinking about it.

JOAN Yes, well, that's all you ever think about, though, isn't it?

SASHA Not necessarily.

JOAN But think is all you can do about it, isn't it? Turn to ice when anyone touches you, don't you?

SASHA *(Turning toward the door.)* I'm leaving.

JOAN Good.

SASHA Good night, Owen, Kenny.

OWEN *(Appearing in the kitchen doorway. He has a beer. He is just tipsy.)* Good night, Sasha.

KENNY 'Night.

SASHA *(Leaves. As she passes Irene.)* Good night, Irene.

IRENE Good night, Sasha. We'll see you tomorrow.

SASHA *(Casually.)* No. Not for a little while—I spend too much time here—I really do—I have a hell of a lot of work piled up anyway.

IRENE OK. Goodnight.

SASHA *(She steps up on the porch and gives Irene a quick, brief hug.)* Goodnight, Irene. *(Exits.)*

KENNY *(Singing, not too loudly.)* There is. A Tavern in the Town.

OWEN Shutup!

KENNY In the town!

OWEN *(To Joan.)* What's wrong with you?

JOAN Mind your own business. What is your business just now, anyway?

OWEN My business is getting drunk.

JOAN Well, skoal!

KENNY *(To the audience.)* That's nearly my last line until the end when I have a little speech. That's the only single time I sing anything. *(Pause.)* I've got a good singing voice, too.

(There is a bright burst of fireworks in the sky off left, with a corresponding sssssss sound.)

KENNY They're at it again!! *(Running out.)* They're at it again! Hey, Owen? Come on!

OWEN *(Starting to run out.)* Tell them to wait!

JOAN Reen's out there, don't go out there.

OWEN *(As the second burst appears.)* Well, so what? *(He runs out, looking up.)*

KENNY Well, just leave her alone.

OWEN What for? *(Outside.)* You see it? Look at that!

KENNY Wow. Only two?

OWEN Watch it. Wow!

(Joan goes into her bedroom.)

KENNY That's all they ever do—boy, some day I'm going to ask them about that. I'll bet there's some great mystery. Hi, Reen.

IRENE Hello. Bright, wasn't it?

OWEN You see them both? *(To Kenny.)* Find out what time it is. Maybe it's the same time every night.

KENNY Roger. *(Runs in to look and back.)*

OWEN Yeah. What are you doing out here?

IRENE Just taking in some air. It's going to be foggy tonight. Sasha should have stayed.

OWEN Yeah. She loves that.

KENNY *(Returning.)* Ten-thirty-five on the button.

OWEN You can still smell it. Sulfur. God, am I drunk. I think I drank all the beer for your picnic tomorrow.

KENNY It's getting foggy, huh? They just barely made it tonight. I'll bet some nights you can't see them if the fog comes in early. Maybe they're signaling some ship out at sea, you think?

OWEN Lost cause tonight if they are. They won't see it out very far.

IRENE It's cold. You come on in. Did Joan go to bed?

KENNY Yeah. *(He goes in.)* It's really cold.

OWEN God, Jill and I used to walk in the fog, remember? It was so thick you could hardly see the rocks. Of course it was dark, too.

IRENE *(Goes up on the porch.)* Come on in.

KENNY *(To audience.)* Actually it doesn't have anything at all to do with the story and then again it does, you know?

OWEN Well, go on in, if you want to.

KENNY *(To audience.)* I'm freezing cold, with the lights even. Just talking about cold just freezes me. *(He wraps in a blanket on the sofa-bed.)*

IRENE The ocean is heavy, too. Hear it? Your father and I used to walk—he loved it. We used to walk along the beach and talk for hours and plan. When I was carrying you. I used to sit out on the rocks with the water splashing around and think about how it'd be; how wonderful everything would be. It was wonderful, with the fog coming in.

OWEN Did you? I wonder what I was thinking?

IRENE Probably that it was cold.

OWEN I don't think anything in the world is as beautiful as a pregnant woman, but I can't imagine you carrying me.

IRENE You kicked like sin.

OWEN I wasn't even born yet. God, how young.

IRENE We're perpetually young, you and me; but I'm afraid that makes us pretty naive and pretty vulnerable.

OWEN God, I'm drunk.

IRENE Come on in.

OWEN Walk around with me for a while and I'll fall asleep in a minute.

IRENE Come on in, Owen. You'll get a cold. Or put on a jacket.

OWEN In a minute.

IRENE Soon then. *(She enters the living room and goes to Joan's room. Opens the door. Quietly.)* Are you awake? *(Pause.)* Good night. *(To Kenny.)* Joan's asleep.

KENNY Yeah. *(He kicks the blanket off.)*

IRENE Don't go to sleep there now.

KENNY I won't. My gosh.

(Owen has been wandering around the yard. As if leading a band, he waves his hands in the air and yells very loud, singing, exactly as the popular recording, with orchestration.)

OWEN Make the world! Go away! *(Now the violins, descending the scale.)* Da, da, da, da, da, da, da, da! I don't! *(Stops abruptly, sits.)*

IRENE *(Comes to the door.)* Owen, you'll wake the whole neighborhood. You're drunk.

OWEN I won't see her again. *(Pause.)* He said I wouldn't see her again. *(Pause.)* Well, do you think Calvin will be back over at least?

IRENE I don't imagine. Go to bed.

OWEN *(Entering.)* When we move up to Fresno, we should—

IRENE Go on, come on to bed.

OWEN I'm dizzy. And I'm sleeping. *(He sits.)*

IRENE Go on to your room now. *(She sits in the chair.)*

OWEN *(Getting up.)* You know what we could do, when we go up to Fresno? We could…

IRENE Shhhhhh. Please, Owen.

OWEN No, really, listen. When, what we should do…

IRENE Shhhhh.

OWEN *(Pause. Shrugs.)* Okay. Listen. What's that?

IRENE The ocean.

OWEN God, it's heavy. Feel how damp it is? It's not like that in Fresno. I remember that, anyway. Good night now.

IRENE Good night.

OWEN Is Joan asleep?

IRENE Yes.

OWEN What's wrong with her, anyway?

IRENE I don't know.

OWEN I'm going to bed. *(Exits to his bedroom.)*

IRENE *(She is seated, her back to Kenny. Pause.)* Kenny? *(Pause. Without looking over to him. This is a prompt. She whispers.)* Kenny? Kenny? You're supposed to—(She looks around.)*

(Kenny is asleep on the sofa. Irene goes to him quietly, shakes him very gently.)

IRENE Kenny? *(Pause. Gently.)* Kenny? *(Hesitantly she pulls the blanket up over him to his waist, tucking it into the back of the sofa and around him. She steps back.)*

OWEN *(Off. Making his bed, faintly singing to himself from the bedroom.)* Fare thee well for I must leave thee

Do not let the parting grieve thee

And remember that the best of friends must sometime part.

Fare thee well for I must leave thee do not let the parting grieve thee;

and remember that the best of friends must part.

IRENE *(Comes timidly, embarrassed, to the audience.)* Ah…*(Almost apologetically.)* This is the end of the play. *(She almost bows to the audience, turns and walks out of the house to stand on the porch, leaning against the house, pulling a sweater around her in the cold air. There is a moment's pause.)*

CALVIN, OWEN, JOAN, SASHA AND CLINT: *(Everyone off stage. Beginning softly, with a slight lilt, hum the first few bars of the song, moving naturally into da, da…until they reach the last line. Singing pleasantly, liltingly.)* And may. The world go well with thee!

(The lights fade out. Curtain.)

END OF PLAY

The Rimers of Eldritch

For Joseph Cino

The harvest is past, the summer is ended, and we are not saved.
—Jer. 8:20

INTRODUCTION

Boy, you go away for a year and everything changes. I came back to Missouri for a vacation; maybe I'd been gone a year and a half. As Alan says in *Lemon Sky,* The color green does not occur in California. Back in Missouri: The bright sun shining through the trees onto an undergrowth of fern and shrubs was so intense, the view so saturated with *green!,* that it hurt my eyes, that first day back, to look out the car windows. My stepfather had been crowded out of his position at the Cheese plant. After twenty-five years in Ozark he had moved to a job in Bowling Green. There were four people from my graduating class still living in town. Bad vacation. I wrenched my neck and spent most of that week in a Springfield hospital, in traction. I went to Chicago to visit friends and ended up staying. The next time I went back home (home is where your mother lives) the folks were living a few miles outside Centerville, Iowa.

I walked from the rented farm where they lived, to what they told me was the closest town. Mystic, Iowa. Mystic was no longer a town, it was a ghost town, built years ago on coal. The abandoned train station, all but falling down, stood, listing badly, in the middle of a vast sunburned field a mile out of town; a ghost of the station-sign, MYSTIC, once white on black, looked like someone had tried to erase it from a blackboard. Maybe twenty people lived in Mystic then; once there had been four thousand. Main Street was abandoned; the back doors of businesses stood open, ledgers fallen across the floors, page after page, volume after volume, of neat rows of debits and credits, brown ink, over the years replaced with black ink, then blue. The floor of the old movie house was strewn with posters, and still-shot photographs, some as late as the early 50s. The whole scene lay in the shadow of huge hoisting derricks, the over-sized corrugated tin buildings of the coal mines, "...rusting away, flaking away." I walked through town, nodding to an occasional person or couple, on a porch or staring from a window. No one spoke or nodded back. But the busted town spoke—of the greed and denial and desire and broken trusts and negated promises of the Midwest, of rural America. Don't talk to me about the South and drugs and Harlem and Appalachia, talk to me about Capitalism and commerce and the Christian Church's denial of the human heart, talk to me about the American way. All my experiences, living among these people, not the good times, you couldn't think of good times in this town, came flooding, painfully, back to me.

Eldritch is not Mystic. I knew nothing of the town, still know nothing. The only parts of Mystic that remain in the play are the coal mines and the cover of the published book, a photograph of a broken window, taken by my friend, Paul Cranefield, after he saw the play and visited Mystic with a camera a few years later. Eldritch is the underbelly of all the Midwestern towns I knew. It is peopled with the sounds and desires I grew up on. In this play I didn't bother to invent anything or anyone; it wasn't necessary. I just turned back the clock, maybe only twenty years, to when there were still young people here in this invented town, and people who still hoped.

I had been having trouble getting the Ozarks, the Midwest, onto the stage. All of the stories I had written occurred in small towns in the Midwest, none of the plays took place there. Four years after I visited my folks in Iowa, I finally wrote a one act play for voices, *This is the Rill Speaking;* a deliberate attempt to unblock the Midwest, just to get down the sound, the rhythm, the town of Ozark. It's a sweet play, mainly sweet, I didn't care what it was, it only mattered that I knew these people and their voices, better than I knew anything, and I had to set them down. But sweet wasn't really what I had to say. My mind went back to Mystic, not as a town, as a symbol, as a presage, as a symptom. I started *Rimers* the week *Rill* closed at the Cino. I couldn't call the town Mystic, that was too nice, at the same time too on-the-nose and still off the mark. I needed a word that sounded like it could have been the Founding Family's name. "Eldritch" is a word of Scottish origin meaning unnatural, hideous, weird. It was probably pronounced something like E-lish, and probably has the same Old English root as elf. I think of it as describing a cry heard on a no-moon night across the moors. I had seen the word once in some essay and remembered looking it up. I used to do that. I didn't change the name of Centerville, it was perfect. With a Midwest accent the T is dropped. They pronounce it "Sinnerville."

All the plays in this volume, except *The Gingham Dog,* are sound exercises. Taking a town, a family, a memory, a summer, and treating it like a faceted sphere, turning it to let a moment, a facet, shine for only an instant, but shine in sound, music—well, like music. I came to New York yelling, Theater should be a three ring circus! I had seen *The Hostage* in Chicago, it set me on fire: the boldness of the theatricality, the collage of sound and time and action, the outrage. of the people and the outrage of the humor. When a friend asked me what I was working on, I described what I knew of *Rimers* (I'm afraid I'm one of those despicable people who shorten titles, even good ones, to nicknames) and he said it reminded him a little of *Under Milkwood.* Well, thanks very much, but I am not a poet and Dylan Thomas is. I was mad for Thomas. I had read everything except his work for the stage. I bought a copy of *Milkwood* and carried it in my hip pocket while I was writing *Rimers,* afraid to read it until I had finished my play, but somehow needing it nearby. (Ibsen wrote with a photograph of Strindberg over his desk.) I knew I would never be able to write *Rimers* if I read *Milkwood*. I read it later—I was right, the two pieces are nothing alike, but I wouldn't have had the nerve. Blessed ignorance. It was enough to remember Joan Littlewood's production of *The Hostage* and be working under the shadow of *that*.

I wrote the entire first act without looking back. During the next week I had to read the script (first time), list all the stories that had been started, and devise plausible endings for them. Some of that was easy because I had based the play on two rather bad stories I had written in Chicago. The actual writing, or wrighting, of the play consisted of braiding those two stories together and into the sound and the other characters and stories of the town. It was découpage, collage; theater, it was music.

The play was done at LaMama. Joe saw no reason why this one couldn't be done at the Cino as well. With a shotgun?! The building would have come down on top of us. Marshall didn't direct *Rimers*. He said he wouldn't do it until he could have that wrecked Plymouth on stage. There was no way we could manage that with LaMama's resources. I directed the play, adequately, with a great cast I had selected mainly because they had the voices I needed. When it was re-staged Off-Broadway my cast was rejected, one by one, for people the director thought looked more Midwestern. At the dress rehearsal he turned to me and said, I think I'm going to get all of your play except the *sound*.

And, actually, he did. And an excellent thing came from that second production. Helen Stenborg was cast as Mavis Johnson. She was wonderful, and is still the best mime I've worked with—I despise mime, but it was useful in that production. Helen has become a good friend (I mean that in the old fashioned way, the kind of friend, we used to say, who is there for you. Rare, rare). She is also a very handy type to have around and one of the best actresses I've had the privilege of working with. I've been lucky enough to exploit her in half a dozen plays since.

PRODUCTION

The Rimers of Eldritch was first presented by Ellen Stewart at La MaMa Experimental Theater Club, New York City on July 13, 1966 with the following cast:

Robert Conklin	Michael Warren Powell
Eva Jackson	Claris Erickson
Evelyn Jackson	Tanya Berezin
Nelly Windrod	Blanche Dee
Mary Windrod	Shellie Feldman
Patsy Johnson	Beth Porter
Mavis Johnson	Kay C. Coulthard
Peck Johnson	Gene Alton
Josh Johnson	Marvin Alexander
Lena Truit	Jane Buchanan
Martha Truit	Ann Harris
Wilma Atkins	Jacque Lynn Colton
Skelly Mannor	Robert Thirkield
Preacher/Judge	George Harris
Cora Groves	Kay Carney
Walter	Frederick Forrest
Trucker	Oliver Dixon

The play was directed by the author; the stage manager was Lola Richardson.

The play was subsequently presented at the Cherry Lane Theater in New York by Theater 1967, directed by Michael Kahn and designed by William Ritman.

CHARACTERS

Robert Conklin (Driver Junior), a boy, eighteen
Eva Jackson, a crippled girl, fourteen
Evelyn Jackson, her mother
Nelly Windrod, a strong woman, middle-aged
Mary Windrod, her pixilated mother
Patsy Johnson, the prettiest girl at Centerville High
Mavis Johnson, her mother
Peck Johnson, her father
Josh Johnson, her brother
Lena Truit, her girl friend, the same age
Martha Truit, Lena's mother

Wilma Atkins, a friend of Martha's
Skelly Mannor, the town character, about sixty
Preacher/Judge, played by the same actor, in mid-fifties
Cora Groves, the owner of Hilltop Café
Walter, her lover
A Trucker

SCENE

The locale of the play is Eldritch, present population about seventy, one of the many nearly abandoned towns in America's Middle West.

The time is the present.

The play takes place during the spring, summer, and fall of the year, skipping at will from summer back to spring or forward to fall and from one conversation to another. All the characters are on stage throughout the play, except twice as indicated, grouping as needed to suggest time and place.

At La MaMa Experimental Theater Club and the Cherry Lane Theater the play was acted on a series of six or eight descending, irregular levels, some with railings to suggest a porch or the witness stand of the courtroom as needed, against a black void. It might also be done with various architectural elements, suggested gables, trees, ruined buildings, American Gothic motifs indicating the various buildings of the town.

The lighting, especially if a bare stage or platforms are used, might be considered the most important single scenic element. In this edition—to assist the readers in seeing the play—it has been indicated at the beginning of each scene where the conversations take place. Some are quite obvious: scenes in the café, court, or church. Others, such as *A street in town,* a director might wish to place elsewhere; they should be thought of only as suggestions to aid in following the printed text of the play. A scene continues—sometimes two or more in separate areas of the stage simultaneously—until the lights dim on the scene and focus attention elsewhere.

THE RIMERS
OF ELDRITCH

ACT ONE

In darkness, Wilma and Martha on the porch of Martha's house.

WILMA Well, what I heard isn't fit for talk, but I heard that Mrs. Cora Groves, up on the highway…?

MARTHA Yes.

WILMA …has taken a boy, she's old enough to be his mother on, and is keeping him up there in her café.

MARTHA In her bed.

WILMA *(With true sympathy.)* That woman went crazy when her husband left her.

MARTHA Oh, I know she did.

WILMA That woman, I swear, isn't responsible for her own actions.

(A very faint light begins to illuminate the courtroom, Nelly standing, her hand raised.)

MARTHA I should say she isn't.

WILMA I hear he does things around the café, whistling around like he belonged there.

MARTHA Have you ever heard anything like it?

WILMA I haven't, I swear to God.

(A sharp increase in the lights.)

(In the courtroom.)

NELLY I do.

(Martha's porch—morning.)

MARTHA Why, she called Evelyn Jackson a liar to her face, and Eva too. Swore things the devil and his angels wouldn't believe it. She'd stand up there and swear black was white.

WILMA And Nelly, poor woman, the life that woman leads. Only God in His Heaven knows the trials that woman has to bear.

MARTHA That she should have to be dragged through this.

WILMA She stood there and told the way it was; I said to Mrs. Jackson—cried the whole time—

MARTHA I know, I saw.

WILMA —Only God in Heaven knows the trials that poor woman has had to bear.

(In the courtroom.)

JUDGE Nelly Windrod, do you solemnly swear to tell the whole truth, and nothing but the truth—

NELLY *(Quietly troubled.)* I do, yes.

JUDGE —so help you God?

NELLY I do.

JUDGE *(Exactly as before.)* Nelly Windrod, do you solemnly swear to tell the whole truth, and nothing but the truth—

NELLY I do, yes.

JUDGE —so help you God?

NELLY I do.

(Martha's porch—night.)

MARTHA So help me God I don't know how we let him hang around here like he did. Not talking to nobody.

WILMA Nobody I know of could live like that.

MARTHA Like that time he scared young Patsy so bad.

WILMA Bad for the whole town with someone like that.

MARTHA Like that way he had of just standing around.

WILMA Around here everybody knows everybody.

MARTHA Everybody was scared of him. Everybody knew what he was.

WILMA A fool like that.

MARTHA Grumbling and mumbling around; standing and watching it all.

WILMA I'd think people'd feel easier now. I know I swear I do.

MARTHA I do.

(In the courtroom.)

NELLY I do.

(Beat.)

JUDGE *(Faintly, fading.)* Now, Miss Windrod, if you would tell the court, in your own words…

(In the grocery where Robert works.)

MARY *(To Robert.)* Now, we have to understand that Nelly is my flesh and blood.

ROBERT I know.

MARY Yes, love, she's my flesh and blood and she thinks she knows but she doesn't know but she thinks she does.

ROBERT I suppose she does if anybody does.

MARY Well, she thinks she does. But I know and you know. I was at my window, watching the moon.

ROBERT Was there a moon?

MARY I said to those people, all those new people in town—there isn't much to know about Eldritch, used to be Elvin Eldritch's pasture till it gave out I guess and they found coal. It was built on coal with coal money and deserted when the coal gave out and here it stands, this wicked old town. All the buildings bowing and nodding.

ROBERT How do you know so much?

MARY And still so little? I would puzzle that if I could. I told them none of the people here now were coal people. The mining people moved off; they raped the land and moved away. There used to be explosives that rattled the windows, oh my, and shook the water in a bucket, day and night.

ROBERT How come you remember so much?

MARY And still so little? The last time I saw you, why, you were just a little baby; you've grown up so.

ROBERT You saw me yesterday, Mrs. Windrod.

MARY You don't know. Isn't that sweet. The last time I saw you, why, you weren't no bigger than that high.

ROBERT You've known me all my—

MARY You've grown up so. I have terrible bruises on my arm there. Look at that.
   (Cora's café. Walter is sitting at the counter.)

TRUCKER *(Leaving.)* I'll see you, Cora.

CORA Can't avoid it, I guess. You watch it now on those narrow roads.

TRUCKER It's push-pull with the load; I'll come back through empty day after tomorrow—you remember to tell me that again.

CORA Stay awake now.

TRUCKER No danger of that.
   (On the porch.)

WILMA I'll say one thing for her. How long has it been he's been there?

CORA *(To Walter.)* Boy.

MARTHA Two or three months now nearly. Walks around the place whistling like he owned it.

WILMA Well, he earns his keep.

CORA Boy.

MARTHA It's not in the kitchen that he earns his keep, Wilma.

CORA Boy.

WILMA Well, I'll say one thing—

CORA —I'm getting ready to close up now.

WILMA —Whatever it is, she looks a darn sight better now than she did a year
ago. Since I can remember.

CORA Boy.

WALTER *(As though waking from a daydream.)* I'm sorry.

CORA I'm fixing to close up. You sleeping?

WALTER Thinking, I guess.

CORA Have another cup of coffee, I got time.

MARTHA That woman isn't responsible for her own actions since her husband
left her.

WALTER Swell.

WILMA It's not for us to judge.

MARTHA That's all well and good but anyone who deliberately cuts herself off
from everybody else in town.

WILMA I don't judge, but I know who I speak to on the street and who I don't.

WALTER Is there work here in town do you know?

CORA Down in Eldritch? Not if you're looking for wages. Not here.

MARTHA It's easy to see the devil's work.

WALTER I had that in mind.

CORA You might try Centerville; Eldritch is all but a ghost town.

WALTER You here alone?

CORA I've managed for seven years; it hasn't bothered me.

WALTER It might not be a bad idea to take someone on yourself.

WILMA It's a sin to sashay through Centerville the way she does, buying that
boy shirts and new clothes. Keeping him up on the highway.

MARTHA I don't go, but I understand he's made a show place out of her café.

WILMA I'd be happier if it was me if they made her close it down.

MARTHA It ought to be against the law serving beer to truck drivers and them
having to be on the road so much.

WILMA The wages of sin lead to death.

CORA Aren't you cold in just that jacket; that's pretty light for April.

WALTER No, it's not bad.

(They regard each other a moment; the light fades on the café.)

MARTHA The wages of sin is death.

WILMA Bless her heart, poor old thing.

MARTHA *(As Mary Windrod passes the porch.)* Good evening, Mary.

WILMA Good evening, Mary Windrod.

MARY *(Stopping.)* You two. I watch you two sometimes. *(Mary talks, almost with everything she says, as though she were describing a beautiful dream to a pet canary.)*

WILMA Aren't you cold in just that shawl, dear?

MARTHA Nights are cold in this valley for June.

MARY It's not bad.

WILMA You'll be catching a chill next.

MARY I was once a nurse and I believe that the constant proximity to sickness has given me an immunity to night air.

MARTHA Never think that.

MARY Us dry old women rattle like paper; we couldn't get sick. I listen to you old women sometimes.

WILMA How's your daughter?

MARY Yes, indeed.

MARTHA I beg your pardon?

MARY The proximity to all that sickness.

WILMA Yes, love.

MARY Immunity to death myself. My number passed Gabriel right on by. It came up and passed right on by and here I am a forgotten child.

WILMA You better get inside, love.

MARY Rusting away, flaking away.

MARTHA You get in, now.

MARY *(Leaving.)* This wicked town. God hear a dried-up woman's prayer and do not forgive this wicked town!
(The Congregation bursts into "Shall We Gather at the River"; after only a few bars, the song stops abruptly.)
(In the courtroom.)

NELLY And Mama came running downstairs and said a man had attacked young Eva Jackson.

JUDGE Would you point out Eva…?

NELLY *(As the light fades.)* There, poor lamb, can't hardly speak two words since this thing happened and I don't wonder—
(On the porch.)

WILMA *(Overlapping a word or two.)* Well, I know I swear I don't know what he sees in her.

MARTHA It's nice of him, though.

WILMA Well, I know but Driver Junior's old enough to be taking girls out; he shouldn't be wandering around with her.

MARTHA It's nice to have somebody to keep her company. Still and all, it doesn't seem natural, I know what you mean.

WILMA I don't know what he sees in her.

MARTHA Poor thing.

(Near Eva's house.)

ROBERT Eva!

EVA Are you glad to be out of school?

ROBERT I liked it all right.

EVA What are you going to be?

ROBERT Who knows?

EVA We had our Eighth Grade graduation in robes! I bet I know what you won't be, don't I?

ROBERT What's that?

EVA A race car driver.

ROBERT Why do you want to say that? You think I couldn't do that if I wanted to?

EVA You don't want to get yourself killed.

ROBERT Driver didn't want it; he just had an accident.

EVA You want to be like him?

ROBERT People don't want to do the same thing their brother did; I couldn't see any sense in it.

EVA I knew you didn't. You aren't going to get yourself killed.

ROBERT Killed doesn't have anything to do with it. Eva, good Lord, I don't want people carrying on like that; honking their horns, coming into town every week like a parade. I never even went to see Driver.

EVA You decided what you want to be?

ROBERT I don't have to decide this minute, do I?

EVA I just wondered.

ROBERT Do you know? You don't know what you want.

EVA Of course I know; you know, I told you. So do you know, everybody knows what they want—it's what they think they really can do that they don't know.

ROBERT Well, I don't have to decide yet.

EVA *(In a sudden burst, as though conjuring.)* When's it gonna be autumn? I love autumn so much I could hug it. I want it to be autumn. That's what I want right now. Now! Autumn! Now!

ROBERT Good luck; I don't see it.

EVA *(In a burst.)* Don't you be derisive to me, Driver Junior!

ROBERT Don't call me that.

EVA Well, don't you go on, Robert Conklin, or I'll call you anything I like.

ROBERT You'll be talking to yourself.

EVA Everybody else calls you that. Don't go away; I won't, I promise. Don't you wish it was autumn? Don't you? Don't you love autumn? And the wind and rime and pumpkins and gourds and corn shocks? I won't again.

Don't you love autumn? Don't you, Robert? I won't call you that. Everybody else does but I won't.

ROBERT I haven't thought about it.

EVA Well, think about it, right now. Think about how it smells.

ROBERT How does it smell?

EVA Like dry, windy, cold, frosty rime and chaff and leaf smoke and corn husks.

ROBERT It does, huh?

EVA Pretend. Close your eyes—are your eyes closed? Don't you wish it was here? Like apples and cider. *You* go.

ROBERT And rain.

EVA Sometimes. And potatoes and flower seeds and honey.

ROBERT And popcorn and butter.

EVA *(Opening her eyes.)* Yes. Oh, it does not! You're not playing at all. There's hay and clover and alfalfa and all that. *(Hitting him, really quite hard, slapping.)*

ROBERT *(Laughing.)* Come on, it's different for everybody.

EVA Well, that's not right; it doesn't at all. Are you making fun?

ROBERT Come on, don't be rough.

EVA I will too; you're not the least bit funny, Driver Junior!

(As he starts to walk on.)

EVA Come back here, Robert! Robert Conklin. Driver Junior! Little brother. Your brother was a man, anyway. Coward. Robert? Bobby?

(In the store.)

WILMA And I'll have some flour and yeast. And three packs of Sure-jell.

ROBERT Right you are. How much flour?

WILMA No more than five pounds in this weather. How're you doing in school?

ROBERT All right.

WILMA I just said to Martha Truit, I suppose Driver Junior will be leaving us as soon as schools gets out next month, like all the young kids now.

ROBERT Not for a while yet.

WILMA Oh, you will; you'll be going off to see the world.

ROBERT I don't know.

WILMA There's nothing for a strong young man in this dead old town. Where do you think you'll be heading?

ROBERT I don't know.

WILMA Des Moines?

ROBERT I don't imagine.

WILMA St. Louis?

ROBERT Who knows?

WILMA Chicago?

ROBERT I might not leave at all for a while.

WILMA Well, your brother stayed and he was wonderful, but we all expect you to be moving along like all the young boys now.

ROBERT I don't know.

(Downstairs in the Windrod house. Nelly has a hold on Mary's arm. Mary is turning backward, Nelly forward, Mary avoiding the raised hand threatening her, much as on a turntable going backward. Just for a moment.)

MARY I know, I know, I know, I know, don't hit me; don't hit me, baby.

NELLY What do you mean telling people a tale like that. You know I bought that mill.

MARY You bought it, baby; I know you bought it.

NELLY Well, they said in town you told I'd killed Dad to get it.

MARY I said he died mysteriously.

NELLY Well, he died of old age, he was ninety-six, for God's sakes.

MARY He died mysteriously!

NELLY In his sleep like you will; died of old age like you will. What in hell do you mean telling something like that?

MARY I didn't mean to, baby. I don't mean to—

NELLY —You're batty as a goddamned loon.

MARY They don't like me is what it is. They know I watch them. They don't like me in town, I knew they didn't. I don't say those things. They tell things on me.

NELLY You're crazy as hell is what it is; you're out of your goddamned mind is what it is.

MARY Baby, don't talk like that. They tell *fibs* on me. They say—

NELLY Showing them bruises and saying I beat you; when the hell did I ever beat you? You know goddamned well how you get those bruises. You fall down! You bruise! You run into things! You're old. You bump things. Who the hell takes care of you and you telling lies on me like that, Mama— what do you mean?

MARY I don't mean to.

NELLY They don't listen to you.

MARY They don't listen to me, Nelly.

NELLY It doesn't do you any good; they come right in and tell me.

MARY Don't hurt me.

NELLY I think you better go up to your room!

MARY No, don't lock the door.

NELLY If I leave the house, I'll lock the door or you'll wander out and get hurt. You'll fall down the stairs and tell I beat you.

MARY I don't want to go up there; the evil town is all around me up there.

NELLY Go upstairs, Mama.

MARY It's painted on the windows—

NELLY Well, pull the shades down if you don't want to see them. *(She leaves.)*

MARY My skin, whole body is just flaking away—this evil town! This evil town!

(On a street in town: Josh and all the young men in the cast except Walter.)

BOYS *(Taunting Skelly, jeeringly.)* Baaaaaaaaaaa! Baaaaaaaaaa! Baaaaaaaaa! Baaaaaaaaa!

SKELLY *(In a deep, mangled, growling, almost drunken voice.)* Get on, you son of bitch. Son of bitches. *(Sounding about like "Geah-own-ya-sansobith! Sansobith!")*

BOYS Baaaaaa! Baaaaaa!

SKELLY Get the hell on, you, get on! *(In a deep, almost terrified growl.)* Go, go on, sonabitch!

(In the courtroom.)

NELLY And I heard something outside—

(The town becomes alive everywhere. Peck, Nelly, Mary, Josh, Martha and the Judge are in the court, Patsy and Lena in town; Evelyn is walking out onto her porch calling Eva, who is approaching the porch. An area may be Evelyn's porch and part of the courtroom at the same time—the effect should be of the entire cast moving in a deliberate direction with lines coming in sequence from all over the stage. Cora enters the café area from upstairs, sleepily, calling softly, exactly as she will when the scene is repeated at the end of the first act.)

JUDGE A travesty of justice.

PECK We, the jury—

CORA Walter?

PECK —find Nelly Windrod—

CORA Walter?

PECK —not guilty.

MARTHA Not guilty.

CORA Walter?

EVA Robert?

NELLY Oh, God; Mama?

EVELYN Eva?

TRUCKER Not guilty.

WILMA Papa?

MAVIS Peck?

JOSH Not guilty. *(He begins whistling softly, calling a dog.)* Here Blackie, here, boy.

WALTER Cora!

CORA Walter?

JUDGE Not guilty.

PATSY I know.

EVELYN Eva? You come on, now.

CORA Oh, God, oh, God, oh, God, oh, God, oh, God.

JOSH Blackie? Here, Blackie?

EVELYN You better get on in here now.

EVA I'm coming.

JOSH Come on, boy.

LENA The poor thing.

PATSY Really, I get so damn tired of all that nonsense.

LENA I know, but they insist I wear it.

(The movement subsides.)

EVELYN *(Continuing.)* You better put a sweater on if you're going to sit out there.

EVA *(Approaching the house.)* I'm coming in directly.

EVELYN Not directly, you come on in now.

EVA All right.

EVELYN Where were you all day?

EVA I was wandering around the woods.

EVELYN Now, you know I don't want you running around alone. What if you fell and hurt yourself and who'd ever know it?

EVA I wasn't alone; Robert and I went walking.

EVELYN Well, don't you go off alone.

EVA I won't.

EVELYN Not all afternoon. Wandering around; God knows what could happen to you.

EVA I know, I don't.

EVELYN You look so fatigued.

EVA I'm not at all.

EVELYN I don't want you spending so much time with that boy.

EVA What boy?

EVELYN That Driver Junior. Wandering around with that boy. Spending all afternoon and evening with him.

EVA Well, who else would I spend it with?

EVELYN Well, why do you have to go off every day of the week? Doing God knows what? You could visit the Stutses, you shouldn't be running around. It isn't good for you; you have to be careful. You're not like other kids; you know how easily you get fatigued; you run yourself out every day; perspiring like you do; wandering off with that boy. If something happened, who'd know? And don't think he's responsible; his brother might have been different; devil and his angels wouldn't know if something happened. I don't know why you can't stay at home like everyone else. Traipsing around the woods half-naked, what do you do out there in the woods alone, the two of you, anyhow?

EVA Nothing.

EVELYN I said you answer me.

EVA *(Rapidly.)* Nothing!

EVELYN I said you answer me the truth, young miss.

EVA We don't do anything. Whatever you think.

EVELYN Don't you talk back to me, what do you do, little miss smarty pants? All day gone from the house, smarty? *(Hits her.)*

EVA We talk.

EVELYN You talk, you talk, I'll just bet you talk; now you get in that house this minute do you hear me!

EVA *(Running to the witness stand.)* I don't know what you think.

EVELYN You get on in to the supper table! You're going to be the death of me. I swear, I swear, I swear.

(Everyone is assembled in court.)

JUDGE —to tell the whole truth and nothing but the truth, so help you God?

ROBERT She didn't see anything.

JUDGE Eva, as a witness to this terrible—

EVA I don't know! I didn't see! I didn't see! I told you I didn't see anything! *(A long run into her Mother's open arms.)*

EVA Mama.

EVELYN Leave my daughter alone! Can't you see she's upset? My God, what are you trying to do to her?

(Simultaneously.)

CORA She told me.

EVELYN *(To Eva.)* Poor baby—*(To Cora.)* You know what I think of you? Before God!

(Simultaneously.)

CORA I talked to her; she told me.

JUDGE *(His voice rising above theirs, simultaneously, trying to quiet them.)* We have all long known Skelly Mannor; we have known of his past—

(Simultaneously.)

ROBERT *(His lines overlapping Cora's.)* She didn't see.

JUDGE —that latent evil in him, that unnatural desire, and we have long been aware that at any time the bitterness in his soul might again overflow. *(General crowd murmur.)*

(Simultaneously.)

EVA I don't know!

JUDGE We let things lie.

(Simultaneously.)

NELLY It's not true, none of it, it's like I said. You're trying to make a murderer of me; it was God's will be done.

JUDGE We took no action to prevent his crime—the pending, at any moment, crime—we all knew it—and the burden must be ours.

CORA She told me!

JUDGE We are responsible for the shock to these two innocents.

(The others have been quieted. General murmur in response to the Judge. Several Amens.)

JUDGE *(Continuing.)* We are responsible for our actions; for allowing the heathen in our fold!

(The Judge's oratory slides into the Preacher. We are at church.)

CONGREGATION Amen!

PREACHER God forgive us.

CONGREGATION Amen.

PREACHER In Your wisdom forgive us. And help these two souls, these two innocent souls forget that dark moment.

CONGREGATION Amen, amen.

PREACHER Blind them to that dark moment and set them free, Lord.

CONGREGATION Amen.

PREACHER Dear Lord.

CONGREGATION Amen.

PREACHER Our Savior!

(In the café.)

WALTER *(To Cora.)* Where do you want the pie?

CORA *(Warmly, chiding.)* On the rack that says "pies."

WALTER And the coffee in the jar that says "coffee" and the typed-up menus in the menu covers? I'll catch on.

CORA You're doing fine.

WALTER Well, for only a week.

CORA You'll catch on.

(In the congregation Martha says, very faintly, "A show place." echoed by "I hear" from Wilma.)

WALTER *(Overlapping.)* And you have to consider that we spend more time upstairs than down, or I'd know a lot more about the restaurant business and a lot less about you.

CORA Now you just clam up before somebody comes in.

WALTER Ashamed, are you?

CORA No, I most certainly am not and you know it, but I don't intend to bother someone else's business with my own.

WALTER Wonder what they think?

CORA You do, do you?

WALTER "No, I most certainly do not and you know it"—I like the way you people talk. You're looking good.

CORA I'm feeling good.

WALTER What would you think about putting an awning over the door so a fellow doesn't get soaking wet with rain as soon as he steps out the door.

CORA Hm. What'd I care if he's going out?

WALTER Oh, it might be that on the way out is when he decides to come back.

CORA You think, do you?

WALTER "You think, do you?" It's something to consider.

WILMA A show place.

(The Johnson house.)

PATSY It's a trash heap is what it is. I don't know what keeps us here; I swear I don't. Maybe it was all right when you were young. The only people who ever comes into town is people to drive around looking around, poking around to see what a ghost town looks like. Movie house been closed down eight years; you want to see a movie you have to drive twenty miles into Centerville. Every building on Main Street closed up, falling down except a store and a grubby filling station. Boys stand out, hanging around, it's a disgrace—

(On her porch.)

EVELYN —Can't be healthy, rats took over the old grainery, all the buildings rotting and falling down, the mine shaft building used to just shine; you could see it miles away; now the way it sags—falling apart, boarded together; everything flapping and rusting, it's an absolute eyesore. Cats poking around through the rotting ruins of all those old buildings, their bellies just busting, it can't be healthy—

PATSY —Dad could get a job in Centerville as well as here; I don't know why we stay here, there's a lot of decent people there, they know how to have fun, but no. We have to stay here. The boys from Centerville *all* have cars, I'm so ashamed getting off that ugly smelly school bus with all those younger kids, squealing; I swear sometimes I think I'm just going to sit there and not budge all day. Just let them drive right into the parking lot and sit there in the hot sun all day broiling rather than get off that bus with the boys all standing around the front of the school watching. I just wish you knew—they're probably surprised I don't smell of cow manure.

PECK Patsy.

PATSY Well, I'm sorry but it's true. I wish you could see the way they dress! In the summertime the boys from Centerville drive by on the highway alongside the field and I'm up on the hay wagon like some common hired hand and they yell and honk and carry on so damn smart I just wish I could die.

MAVIS Patsy June.

PATSY Well, I'm sorry but I do. At night sometimes I just cry my eyes out. Night after night. I just cry myself to sleep; I hope you're satisfied—

EVELYN —Trying to scratch a living together. Trying to keep strong—

PATSY *(Leaving house; to Lena.)* —I'm sorry, but I do—

EVELYN —Sometimes I don't even know why we try.

LENA *(On her porch.)* I said it's warm, for crying out loud; it's May; school's nearly out; I don't know why I have to wear that ugly old thing, you have the nicest clothes. I never have a danged thing.

PATSY Well, all the boys were wearing cashmere sweaters with V necks and I said if they can have them I sure as hell can; the girls in my class just turned pea-green-purple. I said, well, they didn't have what I wanted in Centerville, this two-bit town, so I went along with Dad to Des Moines; you should have seen them.

LENA Peggy was furious.

PATSY Oh, she thinks she's so rich; she has absolutely no taste at all.

LENA I know.

PATSY Black and brown and blue and green; I said the other day, "Why, Peggy, you look exactly the color of Chuck Melton's two-toned Mercury." You should have seen her face.

LENA I wish I could have.

PATSY *(As they walk away from the porch.)* Well, listen; Chuck thinks he's so damn smart himself. Yelling to me, you should hear the things they say. It'd make your ears burn. I told him and he should know, if he wants to come by and come up to the door and knock like some kind of respectable person, then I'd go out; but I'm not going to just fly out of the house like that. He thinks he's so damn smart, I don't care how long he sits out in front of the house in his damn car. Honking. He can honk all night for all I care.

MARTHA *(Coming to the porch.)* Evelyn said a regular show place.

WILMA I heard she closes up at ten every night now.

MARTHA Oh, my…

WILMA *(Leaving porch.)* Ours is not to judge.

MARTHA Still I know what I know.

LENA *(Joins her mother.)* I know he did it. Why would anyone want to poison a helpless dog?

MARTHA He just looked up at me like he knew I'd help him and there wasn't anything I could do this time and I think he knew.

LENA I don't understand somebody doing something like that.

MARTHA There wasn't anything I could do. Just nothing at all.

LENA Why?

MARTHA I don't know, love.

LENA *(Repeating, with same inflection.)* Why?

MARTHA I don't know, love.

LENA Why?

MARTHA I don't know, love.

LENA Just a helpless little dog, he was too old to hurt anybody. There's somebody poisoning dogs around here and that's the lowest, meanest thing in the world.

MARTHA No one should cause an animal to suffer like that.

LENA I know he did it. I know it was him.

MARTHA Well, we can think what we think, but we can't do anything.

LENA I've seen how they bark at him; you know that. A dog can tell an evil person; a dog can tell; they're all scared of him.

WILMA *(Coming to the porch.)* Wickedest man; creeping through town, looking into things.

MARTHA Peeping into girls' bedrooms; standing around looking like that.

WILMA Who know what's in someone's mind like that?

(Patsy screams very loudly, running from her bedroom into the living room.)

PECK *(Startled.)* What in God's name?

PATSY Oh, God, oh, God, oh, God, oh, God. In there.

MAVIS What's wrong, baby?

PATSY I saw him. I saw him. Oh, God, he was looking in the window. His face—

PECK Who was? Answer me.

MAVIS Skelly?

PATSY Skelly. Skelly. Skelly was. Oh, God, you should have seen his eyes! And I was only in my pants. You should have seen him.

JOSH I don't know what he could have seen.

MAVIS That's enough out of you now.

PECK Where was he?

PATSY At my bedroom window, where do you think?

MAVIS You're imagining things; you're dreaming.

PATSY I wasn't alseep, I tell you; I just was getting ready for bed.

PECK It's okay now, I'll go out.

PATSY No, he's gone now, my God, I screamed and he ran away.

PECK *(With some humor.)* Well, I'd think he would.

JOSH Wake the dead; what's he gonna see?

MAVIS Don't you start.

PATSY *(Contrite.)* I'm sorry.

MAVIS For what?

JOSH Sorry he didn't come on in probably.

PATSY For scaring you so.

MAVIS It's all right. My word, something like that, I'd think you would.

PATSY Only I was just so scared.

MAVIS Of course you would.

(Josh is stifling a laugh.)

MAVIS That's enough, Dad said.

PATSY It was horrible.

MAVIS It's all right now.

PATSY I don't think I can go back in my room.

JOSH Oh, good Lord.

PECK Young man.

MAVIS It's all right now.

PATSY Can't I sleep with you tonight?

MAVIS It's all right now.

PATSY Just tonight.

MAVIS No, now, he's gone.

JOSH What are you, some kind of baby?

PATSY I was just so scared.

MAVIS Go on back to bed, honey.

PATSY I'm sorry.

MAVIS It's okay.

PATSY It was horrible. Can't I sleep between you? I'm shaking like a leaf.

MAVIS It was nothing.

PATSY Just tonight?

MAVIS You're too big for that kind of thing.

PATSY Something ought to be done about him.

MAVIS It was your imagination, it was the wind; it was the shadows.

PATSY It was Skelly Mannor! I guess I know him when I see him.

MAVIS Go on back to bed. He's gone.

PATSY I know I saw him.

MAVIS Go on, it's okay now; he's gone; whoever it was.

PATSY Well, it was Skelly Mannor, I guess I know who it was, I saw him.

MAVIS Something ought to be done about him.

JOSH He hasn't hurt anyone—not yet.

MAVIS I suppose you call scaring an innocent girl out of her wits doing nothing. And the whole family too. Everyone knows what he does.

JOSH Well, what could he do but look? He must be over a hundred if he's a day.

MAVIS Just looking is doing; who knows what he might do?

JOSH He's eighty years old.

PATSY He is not. How can you tell how old he is, through all that filth.

PECK Well, I know when I was a young man like Josh or younger we used to
give old Skelly a "baaa" sometimes—

MAVIS Peck, now—

PECK Well, and he looked the same then as he does now, and all the men then said he'd been looking like that for as long as they could remember so he's getting on.

JOSH He's just a curiosity.

PATSY Oh, that's very funny. A curiosity. You're just as bright as the sun; you ought to hide your head under a barrel.

JOSH He's not hurt anybody. Except Warren Peabody.

PATSY Well, Warren Peabody deserved whatever he got, I'm sure.

MAVIS What did he do to Warren, is that Laura Peabody's boy?

PATSY Oh, Lord no; you know he drives an old Chivy, from over at Centerville; part of that river trash bunch. *(Exits, coming to Lena.)*

JOSH Well, he hit Warren in the back of the head with a rock, threw it, I'll bet, thirty feet, and caught Warren running. Knocked him out cold.
        (In town.)

LENA *(Talking to Patsy.)* I remember when Driver was alive.

PATSY Before his accident.

LENA This was a wonderful place.

PECK *(Continuing.)* He's got a good aim, I can vouch for that.

MAVIS I've told you, Josh, I don't want you boys teasing him. You just ignore him, I don't care how old you are. I don't know why you do that. You know he could turn on you any second.

JOSH Oh, I don't bother him.

MAVIS Well, who knows what's in somebody's mind like that.
        (On Wilma's porch.)

WILMA Like that time he scared young Patsy so bad.

MARTHA Bad for the whole town with someone like that.

LENA *(To Patsy.)* Like that parade every Saturday afternoon with Driver spinning through town, laughing; I remember his laugh.

PECK I remember he let Curt Watson have it across the side of the face once. Curt was the fastest runner in town too; let him have it once when Curt gave him a "baaa."

JOSH God knows he's crazy enough to try to do something like that with a sheep.

MAVIS Josh, now.

JOSH Well, I figure maybe he couldn't get a girl.

MAVIS That's enough.

JOSH Well, now; the whole town knows what he did; it's not like it was some secret—it's the funniest thing anyone's ever seen around here.

MAVIS It's not our place to talk.

PECK I don't imagine he did it much more than once and that time he got caught.

JOSH That's about the dumbest thing I ever heard. He must have been really hard up is all I can say.
(On Wilma's porch.)
WILMA To do some bestial thing like that.
MARTHA When I think of the evil in this world.
LENA (To Patsy.) I could just cry.
JOSH Who saw him?
PECK Hell, I don't know. It must have been before I was born.
JOSH Hell, he must be eighty years old.
PECK Well, he's getting on.
PATSY (To Lena.) And Driver Junior. I think he hated his brother. He's just nothing compared. His brother was always so happy at least.
LENA Driver's been dead now three years tomorrow.
PATSY May thirty-first.
LENA Every time I see that car; it just kills me.
JOSH Some dumb old sheepherder. I hear they're all like that.
PECK Well, they don't get into town much. Shit, they sure must be hard up is all I can say.
PATSY (To Lena.) His name is Walter, I found out.
JOSH Shit, I wish I could of seen him. That old son of a bitch. We ought to have him tarred and feathered on Halloween if anyone could find him on Halloween. That old bastard, I don't know how he gets away with the things he does. I know Driver and me was gonna run him out of town once; I think we got drunk instead.
PECK When was that?
JOSH Just before his accident sometime. Shit, we used to run that old boy ragged.
PECK You watch yourself.
MARTHA (To Wilma.) When I think of the evil in this world, I swear.
JOSH Aw, he hasn't hurt anybody. (He leaves Peck and Mavis.)
LENA (To Patsy.) I could just cry.
MAVIS A decent person is afraid to move outside at night; now what kind of life is that?
PECK Well, we'll tell Clevis and see what he says. He can't do nothing; we didn't catch him at it.
MAVIS It'll be too late one day and then who's to blame.
(The light fades on Peck and Mavis.)
(Downstairs at the Windrod house.)
MARY I saw it.
NELLY Sure you did, Mama.
MARY In my dream. Oh, God; it was horrible, Nelly.

NELLY Go back to sleep, Mama.

MARY Someone's going to be butchered in this town. Blood is going to be shed.

NELLY Be still.

MARY Blood is going to be shed; someone is going to be butchered.

NELLY Go on out into your garden, Mama; go back upstairs.

CONGREGATION *(Softly singing.)* "I walk through the garden alone;
    While the dew is still on the roses... *(Fading.)*
    And the voice I hear, falling on my ear—
    The Prince of Peace discloses..."
    (A street.)

SKELLY Hey.

EVA What? What do you want?

SKELLY You tell him—

EVA What? I don't know who you're talking about—what do you want?

SKELLY Your friend.

EVA Who?

SKELLY Him. Robert.

EVA Tell him what?

SKELLY Tell him he's all right.

EVA What do you mean he's all right?

SKELLY He's a good boy.

EVA Well, I imagine he knows that.

SKELLY People talk but they don't know—it's them that's the bastards. He's all right.

EVA You're terrible the way you talk. Nobody makes fun of him. It's you they laugh at.

SKELLY You tell him...

EVA I don't know what you're talking about. I wouldn't tell anybody anything you told me to tell them.
    (In the store.)

CORA He drifted in town and he helped around the café for a while and he drifted on; nothing was holding him here.

MARTHA I heard you started closing the place up at ten in the evening when that boy started working for you.

CORA When Walter came, yes, I did. I closed earlier. I don't know why I used to be open all that late for anyway.

MARTHA I heard you still close it up at ten, though.

CORA Well, force of habit, I suppose.

MARTHA How long is it he's been gone?

CORA I don't know, Mrs. Truit; I suppose a month now.

MARTHA I heard you two made that café a regular show place.

CORA You'll have to come up sometime and have a cup of coffee and a piece of pie.

MARTHA Yes, when you was still with your husband, before he left, I mean, I know you used to make the best pie in the state.

CORA It's still pretty good.

MARTHA *(Leaving the store.)* Yes, I will, I'll come up and see you one day. *(To Wilma.)* "Helped around the store," did you ever hear anything like it? I heard she still closes the café at ten sharp. They say he left without taking so much as a stitch she'd bought him. Didn't leave a note even—
(In town.)

JOSH I hear Hilltop would be an easy place to break into, if you had in mind to steal something.

MARTHA *(To Wilma.)* Leaves the door for him still, every night.

WILMA I hear.

MARTHA Closes at ten.

LENA *(To Josh.)* That's what I heard.

WILMA What Reverend Parker said is so true.

MARTHA Oh, I know it is.

WILMA It's difficult for us to accept.

MARTHA "We must accept the blame upon ourselves. Each and every one of us."

WILMA "It's not Nelly Windrod who is being tried here today."

MARTHA "Nelly Windrod is not the person who is being tried here today."

WILMA —No indeed—

PREACHER *(To Congregation.)* —It is the soul and responsibility of our very community. The laxity with which we met the obligations of our Christian lives. The blindness from which we allowed evil in our lives.

CONGREGATION Amen.

PREACHER Evil in our lives.

CONGREGATION Amen.

PREACHER We watched it fester and grow; we allowed this dreadful thing to happen through shirking our Christian duty. Nelly Windrod—

WILMA —is not on trial here today.

PREACHER —No indeed. That man. May the Lord have mercy on his soul. *(Waits.)*

CONGREGATION Amen.

PREACHER May the Lord have mercy on his soul and mercy on our blindness to His way. It is our responsibility and we must share in that terrible knowledge.
(In town.)

LENA It's not that bad.

PATSY It's terrible, this crummy old ghost town; tumbleweed blowing down the deserted streets.

LENA There's no tumbleweed blowing down the—

PATSY Well, there ought to be, it's enough to give a person the creeps. Everyone from Centerville and all over driving by to see where the murder was committed; it's creepy. Looking at this awful ugly old ghost town, and all the boys know I live here, I swear, I've never been so humiliated in my life.

LENA I know, it's terrible.

PATSY Driver Junior never talks to anyone any more—I haven't even seen him with Eva; of course her—that dumb cripple hasn't said a word since. Everyone staring at her—the whole thing is just the ugliest thing I ever heard about. I knew what was going to happen, I said. I swear Driver Junior is such a creep—never spoke to anyone in his life anyway. Doesn't hang around with us or anyone else his own age; hanging around with her, that girl, I feel sorry for her and all, but I look at her and I just feel my shoulder blades start to pooch out all over, people like that— deformed people, ought to be put out of sight. Like her and Skelly and everybody; I mean people with deformed minds as well, too; don't think I'm forgetting that. It's absolutely creepy the way people drive through here; I've never been so humiliated in my life.

(A street.)

SKELLY You! Hey, Robert, Bobby! Hey!

ROBERT Hay is for sheep.

SKELLY Yeah, uh, you uh—Driver is dead.

ROBERT Well, I guess I know that.

SKELLY You going around like—

ROBERT What? What do you want?

SKELLY He was a son of a bitch.

ROBERT Don't talk like that to me.

SKELLY You don't talk bad.

ROBERT I don't, no, because I don't see any need to talk—

SKELLY Driver was a sonabitch. Walking like some kind of stud horse. He wasn't human.

ROBERT Who are you to tell if someone is human or—

SKELLY You know what he did? I say. You didn't go to the races to see him kill himself.

ROBERT My brother was a very good race car driver and I didn't go because I don't like them; if everyone went and I didn't it's because they like them and I don't.

SKELLY You don't know. I'll tell you what your sonabitch was like.

ROBERT You don't know anything.

SKELLY You hear me talking to people? I *see*. He was a snotnose kid, twelve when you was born. I saw him. And him driving through town like a big shot. With his racing car all green and yellow and rared back there. Lined up after him in cars, trailing after him and honking like a string of geese coming into town. And him telling everybody about it up at the café.

WILMA (*To Martha, on the latter's porch.*) Land, it was wonderful just to hear them cheering.

(*Simultaneously.*)

SKELLY I heard the stories and the shouting and the glory.

MARTHA Another silver cup, another blue ribbon.

(*Simultaneously.*)

ROBERT I don't know what you're talking about.

WILMA First place.

SKELLY I saw him with Betty Atkins—in her bedroom and her crying and crying and how he hit her—you didn't know that! And she cried 'cause he got so mad. He liked to killed her.

ROBERT I thought people made up stories about you peeping into windows—you're worse than they say.

SKELLY I SAW HIM! You're better for a man than he is.

ROBERT You're disgusting; you're as bad as everybody says you are. Dad says you are and Driver said so too.

SKELLY Yeah, because I told him I saw him. Your brother, you know what he did? You know what he did? He had to help himself. Had to help himself out. Out in his car parked on the road and in his room. He had to do it for himself.

ROBERT Shut up!

SKELLY That's what I know.

ROBERT You're disgusting. You should be killed or jailed; my brother was a good person; he was a wonderful person.

SKELLY He beat Betty Atkins and did it by hand. Jacking all on her. I've seen him. I've seen him.

ROBERT Baaaaaaa.

SKELLY That's what I know.

ROBERT You're worse than they say. Everybody knows you spy on them. Who do you think you are?

SKELLY Who do you think your sonabitch brother was? Is what I want to—

ROBERT Baaaaaaa. Baaaaaaa.

SKELLY Now you know! Go on.

ROBERT BAAAAAAAAA! Baaaaaaaaa.

SKELLY Get on—get on—Driver Junior, you like that? I know, I know. You like that? Get on. Hey—

(Robert exits.)

WILMA Such a beautiful man; lived so dangerous; like the world wasn't turning fast enough to suit him.

MARTHA Gave of himself until there was nothing else and got himself killed in an accident.

WILMA The Lord giveth and the Lord taketh away.

MARTHA Poor lad. I swear.

(Silence. Same street as last Skelly/Eva scene, precisely as before.)

SKELLY Boy! Robert!! Boy! Hey!

EVA What? What? What do you want?

SKELLY You tell him—

EVA What? I don't know who you're talking about—what do you want?

SKELLY Your friend.

EVA Who?

SKELLY Him. Robert.

EVA Tell him what?

SKELLY Tell him he's all right.

EVA What do you mean he's all right?

SKELLY He's a good boy.

EVA Well, I imagine he knows that.

SKELLY People talk but they don't know—it's them that's the bastards. He's all right.

EVA You're terrible the way you talk. Nobody makes fun of him. It's you they laugh at.

SKELLY You tell him.

EVA I don't know what you're talking about. I wouldn't tell anybody anything you told me to tell them.

SKELLY You tell him...

(In court.)

PECK We, the jury, find Nelly Windrod. Not guilty.

NELLY *(In court.)* Oh, God, oh, God. Mama?

JUDGE It is not Nelly Windrod who is on trial here today.

(In town.)

PATSY Tumbleweed blowing through town, it's so creepy I don't know how anyone can stand it.

LENA *(To Patsy.)* There's no tumbleweed blowing through...

(On the Windrod porch.)

MARY *(To Eva.)* You talk to him and that's nice. I talk to things too. I talk. I have several tropical fish and a number of small birds that I feed each and every day and take excellent care of them. Talking with them until they die. I like little things, with little hearts beating and little lives around me. Their little hearts just moving away. With short life spans and high temperatures. And I pat out little graves like loaves in the back yard and put little whitewashed gravel, little rocks around each one, and that's my garden. And I decorate the little loaves with flowers when I remember to. Now there's Trinket. That was my rat terrier, died eleven years ago last November, and Bonnie, my cocker spaniel, died four years ago last October, all in the fall; and Gilda and Wanda, the two goldfish, floating on their sides one morning, little loaves, those two. And Chee-chee, my canary, died two years ago last September. And Goldie, my other canary passed on the year after that and Tina, the little blue kitten—beautiful kitten, that one's little too. She prefers violets and Goldie takes daisies and Chee-chee takes dandelions and Bonnie takes roses, and Trinket has daffodils generally—spring daffodils and Wanda tulips; and the flowers dry up and die and I feel I should bury them too. All my children. Gone, gone, gone.

CONGREGATION *(Singing softly.)* "I walk in the garden alone
While the dew is still on the roses
And the voice I hear
Falling on my ear
The Son of God discloses.
And he walks with me—"
(Mary and Eva join the Congregation, Mary by her daughter, Eva by her mother.)

CORA *(Enters the café from upstairs, sleepily, calling softly as if wakened from sleep.)* Walter?

CONGREGATION "And he talks with me."

CORA Walter?

CONGREGATION "And he tells me I am his own."

CORA Walter?

CONGREGATION "And the joy we share."

CORA Walter!

CONGREGATION "As we tarry there!"

CORA Walter!

CONGREGATION "None other. Has ever—"

CORA Walter.

CONGREGATION "Known."

PREACHER Let us pray.
(They bow their heads in silence.)

CORA *(Falling to her knees as though felled.)* Oh, God. Oh, God. Oh, God. Oh, God. Oh, God. Oh, God. Oh, God.

CURTAIN

ACT TWO

Patsy and Lena are on the Johnson porch.

PATSY It wasn't really sudden. I knew he wanted to, he'd let on, you know, in little ways. He said would I mind not being in school; he'll graduate, of course 'cause this is his last year—and I said would I *mind?*

LENA That's just incredible; when's it going to be?

PATSY We aren't messing around; he said two weeks from this Saturday. He didn't want to have a church wedding at first—you know how he is—and I said, Chuck Melton, if you think I'm going to just run off to a preacher and practically elope you got another thing coming. So it'll be the First Presbyterian of Centerville, but I want it to be just simple. I said I wanted a street-length dress—I know, but that's what I want and I'll have a veil, a little pillbox hat, I love those, and a veil and probably roses, if it's not too early for roses—

(In the Windrod house.)

MARY *(Over.)* —Bonnie? Here girl. Bonnie? Here kitty, kitty—

LENA —I'm just so surprised.

PATSY Well, it wasn't really sudden; I knew he wanted to, he'd let on. I love the First Presbyterian. I only hope the trial and all is quieted down. That could just ruin it all.

LENA Oh, it will be.

PREACHER *(Over.)* Now you know I'm aware we all want to get this settled and go home and forget about it.

PATSY It's a beautiful church.

LENA I really love it; it's just beautiful.

PATSY And my aunt's gonna give the bride's breakfast.

LENA Aren't you excited?

PATSY I imagine we'll live in Centerville. You know, till we have enough money to get a place or maybe move somewhere. Probably right in town; there's a wonderful place over the barbershop, the Reganson one on the corner with windows on both sides that's been empty for weeks. I only hope someone doesn't beat us to it. I want to tell Chuck to put some money down on it. I don't want to live with his folks. I just can't stand them and I don't think they think too much of me either. They're so square and old-fashioned. They really are. They don't even smoke or believe in make-up or anything.

LENA Chuck is wonderful, he really is. I'm just so surprised.

PATSY *(Beginning to cry gently.)* He was so cute; he said would I mind not being in school next year, junior year, and I said of course I'll miss my friends, but would I *mind?*

LENA It's so beautiful. It's a beautiful church for a wedding.

PATSY Isn't it?

LENA Aren't you excited? What's wrong?

PATSY Well, of course I am, silly.

LENA I don't think Josh and me want to get married, though, until after I'm out of school.

PATSY Oh, my God, you don't want to marry Josh. My Lord, I can't imagine it. You're not serious about him. Lord, he's so childish.

LENA He isn't. He's six years older than you are. He's worked for two years.

PATSY Well, I know, but you don't want to marry him. Age doesn't have anything to do with it. He's all right and he's sweet and all, but I mean to go to the show with and hold hands. I don't know how you can bear to ride into town in that garage tow truck, though.

LENA I drive it sometimes; it's not bad.

PATSY Well, I know, but Josh! Lord, Lena, I've got so many things to do yet. You know the thing I think I like most about Chuck is that he's so clean and neat and all. The way he takes care of his Mercury. It's always like spanking new.

(In court.)

ROBERT And he took us by surprise.

(In the café.)

CORA *(To Walter.)* You seem uneasy.

WALTER I'm not really.

CORA I depend on you too much probably.

WALTER Huh? No, nothing's wrong.

CORA I've always had a dream, an idea, of maybe leaving here.

WALTER You have?

CORA Would you like that?

WALTER And go where? Hawaii?

CORA Well, no, not quite Hawaii. I don't know. It's sometimes somewhere and sometimes somewhere else. Somewhere. St. Louis maybe; Des Moines, Chicago. Anywhere.

WALTER What would you do there?

CORA The same, of course. Only a nice place maybe. I know the business, if I could sell this place.

WALTER You wouldn't want to do that, would you?

CORA Wouldn't you like that? St. Louis maybe, or anywhere. I thought you'd like that. Have a bigger place. Maybe hire someone to run it for us so it doesn't take up all our time.

WALTER That's an idea. I can't say I like St. Louis much.

CORA Have you been there? Well, Chicago then.

WALTER Chicago's nice.

CORA I have a uncle in Chicago; he might help us get started. What's wrong, anything? You seem uneasy.

WALTER I'm not. Why don't we close early.

CORA I'd be agreeable to that.

MARTHA *(Coming to Eva's porch.)* Is she any better?

EVELYN Oh, I don't know. Who can tell?

SKELLY *(Entering his shack; alone.)* Hound? Hey, hound. What are you shaking about, huh? Get your tail up in the air and out from between your legs like a hunting dog. No, you wouldn't be any good for that, would you? What kind of dog are you? Huh? I got a roast bone from Cora's for you. Here. There you go. Go to it. Those guns scare you, do they? Those hunters? Eh? Oh, they strut around and shoot around after their quail and their duck and their pheasants. They scare you, huh? If you wasn't wild, you could sit out on the steps, huh? No, they'd shoot off one of those duck guns or a firepopper and off you'd go back in under the bed, huh? Under the steps. And they're wasting their shot anyhow. Couldn't hit the broad side of a barn ten feet off. You should have seen it with the mines running. With the mines working and the dynamite and the what-you-call-it booming around everywhere underground fifty times a day or more. Boom! *(Laughs.)* Boom! *(Laughs.)* Every hound…*(Coughs.)*…every hound in town kept out of sight from seven in the morning till seven at night. Under every bed in town. That'd make you shake. Eat it. That's roast bone. You. *(Laughs.)*

  You good for nothing. Oh, hell, yes. They was fancy people; butter wouldn't melt. Old Man Reiley bought the Eldritch place up on the hill, wouldn't no other place do for him, and carried on with their miners drinking parties and societies if you please. And Glenna Ann sashaying around serving tidbits on a platter; oh, well-to-do. Blast all day in the mines all day and blast all night at home. Old Man Reiley called me every name in the book. Fit to be tied. She was a pretty one, too; only eighteen, the both of us and her wearing dresses to the ground and bows and her old man called me every name in the book. Chased me off the place with a crowbar. *(Laughs.)* And we done it in the old man's woodshed. Oh, sure. I sneaks back the very same night and we done it out in the woodshed there. Everything smelling of hickory and cedar for their fancy fireplaces. Oh, yeah. And, oh, how she did squirm! Oh, Lord. Saying to me, "Oh, I love you. Oh, I love you, oh, really I do, Skelly." Oh, shit. *(Coughs.)* Till I thought she was gonna croak. Oh, Lord. Never let on she even knew me.

Sashsay around town with her big hats. Glenna Ann. Pretty girl. Oh, yeah. No girl in town so pretty. Then or now. None in between. How she did claw and bite. No bigger than a mite. Hound. Where'd you go? Don't you bury that. You eat that now. That's good. You no good. Old Man Reiley moved off; she moved off, whole family, lock, stock, and petticoat. Mines give out, off they git. How she did squirm. "Oh, I love you so much." Oh, sure. Pretty girl too. Right in the woodhouse the very night her old man chased me off with a crowbar. And we sat up against the wall there, playing in the shavings on the floor. Till morning, near. Sure. All blue. The bluest blue in the morning. Blue light on her gown there. Sticking her feet into the shavings—digging. Holding hands, panting. Where's that tea kettle, huh? Where'd it go? Make some sassafras. Yeah, wouldn't eat it if I gave it to you, would you? Don't know what's good, do you? Beautiful tits; no tits like that then or since. I guess you know Peck Johnson fairly beat the shit out of that girl on his last night. Whipped her good. Never seen anything like it. Thought she was dead. Patsy. Little whore she is, too. Thought he near to killed her. The old lady standing there with her teeth clenched watching, white as a ghost…mad as the devil. Good! I say good! What she done, I say good! She deserved it; little whore. Here, you whore. Go on with you! get on out with you. Filthy brother; whole family right along brother and sister both. Beat her till she nearly bled. Thought he was gonna kill her. People don't care! What kind of thing goes on. What kind of devilment. Where'd you go to? Hound? What-are-you-not eating? If you was tame, you could come out and sit on the street. Catch a rabbit, huh? You scared of rabbits? Are you? That's a good girl. You're okay. Bluest blue you ever saw in the daytime. Cold too and her in a nightgown; run right off of the house when I called up and off we went. *(Laughs.)* Oh, boy! Arms is no good. Can't lift 'em even over my head. Look a-there. Oh, boy. Red thing over her nightgown there. Barefoot. Grass sticking to her feet from the fresh-cut lawns with their lackeys there, mowing and clipping and futsing. Barefoot. Right across the dew and all.

That crippled girl, Jackson, she's got her leg shorter, one than the other. Cries. You never saw anything like it. Dances around her room in the window curtains, all lace, wrapped around her whooping, dancing around like a banshee. Oh, he's all right. Tell him I said he's all right. Well, I guess he knows that. No, he don't know it, now, there! Better'n his no good brother everybody yelling about doing it by hand. Hitting girls around. People don't care! They don't see. What. What they want to think they think; what they don't they don't. They don't care anyway; what kind of devilment. What goes on. Her old man, Old Man Reiley; never did know. No, no. Never did know. I weren't the only one either, you can bet. Get some water boiling; make some sassafras; good for the stomach. Cedar. All in the air. Bluest blue in the air. Hickory and cedar cedar cedar cedar cedar in the air. Sang. *(Laughs.)* All manner of songs there. Soft so's it wouldn't carry to the lackey's house there. Carrying on, scratching, biting, thought she was gonna croak. "Oh, really, oh, I love you so!" *(Laughs.)* Pretty girl. Beautiful tits. Beautiful tits. Oh, yes. Oh, sure.

(On Eva's porch.)

MARTHA Is she any better?

EVELYN Oh, I don't know. Who can tell?

MAVIS Has she said anything?

EVELYN The doctor said it was just shock.

MARTHA Well, I'd think so.

WILMA I've never heard anything like it.

MARTHA Like when he scared young Patsy so bad.

WILMA Bad for the whole town.

MAVIS It's awful.

PATSY I feel so sorry for her.

WILMA How's Driver Junior?

EVELYN He hasn't been over. I don't know what to think about that. I'd told her not to go off; well, I won't say anything.

MARTHA Such a shock. For us all.

MAVIS A terrible thing.

EVELYN She's always been so easily upset.

LENA Well, she has cause.

PATSY I just wish he was still alive! That's what I wish.

WILMA When I think of the evil in this world.

EVELYN The doctor said she just needs rest.

MAVIS If he'd of lived he'd not have seen the light of day tomorrow.

WILMA That poor girl.

MARTHA And Nelly, that poor woman, the life that woman leads.

WILMA *(Leaving.)* I said to Eva's mother—cried the whole time—

MARTHA I know, I saw—

WILMA Only God in His Heaven.

(In court.)

MARY It appeared to me that both the men were hitting her.

(Tremendous crowd reaction.)

JUDGE Order!

MARY It appeared to me.

JUDGE Now you have testified, as a witness, Mrs. Windrod.

MARY I was at my window, watching the moon.

ROBERT *(To Mary, but not in court.)* Was there a moon?

MARY A crescent moon that night, I know for sure.

JUDGE You have testified that you saw—

MARY Blood, everywhere; all over. It was terrible. On the porch, rivers and I
was mopping and it spread with the water, all around, all over.

JUDGE —Driver Junior and young Eva clearly.

MARY I didn't say "clearly," I couldn't see clearly; I don't see well.

JUDGE You testified you saw—

MARY In my dream.

JUDGE You were asleep?

MARY Weeks ago and I told Nelly that blood was going to be shed, and I was
wiping and it spread with the water, all around on the porch—*(She leaves
the stand.)*

NELLY *(Taking the stand.)* And Mama said someone was in the back yard and I
took up the gun that I keep by the door, the shotgun; and checked to see
if it was loaded and it was and I opened the door.

MARY *(Over.)* —Bonnie? Here, kitty, kitty, here, girl.
(In the café.)

CORA *(To Walter.)* Did you go into town?

WALTER Yeah.

CORA Into Centerville?

WALTER No, no, only into Eldritch.

CORA Did you? Well, what do you think?

WALTER Well, what can I tell you, it's a ghost town.

CORA I told you.

WALTER What was that big building?

CORA The movie house?

WALTER On the corner.

CORA Oh, there was a drugstore, and an exchange. And a lawyer's office and a
couple of doctors up above had their office in that building. A dentist, I
think. That was the first building to shut down.

WALTER Some people said hello like they knew me.

CORA Well, they do know you from here.

WALTER Wonder what they think?

CORA You do, do you?

WALTER Sometimes.

CORA Peck Johnson said the new boy "helping" me appeared to be a genuine
good worker.

WALTER What did you say to that?

CORA Well, I said, oh, yes, yes, he's a genuine good worker.

WALTER *(Laughing.)* I like some of them all right. The truck drivers are all right, anyway.

CORA Oh, they're from all over; they support the place. Have for years.

WALTER Some of the people from Eldritch aren't so bad.

CORA I think a couple of the girls have a crush on you. Well, I don't blame them.

WALTER They're young.

CORA Well, they're not all that damn young.

WALTER It's gonna be a nice night.

CORA It's gonna be a nice summer.

(Josh and the Trucker walk casually to Skelly.)

EVA *(In the woods.)* No, in the wintertime and in the autumn especially. It's so nice; it smells so clean.

ROBERT *(In court.)* He came from nowhere!

EVELYN *(On her porch.)* I said she shouldn't be out gone from the house like that!

JOSH *(To Skelly.)* What are you standing on the corner about? Why aren't you back to your grubby house? Where do you sleep now your stinking shack burned down? Or do you sleep? Do you sleep? Sleep with sheep, huh?

SKELLY Get on.

TRUCKER What'd you say?

SKELLY Mind your own business.

JOSH Which old damp rotting cellar do you haul up in now your dry old shack's gone? Huh? I bet you eat worms, doncha.

SKELLY Go on, you.

JOSH What d'you eat? Won't tell anybody where you live, will you? 'Cause you know what'd happen if you closed your eyes there, don't you?

SKELLY Yeah, you sonabitch, you mind your own—I don't say whether I got ary a bed or no now.

JOSH What'd you call me?

SKELLY Go on with you.

JOSH I said what'd you call me?

TRUCKER Ought to kill him, Josh.

JOSH What'd you say? Shit, he ain't worth it.

SKELLY Get on.

JOSH Just don't let anybody follow you home.

(Skelly leaves.)

JOSH You get on now. You're the one who had better get on, not me. You'll wake up to a hot bed one of these days again. *(Laughs.)* Old bastard. Baaaaa! *(Laughs.)*

TRUCKER Son of a bitch shepherd!

(In court.)

ROBERT He was just there all of a sudden from nowhere and he took us by surprise and he pushed me—he hit me from behind; I don't know if I passed out or not.

(Crowd murmur.)

ROBERT He's immensely strong.

(Crowd murmur.)

MARY *(Overlapping crowd murmur, in her house.)* Nelly, Nelly, there's someone out back, honey, having a terrible fight. They came through the woods and started yelling all kinds of things.

NELLY *(To Mary.)* Where was you? I thought you was in bed.

(Simultaneously.)

ROBERT And I heard a ringing in my ears—

MARY You better go out and see, honey.

(Simultaneously.)

ROBERT —and I saw what he was trying to do and everything went white.

(Crowd reaction.)

PATSY *(To Lena; in town.)* I mean he's out there polishing the chrome and dash and all.

(Simultaneously.)

ROBERT And he pushed me!

(Crowd reaction.)

LENA I know, it's amazing.

(Some of the crowd reaction has been to Eva, who has been moaning throughout Robert's testimony. Now she screams—a huge ear-splitting scream, and I mean it.)

EVELYN Oh, God, baby, my baby—

EVA —No, no, no, no, no!—

EVELYN See her crippled body. See her broken back; why, why has God cursed me with this burden. I don't complain. I ask why? We love Him. We bless Him. Praise Him. And this monster! I mean Skelly! My daughter is weak; you're trying to kill her! Look at her! Is that what you want? I only ask why?

PREACHER *(Overlapping.)* The Lord works in—

EVELYN *(Overlapping.)* Why? I said, why? I have a right to know; I'll repent if I've done anything; if I've sinned—

CORA *(Overlapping.)* —Eva said to me—Eva, you know what you said. Skelly worked for me sometimes; none of you knew him. He was honest.

EVELYN *(Overlapping.)* My daughter has never spoken to you; my daughter has never spoken to a person like you; my daughter has been scarred, permanently scarred by this. She's crippled already. She's weak. She can't stand up.

CORA If you'd listen to me.

EVELYN No, no. I won't listen to you; I won't trust the word of a woman like you.

CORA And what are you?

(Crowd reaction, which continues until singing begins.)
(Simultaneously.)

EVELYN *(Screaming wildly.)* My daughter is a virgin! She's pure! She's a Christian, from a Christian home; a daughter of God and you'd put your word against the word of a virgin. A beer-swilling harlot. Everyone knows.

CORA I talked to her because I knew Skelly would never never harm anyone. If you'd listen to me.

(Simultaneously.)

EVELYN A drunken Whore of Babylon! Harlot! Daughter of Babylon! Go back to your beer parlor; your house of sin. You couldn't keep your husband and you couldn't keep your whore boy friend.

JUDGE *(Begins pounding steadily with the gavel.)* Order. Order. Order. Order.

(Simultaneously.)

EVELYN In the name of God before this court I call you that. Liar. You're the liar. Before God I call you that. On His word. His holy word. Yes! Put her on the stand. Let her talk. We have nothing to hide. Ask her if she didn't keep a whore boy friend up to her place. Ask her what kind of woman she is…

(The Congregation begins singing "When the Roll Is Called Up Yonder," to the rhythm of the gavel. The Congregation drowns Evelyn out with the loud, joyous hymn, the pulpit beaten now, in time to the song. The song is sung to its finish. Everyone moves into small groups. Worried, quiet.)
(A long pause. Silence.)

PATSY *(Very upset; quietly to Walter.)* Pretty sure.

WALTER *(Beside her, after a pause.)* Are you sure it's me? *(Pause.)* You're not sure are you? *(Pause.)* It could be somebody else. It could have been what's-his-name. Chuck. *(Pause.)*

PATSY Well, it was somebody! *(Pause.)* Oh, God.

WALTER I don't know what you want from me.

PATSY I'll tell your precious Cora what you're like. Then we'll see how high and mighty you think you are. No, you wouldn't like that very much, would you?

(A street in town: the Judge, Peck, the Trucker, and Josh in a group. They speak with deliberation.)

JUDGE The oats was late 'cause of the spring was so wet.

PECK Me and the boy couldn't plant till late May. Eighteenth of May. Up till then the ground was so wet we couldn't get at the field even.

TRUCKER And then that cold spell.

JUDGE Ground was solid out our way till almost April.

JOSH Hell it was.

JUDGE Almost April. You couldn't stick a fork into it. Hard as a rock.

PECK 'Course you're high; it wasn't near so bad along in the valley.

TRUCKER Oh, no, It wasn't near.

PECK Along the valley there I don't imagine there was more than six-ten cold days. Days it was froze solid. River wasn't more than three inches ice.

JOSH I don't believe it ever froze clear across.

PECK No, it never froze across.

JOSH There was some running out aways right through the winter.

PECK 'Course you're up on the hill there. You're not protected.

TRUCKER Yeah, it was froze solid right up through April.

JUDGE 'Course the rains was bad for you. In the valley there.

JOSH Oh, yeah.

TRUCKER I don't believe I've ever seen the rains so bad.

PECK Yeah, the river swelled up there along in March, I can't remember it that bad before. I said to Josh, I couldn't remember it that bad. There was that.

JOSH Most of the field was under six-ten feet of water along in the spring.

PECK April it was.

JOSH Yeah, I believe it was April.

PECK Wasn't able to set a plow till late in the month. Plowed for the oats finally in May. Eighteenth of May; that's the latest I can remember. I believe it was the eighteenth.

JOSH It was, I remember.

PECK Latest I remember.

JUDGE Well, you're in the valley there; you're not protected.

TRUCKER The floods was bad for you.

PECK Yeah, I'll say. It's rich soil, though. Good bottom topsoil.

TRUCKER Yeah, it's rich bottom land.

PECK It's good bottom land.

TRUCKER It's good for corn.

PECK Oh, yeah.

JUDGE It's sandy for oats though.

JOSH Yeah, the oats idn't doing well.

TRUCKER Well, it's been dry the past month.

PECK Radio says we might be heading for a drought.

JUDGE I been thinking I might have to irrigate. Later on. If it doesn't get wetter.

JOSH Yeah, we had all our rains right there together.

TRUCKER Not what you'd call a deep rain though.

JUDGE No, it run right off, much as there was to it. Could sure use some of it now.

PECK Oh, yeah.

JUDGE The corn's beginning to curl; I noticed this morning.

(Josh leaves, goes to Lena's porch.)

TRUCKER It was dry this morning. Almost no dew even.

PECK There wasn't much even low like I am. Course you're up on the hill. You must be getting the worst of it.

JOSH *(To Lena.)* Just got off work.

LENA You look it; you didn't even wash up.

JOSH I did, but it'll have to wear off; it's ground right in, I think.

LENA Where did you want to go tonight?

JOSH You mind eating up at Cora's or you want to go into Centerville?

LENA It doesn't matter, whatever you want.

JOSH We might as well go on into town to the drive-in.

LENA Oh lets, 'cause Patsy'll be there and I wanted to see her.

JOSH You're seen her this morning.

LENA Yes, but she said she had a surprise she wanted to tell me.

JOSH I don't know what she thinks is a surprise. Then we'll go into the movies, all right? Or would you rather just drive?

LENA I'd kinda like to see the picture.

JOSH Whatever you want.

LENA *(Going to Patsy.)* She's gonna be with Chuck so you be nice to him.

PATSY Don't you think he's cute, though?

LENA I guess.

PATSY Was he really at the drive-in with her? That's so funny. His name's Walter I found out. But I can't imagine. That's the funniest thing; I just wish I'd have seen it.

LENA It's not so bad.

PATSY But, she's so old for him. My God, she's thirty-eight.

LENA She isn't, is she? Mama said thirty-four.

PATSY Well, she's older than any thirty-four, and besides that's bad enough.

LENA That soldier you went out with last year was that old.

PATSY He was not.

LENA I'll bet he was. He was balding.

PATSY He was not, what do you think I am, he had a crew cut; besides he was twenty-six, I saw his ID.

LENA Oh, he wasn't any twenty-six.

PATSY I saw his draft card, Lena. Besides, my God, it's different with a boy. He was very nice. Besides, I only went out with him twice. I felt sorry for him. We didn't do anything.

(On Eva's porch.)

CORA That's hard for me to believe, Eva.

EVA You ask Robert; what difference does it make?

CORA 'Cause he worked for me; he used to pick up the garbage for his hogs. He lived out back of the café for years, till they burned that shack down. I still say it was Driver Junior's brother and Josh did it, burned that shack down.

EVA We come into the clearing back behind Nelly Windrod's house, by her mill there, and I heard something, and he said he'd show me what.

CORA Skelly did? He did not.

EVA No. He didn't say.

CORA Eva if that's not the truth, you better say how it really happened.

EVA I said it happened like Robert said. It's like that and I don't care if you knew him or not. Mama said the preacher said a sermon about the evil in people like him and that we should have killed him or something before he had a chance to take advantage of me. I've been cursed and scarred.

CORA You can't lie under oath, Eva.

EVA *(Running away.)* You're the one who's going to hell. Not me. I didn't do it, anyway; Nelly did it.
(In the café.)

CORA It wasn't Skelly.

TRUCKER *(Leaving café.)* Well, who do you think it was?

CORA She told me.

TRUCKER If he hadn't of died, I know he wouldn't have seen the light of day the next morning. *(Goes to Josh.)*
(A street in town.)

JOSH *(Almost good-naturedly.)* Damn that mutt anyway.

TRUCKER Good watchdog, is he?

JOSH That old bitch of a dog, I'll kill that bitch.

TRUCKER Wakes up the folks does he?

JOSH Every damn time we drive up it starts up a racket. Son of a bitch, every light in the house goes on. She has to run on in, the noise that dog raises, every goddamned night. I don't care how easy I drive up. We started parking on down the block, she still starts up as soon as Lena steps a foot on the porch.
(On Martha's porch.)

MARTHA When I think of the evil in this world.

WILMA To do some bestial thing like that.
(In town.)

PECK *(To the Trucker and the Judge.)* Well, I never figured him to actually hurt anybody.

TRUCKER Hell, we all knew he was loony.

JUDGE Someone like that—we all knew he was capable of any kind of thing.

PECK Capable, yes, but I never figgered him for actually hurting anybody.

TRUCKER Well, when somebody lives like that—away from everybody.

PECK The boys give him a hard time but he can take care of himself.

TRUCKER Should have been put away the way he looks at everybody.

JUDGE Should have been shot—just shot in the woods; nobody the wiser.

PECK I just never really figgered him to do anything. Capable, yes, but I have to admit I'd never thought he'd do anything. Outright, I mean.

MARTHA *(On her porch.)* Why, she called Evelyn Jackson a liar to her face, and Eva too. Swore things, the devil and his angels wouldn't believe it. She'd stand up there and swear black was white.

MARY *(In her house, upstairs.)* Nelly, Nelly, there's someone out back, honey, having a terrible fight; they came through the woods and started yelling all kinds of things.

NELLY *(As she exits to a street in town.)* Where was you? I thought you was in bed.

MARY You better go out and see, honey.

MAVIS Morning.

NELLY Good morning.

MAVIS We don't see you to talk to much.

NELLY Well, summer is a slow time; I've been saving up strength for Peck's corn crop this year.

MAVIS It's sure looking good.

NELLY I drive past; I've been keeping my eye on it.

MAVIS How is the mill?

NELLY Well, summer is slow.

MAVIS We see you drive by.

NELLY Evenings I've been going into Centerville; talking to the farmers over there; say we might be into a drought.

MAVIS We saw you, I believe going into the movie house there.

NELLY Yes, I don't get a chance to go often.

MAVIS Well, we don't go.

NELLY I've seen the girl there.

MAVIS Patsy? Oh, yes, Patsy enjoys it. She goes with Chuck; awfully nice boy; I guess you know we're planning a wedding; I said it wasn't any use having a church wedding, all amounts to the same—Patsy wouldn't hear of it, of course, so I suppose we're going all out.

NELLY He's an awfully nice boy, I hear.

MAVIS Do you? I'm glad to hear it; we hardly know them really; but he does seem sweet; his family has a lovely farm, we visited. Last Sunday. They grow up so fast.

NELLY Quite a nice young lady.

MAVIS We're proud of her. How's your mother?

NELLY Oh, Mom's the same; her mind's gone. I hate to leave her alone nights. Just like a child.

MAVIS Well, you have a life of your own; you have to get out.

NELLY Yes, I do. I hate to leave her, though, just the same.

MAVIS We see you driving into Centerville.

NELLY It's good to get away from the mill; Duane nearly runs it for me now.

MAVIS I was talking to your mother; poor thing.

NELLY Yes, it's sad.

MAVIS I remember she had a fine mind.

NELLY Yes, she did. One of the first registered nurses in Des Moines. Long time ago now; when she was a girl.

MAVIS She goes on terrible about you; poor thing.

NELLY I know, she doesn't know what she's saying half the time.

MAVIS Still she tells things; it must be terrible for you.

NELLY I'll take care of her, Mavis, as long as my strength holds out.

MAVIS Martha Truit said, the life you have to bear.

NELLY It's my cross, Mavis.

MAVIS I know, I told Peck...

NELLY How is Peck?

MAVIS Oh, he's all right; his back is giving him trouble again. It's just nerves I keep telling him, but I don't know. Between you and me I don't know.
(On Martha's porch.)

WILMA Who knows what's in somebody's mind like that.

MARTHA Like that time—when was it, last summer.
(The people have wandered to random, scattered positions about the stage. They stand still and isolated, Robert and Eva moving about them as though walking through the woods.)

EVA No, in the wintertime and in the autumn. It's so nice, it smells so clean.

ROBERT Okay, the fall then.

EVA Yes. And it's heavy, heavy frost and it covers everything and that's rime.

ROBERT And it's just frost? Is it a hoarfrost?

EVA That's it, hoarfrost is rime. And it covers everything. Every little blade of grass and every tree and houses and everything. Like it's been dipped in water and then in sugar.

ROBERT Or salt. Yeah, I know what it is.

EVA It's better than ice storms or anything like that. And everything is white and sparkling so clean when the sun comes up it nearly blinds you and it's rare! It doesn't happen every year. And that's what I'd like to be. What I'd like to do. I have a book with a picture of Jack Frost painting rime on a windowpane with a paintbrush. Do you fly? Do you dream you fly?

ROBERT When?

EVA Ever?

ROBERT I guess. I haven't thought about it.

EVA How high? Think about it. It's important. Everybody flies, it's important how high.

ROBERT I don't know. Just over the ground.

EVA Really?

ROBERT I guess. As high as my head. I'm always getting tangled up in wires and all.

EVA I'm way over the treetops, just over the treetops, just brushing against the treetops, and I fly right over them, just brush them with my arms out. Over the whole town like an airplane. Spreading this salt frost in the autumn. I love autumn. And when the sun comes up—

ROBERT Right.

EVA It'll blind you!

ROBERT I've seen it.

EVA It's so bright it blinds you. I want to fly like that, all over the town, right over everybody. It's beautiful.

(Skelly takes a step forward, among the silent people.)

EVA Listen! Listen. Did you hear something?

(The people move from their still positions into small groups. Skelly comes to Cora and Walter.)

CORA Are you out there?

SKELLY Here. Yeah.

CORA Can Walter help you? You know Walter.

SKELLY Yeah, I know.

CORA We're gonna be turning in, but he can help you with it.

SKELLY The white one, with the spots?!

CORA Spotty?

SKELLY Had a litter.

CORA She did?

SKELLY She had four but she ate one.

CORA Skelly, you just let them go wild, that's terrible, you should take them away from her.

SKELLY The runt, the last one.

WALTER She what? She ate one of them?

CORA Pigs do that sometimes; they're terrible. A runt or something that they think is weak, they will.

WALTER Couldn't you stop her?

SKELLY I didn't see it.

CORA Oh, he lets them just go wild, you can't get near them; one of them's all right, the brown one.

SKELLY She's good.

CORA One of them is tame and nice, the rest you can't get near them. He has four. So that makes seven now, doesn't it? You're getting to be a regular rancher.

SKELLY The brown's a good one.

CORA He has an old hound dog he keeps too; he's good with them but they just run wild. *(She leaves.)*

WALTER You want me to help you?

SKELLY I'm all right. You like her?

WALTER Do I like? What? Who?

SKELLY Johnson. *(Pause.)* That Patsy Johnson. Cora ain't good to you?

WALTER Cora? I imagine she's good to everybody.

SKELLY But you. She's good to you. I seen you with Patsy Johnson. You like her? You like that carrying on?

WALTER What? I thought you were talking about your brown sow; I've not seen her.

SKELLY I said, if you think you're a big man and you play around here and you play around there.

WALTER You want me to help you slop the hogs?

SKELLY I'll be all right.

WALTER Well, if you make it your business to know what everybody is doing, I see why Cora makes sure we pull down the shades at night, and turn off the light and listen to hear if anyone's about. If that's your business, I guess I don't have to tell you what Patsy Johnson is like.

SKELLY She's a bitch.

WALTER Patsy? And them that lies down with...

SKELLY Cora's a good woman.

WALTER Yes, well, you slop the hogs and carry off the garbage and I build the fence and paint the café; we're none of us freeloaders, I don't suppose. I don't imagine I owe anyone anything except money. I don't owe anybody time. I can't say that I see it as any of your business anyway, Skelly. You don't have to worry about her; she's managed seven years without you or me either. Don't you think? *(Pause.)* Wouldn't you say? *(Pause.)* You go on and slop you hogs. *(Pause.)* Go on, get on, be thankful she gives it to you for the price of carrying it away. *(Pause.)* Hey. What do you do with those hogs anyway? How come they're so wild? *(Pause.)*

SKELLY I feed 'em, they run wild.

WALTER Go on, I didn't mean anything by it. Good night.

MARY *(To Mavis.)* I have a bruise there on the inside of my elbow, she holds onto me there, she pushes at me terrible, she can't help it.
(A street in town.)

EVA If you had a car, you could drive all over.

ROBERT What do I want with a car?

EVA Are you afraid?

ROBERT What for? So I can drive around the square. Around the square, around the square. It's all they ever do; all the boys with cars. Around the square and over into Centerville to a drive-in to eat and a drive-in to see a movie.

EVA You just don't want to be like—

ROBERT Everybody doesn't have to have a car. Everybody talks like that's all there is. The guys at school spend their whole lives in or on top of or under their cars. They eat in them and sleep in them and change clothes and drink and get sick and vomit and make out with their girls—it's all they even ever talk about. Evolution's gonna take their feet right away from them. Make turtles with wheels for legs out of them.

EVA I think you're afraid 'cause of Driver.

ROBERT Well, that's another thing I hadn't thought of. They die in them too. Live and die without ever stepping outside. Why would I want that?

LENA *(Offstage.)* Sometimes I think life is so short and we should enjoy it for the time we're here and then I think I should work really hard so I can be comfortable, you know, after I've made some money, and then I think how awful working all that time would be and most of my life would be gone by that time and I'd have wasted it, you know what I mean? No, no, don't, Josh!

JOSH *(Offstage, to Lena.)* You said you would.

LENA Sometime, I said.

JOSH You don't want to?

LENA It isn't that. You know. Don't now!

JOSH What?

LENA You know. If something happens, you don't know what can happen. And there's no assurance—of what can happen.

JOSH Nothing can happen, I told you.

LENA Come on. Don't now! I'm not kidding now.

JOSH Just see.

LENA You don't like me really or you'd respect me.

JOSH What? I don't like you? Why do you think I want to?

LENA You know what I mean.

JOSH Just see. Just see. Just see. Nothing will happen; just see.

LENA No, I said, now. Come on.

JOSH Jesus Christ, Lena.

LENA Well, don't be mad.

JOSH Well, you let me go so far and then say no, I don't know what you expect.

LENA It's all right, isn't it? Josh? Well, don't just sit there. I said sometime. Sometime, really. I mean it. Just not tonight. Okay? I want to, too; I just said not tonight. Really. It just scares me. Okay? Okay? *(Pause. Then rapidly.)* Josh! Damn it, now, come on. No! I said and that means no! Good Lord. *(Sound of someone being slapped. Pause.)* Now you're mad, aren't you?

PREACHER *(To Congregation.)* No, sir, it is the soul and responsibility of our very community. The laxity with which we met the obligations of our Christian lives. The blindness from which we allowed evil in our lives. We watched it fester and grow; we allowed this dreadful thing to happen through shirking our Christian duty. Nelly Windrod is not on trial here today. That man, may the Lord have mercy on his soul damned eternally to hell, and our blindness to His way. It is our responsibility and we must share that terrible knowledge. As you go your ways tonight. As you leave and walk and drive to your homes, realize that the burden must be ours and ask the Lord for his grace. Pray for these two souls as you pray for the lost, the outcast, as you pray for the soul of the damned, and the care of our boys overseas; Pray to the Lord to unlock the bitterness in the hearts of those like him in the world today and pray that they may see the light of His holy way.

CONGREGATION Amen.

PREACHER Amen, the Lord be with you.

(The Congregation walks slowly, as if coming from church, to the positions of the woods.)

JOSH Had the Olds out last night.

TRUCKER The old man's Olds?

JOSH Took it out onto the Old Sparta Road and opened it up.

TRUCKER Gene was out there last week.

JOSH Pegged it. Hundred twenty. That old needle was bouncing against the peg and half the way back again. Two miles or over, then I eased it down.

TRUCKER We'll have to take 'em out Sunday.

(In the woods—precisely as before, a rerun.)

EVA And it covers everything and that's rime.

ROBERT And it's just frost? Is it a hoarfrost?

EVA That's it, hoarfrost is rime. And it covers everything. Every little blade of grass and every tree and houses and everything. Like it's been dipped in water and then in sugar.

ROBERT Or salt. Yeah, I know what it is.

EVA It's better than ice storms or anything like that. And everything is white and sparkling so clean when the sun comes up it nearly blinds you and it's rare! It doesn't happen every year. And that's what I'd like to be. What I'd like to do. I have a book with a picture of Jack Frost painting rime on a windowpane with a paintbrush. Do you fly? Do you dream you fly?

ROBERT When?

EVA Ever?

ROBERT I guess. I haven't thought about it.

(They walk about the forest, walking slowly through the people.)

EVA How high? Think about it. It's important. Everybody flies, it's important how high.

ROBERT I don't know. Just over the ground.

EVA Really?

ROBERT I guess. As high as my head. I'm always getting tangled up in wires and all.

EVA I'm way over the treetops, just over the treetops, just brushing against the treetops, and I fly right over them, just brush them with my arms out. Over the whole town like an airplane. Spreading this salt frost in the autumn. I love autumn. And when the sun comes up—

ROBERT Right.

EVA It'll blind you!

ROBERT I've seen it.

EVA It's so bright it blinds you. I want to fly like that, all over the town, right over everybody. It's beautiful.

(Skelly steps forward.)

EVA Listen! Listen. Did you hear something?

ROBERT No. What?

EVA Like something rustling in the leaves?

ROBERT No. What? It was probably a rabbit.

(Skelly steps forward again.)

EVA Listen.

ROBERT I don't hear anything.

EVA Maybe it was the wind.

ROBERT There isn't any; maybe it was a fox.

EVA Don't.

ROBERT Or a wolf.

EVA Ted Caffey trapped a wolf in his barn last year.

ROBERT Shot its head off too.

EVA Oh, he did not—are you trying to scare me?—it got away.

ROBERT Shot it and killed it; took its pelt into the county agent in Centerville and got twenty dollars for it.

EVA It wasn't anything; we better get back.

ROBERT It was probably the mate looking for the one Caffey shot.

EVA Don't say that, it wasn't—

(Skelly moves again.)

EVA Listen!

(They stop still.)

WALTER *(Turning from his tree position.)* What's that junk heap of a what was it a Plymouth?

CORA At Church Street? That's Driver's car. Driver Junior's older brother. Drove it in stock car races; over in Centerville they have a track. The whole town went; used to, when he drove. I suppose they think it's bad luck now, he had some kind of accident; smashed it to hell, it looks like, doesn't it?

WALTER He get killed?

CORA Oh, yes, killed instantly. They hitched up a chain to the car and pulled it back here.

WALTER And dumped it in the middle of the street? The grass and weeds almost cover it; I didn't know what it was at first.

CORA Well, that's where the chain broke and the axle broke and every other damn thing broke, so there it sits. Not a very pretty sight.

(The following is from all over the stage. The characters may move from their stationary positions for a few steps and return to them. The woods become alive with their voices. The sequence should begin softly and build, becoming faster and more forceful toward the end.)

MARY Rusting away—flaking away.

EVELYN Falling apart, boarded together, everything flapping and rusting.

MARY All the buildings bowing and nodding.

PATSY Movie house been closed down eight years.

TRUCKER It was dry this morning; almost no dew even.

NELLY You fall down, you bruise, you run into things, you're old.

PATSY Tumbleweed blowing down the deserted streets.

MARY And the flowers dry up and die.

SKELLY You didn't go to the races to see him kill himself.

EVA And it covers everything and that's rime.

LENA I remember his laugh.

CORA Eldritch is all but a ghost town.

WILMA The wages of sin—

MARTHA I don't know, love.

EVA And when the sun comes up it blinds you!

EVELYN The mine shaft building used to just shine.

SKELLY All in he air.

JOSH Just see.

LENA It's a beautiful church.

WALTER Wouldn't you say?

MAVIS A decent person is afraid to move outside at night.

PREACHER As you go your way tonight.

CORA You seem uneasy.

EVELYN The doctor said it was just shock.

PECK You watch yourself.

MARY Gone, gone, gone.

EVA Like it's been dipped in water and then in sugar.

MAVIS And not seen the light of day tomorrow.

MARY All my children.

EVA And that's what I want to be.

(They are still, trees again.)

MARY Gone, gone gone.

EVA *(Continuing in the woods.)* You know what my mother says?

ROBERT What?

EVA When I come in?

ROBERT What?

EVA She says you're unresponsible, and she asks me things like where we go and all, everywhere we go every time I go anywhere with you. Everything we do.

ROBERT Where does she think we go?

EVA Oh, I tell her we just go walking in the woods; talking. She knows that but she thinks we do other things too.

ROBERT Like what?

EVA You know.

ROBERT Like what?

EVA You know. Dirty things.

ROBERT What does she think that for?

EVA I don't tell her, though.

ROBERT What would you tell her?

EVA About that. About when I have to pee and things.

ROBERT Well, there's nothing dirty about that.

EVA Well, don't you think I know!

ROBERT She means other things.

EVA What?

ROBERT Never mind.

EVA Well, don't you think I know? I know. You don't do things like that, you don't even look! I can, though; I know.

ROBERT You don't know anything.

EVA I DO TOO! I've seen. You think I'm so young because I'm so little. I'm fourteen; I can have babies already; and I've seen cows do it when they're in heat. But you wouldn't do something like that.

ROBERT Let's go back.

EVA Let's do. I know how; I can.

ROBERT When cows are in heat, that's one cow jumping on another; you don't know anything.

EVA You're ashamed; you're not old enough to.

ROBERT You don't know what you're talking about.

EVA Boys have to be older. But I'll bet your brother could anyway. I might as well because she thinks we do anyway. You're the one who doesn't know anything about it.

ROBERT I should, just to show you—don't—you don't know what you're talking about.

EVA What?

ROBERT Anything. Because you don't know anything about it.

EVA I do too. You're afraid.

ROBERT You don't know what you're talking about even.

(Their lines begin to overlap.)

EVA Only not here.

ROBERT Why not? What's wrong with here?

EVA You have to be in bed, stupid!

ROBERT If you think you know so much. *(Grabbing her.)*

EVA *(Violently.)* Let go of me! You leave me alone. I will if I want to.

ROBERT You want to get it in you so bad! You think I can't.

EVA Stop it.

ROBERT You think I won't do it.

EVA Leave me alone. I'll tell.

ROBERT No you won't; you asked for it.

MARY *(To Nelly, from upstairs at the Windrod house.)* Nelly, Nelly, there's someone out back, honey, having a terrible fight; they came through the woods and started yelling all kinds of things.

(Simultaneously.)

EVA Leave me alone.

NELLY Where was you? I thought you was in bed.

(Simultaneously.)

ROBERT *(Throwing her to the ground.)* You think you're so smart; I'll show you. Shut up now, shut up or I'll kill you anyway; you asked for it.

(They struggle violently on the ground. Eva saying "No, stay away, leave me alone." S creaming.)

ROBERT You little whore; you think I won't. Stop it.

MARY You better go out and see, honey.

(Nelly takes up a shotgun, throwing open the door.)

(Simultaneously.)

SKELLY *(From the woods, breaking toward them. His lines are simultaneous with the above struggle.)* What do you think—leave her alone. Don't hurt her. Robert. Don't hurt her.

NELLY What's going on? Who's there?

(Skelly throws Robert off her. Eva screams. Skelly, seeing Nelly, looks up and runs toward her instinctively.)

SKELLY Help her!

(As Eva screams, Nelly levels the shotgun at Skelly's chest and fires first one, then the other, barrel. Skelly falls, violently spun about by the force of the gun. In production it is important that the blanks for the shotgun be very loud, about half as much power as in actual shots; the powder from the gun smokes the entire stage until the end of the play. The Congregation moves from their stationary position as Skelly hits the floor. They mill a brief moment. The gun is passed, without much interest from one to the other of the men: Judge, Josh, Peck, and the Trucker. The cast assembles at the court, blocking Skelly from the audience's view.)

JUDGE *(Immediately after the Congregation begins to move.)* State your name.

ROBERT *(Moving into the witness stand.)* Robert Conklin.

JUDGE Do you swear to tell the whole truth and nothing but the truth, so help you God?

ROBERT I do.

JUDGE There's nothing to be nervous about, Robert. We want you to tell the court, just in your own words, what happened on the night in question. Can you do that?

ROBERT Yes, I think.

JUDGE We know this has been a terrible shock to you—

ROBERT —I'm okay. I think. See—Eva and I were walking. We do quite frequently. Just wandering through the woods, talking. And we noticed that it had begun to get dark so we thought we had better start back—and we were heading back toward the main street, that would be west. And Eva thought she heard something behind us and we listened but we didn't hear it again so I assumed we were hearing things. Or it was our imagination. And it got dark pretty fast. And we were just coming into the clearing right behind the mill. Windrod's mill. And uh, we heard something again and this time we saw something behind the trees and we started running. More as a joke than anything—and then he started running too. And it was Skelly, and I wasn't afraid of him, but I knew he'd never liked my brother, and he started running too. He must have been following us all the time; everybody knows how he spies on people; I guess just as we broke into the clearing—and he came from nowhere.

(Crowd reaction.)

ROBERT And he took us by surprise and he pushed me—he hit me from behind; I don't know if I passed out or not.

(*Crowd murmur.*)

ROBERT He's immensely strong.

(*Crowd murmur.*)

ROBERT And I heard a ringing in my ears and I saw what he was trying to do, and everything went white. And he pushed me.

EVA (*Screams as loud as possible.*) AHHHHHHHHHHH! AHHHHHHHH-HHHH! AHHHHHHHHHHHHH!

EVELYN Oh, God, oh God, baby, my baby.

EVA No! no, no, no, no, no.

EVELYN See her crippled body. See her broken back; why? Why has God cursed me with this burden? I don't complain, I ask why? We love Him. We bless Him. Praise Him.

(*Everyone freezes. Tableau. Silence.*)

PATSY (*Off.*) You know I saw you the day you first came into town, I'll bet. I've seen you a lot. Up at the Hilltop. I told Lena I liked you. No, no, come on. Yes, it's all right; I want you to. You know I do.

WALTER (*Off.*) I've got nothing with me.

PATSY (*Off.*) I know, it doesn't matter. You wouldn't wash your feet with your socks on. Be easy. Did you know I'd watched you? Huh? Did you? Huh? Did you know I had?

WALTER (*Off.*) No. I've seen you a couple of times.

PATSY (*Off.*) I told Lena I liked you. I don't like any of the boys here; they're terrible, shiftless; oh, they're all right. But nobody wants to spend their life here; not here in this place rotting away. Walter! You're name's Walter, isn't it? I found out. Oh. Oh. I love you, Walter, I do. I really do. I love you. Oh, I do. Really. Did you know that? I have since I saw you that first time. I do. I really do. I love you so much. I love you, oh, I do, I love you. I do. Oh, I love you, Walter. You're the only one I love; I do. Really, I do.

(*Pause. Silence. The people mill gently leave the stage slowly, silently, a few at a time. Skelly lies on stage where he fell. Curtain.*)

END OF PLAY

The Gingham Dog

INTRODUCTION

I'm leaving this play essentially as it was. I was going to rewrite it, doing what? maybe making it more politically correct, but to hell with it. This is where we were in 1969, I know it's unbelievable, but this is where we were.

This is the original introduction, the only one I wrote for one of my published plays.

When *The Rimers of Eldritch* was published I sat in front of the typewriter a long time (days) trying to work on an "Introduction" for the book. Too many things had happened that month; the air was waterlogged. At least in my room. The dedication was all that was left by the time I finished. I was going to write about Joe Cino. I don't think I ever will now. He kept appearing in my head saying, "Oh, come off it."

I once started a poem that began: "What do I owe, and to whom?" and Marshall Mason remarked: "That promises to be a long one."

Yeah.

I think of a hundred incidents at once this morning. This morning after a long useless night of trying to work on someone's screenplay (screenplay?) I sit at the typewriter again, wondering whom to credit for the first production of this play that was written so many years ago and has gone through so many drafts and hands and productions before it finally gets committed (sentenced) to print here.

What do I owe and to whom?

Would I hurt the Washington Theatre Club by admitting that a very good staged reading was presented prior to their "premiere?" Could I discredit my friends who were in the reading at the New Dramatists Workshop by admitting that the first "professional" production of the play was presented in Washington, D.C.? And wouldn't it look a lot cleaner just to list the Broadway cast? And what about that reading at the Clark Center in 1965? And I know it doesn't make any difference at all; probably none give a damn really and neither do I.

And there's that matter of dedication. B.H. or E.F., or G.F. or T.B. or R.L., or pick a letter—probably they had a place somewhere. Something they said once, something I overheard and never even remembered I remembered.

And of course Cino without whom, etc., and is it fortunate that I can think of him less often—finally. And Ellen and Michael and Bob. What and to whom? And of course there's that "What."

What. Well, certainly not just this. Surely not. Later, then.

And to whom? An actress whom I never saw (but lied and said I did) for whom I wrote the role of Gloria—imagining the performances as they were related to me by friends, trying to create a role worthy of those glowing reports. And to Vincent. Later, Vince: I'll get to it. And shouldn't I say something to the exaltation of Broadway reviewers?

No.

And how do you wind through all the wind? (Cubed.)

I suppose I'm so oddly unbitter and so nostalgic only because the play has a longer history than any of the others—from finished script to binding. I've seen three very good very different productions. And so much has happened in between. For one thing, I don't much write like this anymore. It should have been obvious to a number of people—but it didn't matter.

The play began with the people—the only place I ever seem to begin. And soon after, the shape. Before it was really begun I knew I wanted the shape to be what it is now. No audience has seen the second act acted much differently from the way I intended it. I thought it was going to be difficult. I suppose it was, but the actors made it look easy. It didn't mean anything to many people. It means a great deal to me.

And what has that big Golden Theatre (which is small) on Broadway (which is on 45th Street) to do with the Caffe Cino? Or the stage of the gym at Ozark High? Actually it wasn't any different. Not a bit. I was working with great people. What came of it? Who knows. I said once somewhere that theatre was in for a big boost—when the Off-Off-Broadway writers and directors began to work in the uptown theatres. I'm not so sure. This year I've seen all the hits. Most all the shows. (Plays, whatever.)

I like *The Gingham Dog* better.

It occurs to me that in its brief run it was seen by more people than have seen any of my other plays. Now, that should mean something. It doesn't seem to, but it seems it should.

Who saw it?

Who are we out there in the audience? Today, I mean.

What do we do?

Traveling across the country—meeting people and seeing places; isn't it unbelievable? It always seems people are telling us that we have the best damn standard of living in the world. You know, without checking the statistics, I'll bet that's a lie. Sweden, Denmark, Holland—looked very familiar. Looked fine. Germany, England. But it isn't that we're always bragging or that politicians at the same time compliment our wealth and credit themselves for it. What do we do? The young people of my country are alive—they're living. I don't know how. It isn't just that they are living, they are refusing to die. While the country dies and dries and blows away from under them. How do they do it. They scream in anguish—bitterly angry and desperately sick because they love this country unbearably; and can't bear it. We're raping our land. Ignoring (deeply, truly) the Indian, the black man, and each other. I listen to the opinion of my country—the voice of the people is reported into my room on the TV in interviews and how can you keep from crying? We are wonderful, beautiful, tall, strong, generous, loving, gentle, kind, concerned, and passionate monsters. What do we do? Many people believe they are better than other people, *innately;* deserve to keep their wealth, or equal someone's possessions regardless of what it costs—what it costs *them;* their children; and the land. I mean the earth. Dirt. The very soil is dying. The water and wildlife are poisoned and it's like smoking: it's a habit and it's killing us and we know it, but what can we do, we can't stop.

What do I owe and to whom?

(Everybody sing: To the girl who at the age of eight

taught me how to copulate

imitating her dad's eight-pager

that we found in the bottom of the dresser.)

Just for now, at least: (it must be noon, it must be two) I'll list on the next page the three productions chronologically; dedicate the play not to those people from whom I learned it, but to my parents from whom I learned (but did I?) so much more. (It's about time I gave you something.) And for now apologize to Mr. Katz whom I promised (six years ago) to take to the opening of my first Broadway play—I came by the hotel and they said you weren't working there anymore. That's all for now. No more apologies.

I don't often start poems and I very seldom finish them and when I do I never much like them. The one about owing and to whom—yes, that would be a long one.

That will be one I never finish.

LANFORD WILSON

July 14, 1969
New York City

One historical curiosity: later on the day the above introduction was written, about a hundred people, actors, directors, designers and writers that Marshall Mason had called together—met over a Thom McAn shoe store on upper Broadway in New York City and formed a theater called Circle Repertory Company.

PRODUCTION

The Gingham Dog was presented by The New Dramatists Committee Workshop, New York City, February 26, 1968. Direction and design by Marshall Mason. Stage Manager, David Rapp. Lighting by Harry Pinkerton. The cast was as follows:

GLORIA ....Lea Scott
VINCENT ....Michael Warren Powell
ROBERT ....David Gallagher
BARBARA ....Gretchen Walther

It was subsequently presented by The Washington Theatre Club, Washington, DC, September 27, 1968. Directed by Davey Marlin-Jones. Production design by James Parker. Lighting by William Eggleston. Production Stage Manager, Ralph Strait. The cast was as follows:

GLORIA ....Micki Grant
VINCENT ....Robert Darnell
ROBERT ....Bob Spencer
BARBARA ....Diane Gardner

It was subsequently presented by Haila Stoddard/Mark Wright/Duane Wilder/Harold Scott at the John Golden Theatre, in New York City, on April 23, 1969. It was directed by Alan Schneider; the setting was by William Ritman; costumes were by Theoni V. Aldredge; and the lighting by Tharon Musser. The Associate Producer was David G. Meyers. The cast, in order of appearance, was as follows:

GLORIA ....Diana Sands
VINCENT ....George Grizzard
ROBERT ....Roy London
BARBARA ....Karen Grassle

CHARACTERS

Gloria, a black woman, 27, attractive without being devastating
Vincent, her husband, 28, strong, handsome, white
Robert, a neighbor, about 25
Barbara, Vincent's sister, 18, attractive

SCENE

Gloria and Vincent's apartment on the third floor of a new building in New York's Lower East Side, "East Village." The building is fresh, cold, sterile, hard and thin-shelled; the walls and ceilings are refrigerator white. Long expanses of flat walls, very sharp, unmolded corners, door frames, etc. Parquet floors. The limitations of the architecture have been rather lovingly overcome by comfortable, tasteful, practical furnishings.

We see the living room, kitchenette and doors to the hall, bath and bedroom. A window overlooks the street below. On the long window ledge are rock specimens: quartz crystals, tourmaline, an amethyst geode, etc. Among bracketed hanging bookshelves are components of a rather elaborate stereo outfit. The room also has served as Vincent's studio; there is a drawing board with blueprints spread out over it; a small tabouret beside it. The stove, sink, and refrigerator should be practical. It is 1968.

THE GINGHAM DOG

ACT ONE

At rise, although the apartment is almost compulsively clean, there are piles of clothes in the kitchen, a footlocker beside them, several boxes are packed or ready to be packed and a suitcase is near the door. Gloria is going through a pile of clothes distractedly, dumps them finally, pushes a box aside with her foot, and wanders to the window, a sponge in hand, looking as if to clean without knowing where to start or what to put away. The door is ajar. Gloria is a well-educated, if somewhat vulgar, graduate of New York University. She must have a personal charm, an energy that outweighs a kind of frantic, superficial vulgarity, a detachment from most things and a driving passion for others. Vincent enters, Gloria does not look around. He comes bustling in, a little winded from the stairs. He is in shirt sleeves, suit pants, a tie slack at his throat. Vincent is a strong, good-looking man, though he looks now, sometimes, rather like a tired young executive. He goes to the drawing board and begins packing whatever chalk, pencils, etc., that he might want to take. There is a tension between them as though they have been arguing for some time.

GLORIA *(Lifts a rock from the window ledge, sets it down.)* Do you want this?

VINCENT *(Without looking up.)* What?

GLORIA This slag glass or rutilated quartz or whatever-the-hell it is.

VINCENT Is this the mail?

GLORIA Well, what does it look like?

VINCENT The mail. Is this all there was?

GLORIA Uhm. *(There is a mumbling groan characteristic of Gloria, a comic understatement, rather like saying, "I pass.")*

VINCENT Not a damn piece of mail in five days that isn't advertisements.

GLORIA *(Has wandered back to the pile of winter clothes.)* Do you want these in the footlocker?

VINCENT What are they?

GLORIA Well, turn your curly head around and see. All these winter clothes. Do you want them sorted or what?

VINCENT I don't care. Just let them do it when they get here; they're paid to pack things.

GLORIA I might want to clear some of this crap off the floor so I can get started cleaning the place up. Well, I can't do this jazz alone. Fuck it. *(Kicks the pile.)* I said fuck it.

VINCENT This minute?

GLORIA Funny.

VINCENT I don't want any of it. Just throw it all out for all I care.

GLORIA You'll want "any of it" next winter.

VINCENT I may not even be in this temperature zone next winter, how do I know?

GLORIA What, are you going "on the road?" Vincent the vagrant. A little late in the spring to start a new life as a box-car hopper, don't you think?

VINCENT "A little late in the spring." That's very good. You're working at it.

GLORIA Of course you've hopped everything else. Bandwagons—

VINCENT —You!

(She nods an acknowledgment and heads toward the bookcases.)

VINCENT Now just stay the hell away from the goddamned record player. Just leave it all alone. They'll pack it.

GLORIA I'm not touching the goddamned Garrard record player. I wouldn't go near it.

VINCENT OK, OK.

GLORIA —Pickering cartridge, Janzen speaker, Telefunken turntable; I wouldn't go near it. It can rot there for all I care.

VINCENT It won't rot there.

GLORIA What, are you giving it away?

VINCENT I am certainly *not* giving it away.

GLORIA Taking it along with you? Hopping box-cars with a pack over your back like Santa Claus, for Christsake. Handing out Deutsche Grammaphon records to all the good little kiddies. If they've been real good little mama's helpers they get *Till Eulenspiegel's Merry Pranks,* only just so-so, maybe *Saint Matthew's Passion, Condensed.*

VINCENT If you'll be quiet and let me think, I'll get out of your bumbling way. You bumble around the room like a bus.

GLORIA Are you going to help me take down those shelves or not? Well, never mind, you obviously aren't, I don't know why I asked.

VINCENT I don't want them. I don't even want them stored. They never work, they fall off the damned wall, they can be thrown out.

GLORIA Well, whether you want them or not they still have to come down. *(Out of desperation finally, she settles at the pile of clothes and begins packing them in the footlocker. She folds things, rather than wadding, pressing them with her hand. Even when she is flailing about, you have the feeling that she is packing the trunk neatly.)*

VINCENT I don't know why you've suddenly decided to move off just because I am. You aren't going to find a better place around here.

GLORIA Who said I wanted to live around here? You think I'm passionately in love with the Lower East Side? What, have I suddenly got the hots for the electric sitar?

VINCENT I'd leave all this stuff with you. I don't want it; it would save everyone a lot of headaches.

GLORIA No, thank you no. You just store it up, you'll find a use for it. I don't need it thank you.

VINCENT Were you here on Thursday?

GLORIA When was Thursday?

VINCENT Day before—

GLORIA No, why?

VINCENT Because I called here—

GLORIA *(Overlapping.)* Robert said you called and asked for some of your stuff. I told him I didn't know anything about it—

VINCENT —It's been right here for five days—

GLORIA —I don't know anything about it. I haven't looked at it or gone near it—

VINCENT —You knew what I wanted; you might have been considerate enough to do this one thing; it's not like I—

GLORIA —It's your work and your blueprints; I told you I'm not interested in it—

VINCENT It never occurred to you that I wouldn't have called here unless it was impossible—

ROBERT *(Calling from downstairs.)* Vincent.

GLORIA *(With a glance to the open window.)* —It occurred to me that if you were that desperate for them you could come and get them yourself. You must have managed somehow.

ROBERT *(Off.)* Gloria.

VINCENT Yes, sure, by drawing out the file copies—which have "File Copy" stamped across them and is strictly against company policy.

ROBERT *(Off.)* Vincent.

GLORIA *(Moving to the window to look out.)* I promised to burn the damn things and you don't know how close I've come.

ROBERT *(Off.)* Vincent.

VINCENT *(As Gloria looks out the window.)* I don't know what you think that would get you.

ROBERT *(Off.)* Hey!

GLORIA *(Moving back to the kitchen.)* Someone's calling you.

VINCENT What the—*(Looking out the window.)* It's Robert—looking like a lost duck—*(Calling.)* Yeah?

ROBERT *(Off.)* You got my other set of keys? I can't find my keys.

GLORIA What does he...

VINCENT His keys—Where are Robert's keys? Where—

GLORIA *(Has reached into the cabinet.)* Here! And you can tell him to keep them. *(She tosses him the keys.)*

VINCENT Hey! *(Soft.)* Dumb ass look up. Do you want them or not? *(He drops them out the window.)*

ROBERT *(Off.)* Kill me why don't you.

VINCENT *(Moving back to his drawing board.)* Nut.

GLORIA When's your sister coming over?

VINCENT How do I know when she's coming over? She said this morning. She thought she could be of some help.

GLORIA I'll bet. She could be of some help by staying away.

VINCENT Please don't start in on Barbara. I know she's useless and you know she's useless, but Barbara at least thinks she's helpful.

GLORIA I'm hip.

VINCENT It's no good, really; cleaning the apartment, you know.

GLORIA Yes, well, I'm going to clean it up if I have to clean around both of you. I don't know why you even came back if you hired movers to do everything for you—just so you could be compulsive all over the living room.

VINCENT *I'm* being compulsive?—if that's not the pot calling the kettle—

GLORIA Black.

(Gloria joins Vincent in speaking the bracketed words.)

VINCENT If you clean it up, they'll only say "What a pretentious [educated nigger,] she only cleaned up her filth to prove [how white she was.]" If you leave it dirty they'll say "[what would you expect?]" They'll disinfect the place before any kind of tenant will live here anyway.

GLORIA I don't care if they come in here with gasoline and burn out the walls and ceiling. I said it was clean when we moved in and I'll leave it that way.

VINCENT "*I'll* leave it that way." What a martyr you are.

GLORIA *(Helping out.)...Black* martyr.

VINCENT What a black martyr you are.

GLORIA I'll say *we'll* leave it clean when you get off your white ass and help me clean it.

(Robert enters. He is carrying two large bags of groceries, holding them against

his chest, his mail in one hand and the other extends—as much as it can—a brightly colored advertisement. Robert is thin, blond or red-headed with a kind of haggardly interesting face. He wears glasses and is all angles and is rather clumsy. A kind of high voice, nervous and cynical.)

ROBERT Hey, Gloria—Knock knock—You kids want to stop fighting long enough to take this? It was in my box by mistake.

GLORIA Thanks. You want me to help you?

ROBERT No, don't touch anything, I got it balanced now. This one's ripped from top to bottom—I think, I can't look. So how's the Master Builder?

VINCENT Come on, knock it off.

ROBERT Okay, Jesus. When did you get back?

VINCENT About half an hour ago or so.

ROBERT I gotta dump this stuff—I brought you some goodies. *(Robert exits, but continues to yell at them as he takes the groceries to his apartment directly across the hall.)*

VINCENT Goodie!

ROBERT So why don't you let a fellow know where you are, for Christsake? I was going to call your office but it slipped my mind.

VINCENT *(Yells to him.)* Thanks.

ROBERT *(Off.)* Well, then you called here so it wasn't necessary. You know you sound like every other Young Man On His Way Up Coming Down From a Six Day Binge over the phone? You get those plans all right?

GLORIA You get those plans all right?

ROBERT Well, anyway, I just assumed you were out on some really knocked out trip and would return to earth when you returned to earth—*(Re-entering with a smaller bag.)* You get those plans all right?

VINCENT What plans?

ROBERT How do I know what plans, the plans you wanted, the blueprints.

VINCENT We used an office copy.

ROBERT I mopped you some staples from the cafe. There's sugar, some tea and a ten years' supply of mayonnaise.

VINCENT Tea?

ROBERT Drinking tea.

VINCENT Oh.

ROBERT English breakfast. Would it were Acapulco Gold but that's the breaks.

GLORIA Oh, thanks, I guess…I don't…

ROBERT Take it, it didn't cost me. *(Turning to Vincent.)* So how come all the stuff in the car? And don't say *what* car—your car downstairs in front of the building with all the stuff in it.

VINCENT I'm leaving, obviously.

ROBERT For good? I mean that not as opposed to "for bad."

VINCENT Probably for good. Who knows?

ROBERT *(Slight pause. Change in tempo. Robert is slightly more serious for a second or two.)* Well. Condolences, I guess. Really. And here I stand with a welcome home house warming gift. Well, do we hang the door with black crepe or, sorry doll, or throw a party or what?

GLORIA Either one, we won't be here.

ROBERT It must take a hundred times as much gall to break up as it does to get married.

GLORIA Don't trouble yourself with it.

ROBERT *(Overlapping some.)* Oh, don't tell me, I'm not involved. I only dropped in on my way to work to pick up a few pointers on marriage. I'd think I might at least close the door, I could hear you all the way down stairs—unless you *want* everyone in the building knowing your affairs— which is possible—

GLORIA Let them snoop, who cares?

ROBERT They don't have to snoop, you're drowning out their television sets. *(To Vincent.)* So where'd you go on your six-day binge?

VINCENT Five-day—

ROBERT Five-day.

VINCENT Uptown. With friends.

ROBERT Why, you haven't any friends in the Village? Well, that's easy enough to understand. New suit?

VINCENT Yes.

ROBERT That'll teach you to run off without a change of clothes. You're looking very "Uptown."

VINCENT Thanks.

ROBERT It isn't a compliment exactly—

VINCENT —I know, I know.

ROBERT So when are you leaving?

VINCENT Jesus Christ!

ROBERT OK, OK.

VINCENT Well, for someone who's not involved.

ROBERT OK. I try to be friendly and I'm misunderstood. I should learn. Are we going to see you kids on TV? On *Divorce Court?* I understand you get paid for it now.

GLORIA No one has said anything at all about divorce; Vince and I aren't discussing it and I don't see any reason for you to.

ROBERT *(Slowly.)* Oh. I get it; you're "separating." *(Pause.)* That's sort of the opposite of engagement, huh? I'd think you two would have enough balls to just give it up. I mean you've been fighting for a solid year now that I know of.

GLORIA Well, that's our problem.

ROBERT You're telling me. *(Beat.)* So what are you doing about your lease?

VINCENT Gloria might be staying.

GLORIA No, Gloria is not staying. *(To Robert.)* You want a stereo? Vince is giving his stereo away.

VINCENT No, Vince is not giving it away.

ROBERT You selling it? How much you want? I might know someone—

VINCENT No, I'm not selling it.

GLORIA He's dragging it cross-country.

VINCENT I'm crating it up with everything else and storing it in Stephen's basement.

ROBERT Where you going to be staying?

VINCENT Uptown. Temporarily anyway.

ROBERT With friends. What's her name, you can tell me—almost.

VINCENT *(Reluctantly, an irritated edge to his voice.)* The "Y" uptown probably. It's close to work.

GLORIA That's convenient.

ROBERT And they'll let you set up a stereo?

VINCENT I didn't say I'm taking it along, I said I was storing it somewhere for a week or so temporarily.

GLORIA He could set it up there, though, no one would hear much of anything the way he modulates it.

VINCENT I do not modulate.

GLORIA You should let him play a record for you on that precious Telefunken turntable of his. He sits on top of the amplifier practically, adjusting his tracking force pick up and blowing on his sapphire stylus. He turns down all the *crescendo* so it doesn't get to maximum and boosts up the *piano* so it doesn't get too minimum. *Bolero* starts out on ten and ends up on one.

VINCENT I don't own *Bolero*.

GLORIA And he's a snob to boot.

ROBERT I'm surprised you're leaving again. I kinna thought you were back and everything was all right when I heard you fighting—but then I have this silver-lining view of life. I suppose it's a communication problem—

VINCENT A what?

ROBERT Were you not listening or not understanding?

VINCENT Either one.

GLORIA You're right; we speak different languages. It's the Fabled Tower of Babel in a heap right in our own living room. Rubble. I thought this was only a mess around here—wadded up drawing paper and all your old shoes. I thought I was walking on a cloud of crap—it's not crap. It's rubble.

VINCENT Right.

GLORIA Ruins. We couldn't build anything if we worked a hundred years. Not you and me. You give me a headache.

VINCENT You give yourself a headache.

ROBERT Where was the hutch?

GLORIA What hutch?

ROBERT I don't know, I'm asking you—the place you called the hutch.

GLORIA Over on Sixth Avenue; we don't talk about it.

ROBERT I'd think you would.

VINCENT It was different.

ROBERT Haven't you ever wondered how?

GLORIA *(She looks around. Beat, beat.)* I thought I'd have a chance to clean this place up before I left; it's going to be great fun with a mob of truckers tearing everything apart.

ROBERT Very well. You don't talk about it. God, are you nervous.

GLORIA No; not especially.

ROBERT You want a Miltown?

GLORIA Robert, I told you those things aren't any good for you; you don't need them, you just think you do.

ROBERT Oh, I know—alone in my room, I'm perfectly calm, but I step a foot outside and all my friends are tearing each other apart—want one?

GLORIA I said I wasn't nervous.

ROBERT Okay, you're not nervous. You're tense.

GLORIA It's going to be great fun with a mob of truckers running in and out of here.

ROBERT Vince, you want one?

GLORIA I hope you can decide by now what you want of this stuff or I'm just going to put everything in the footlocker.

VINCENT Do what you want with it.

ROBERT You'll understand if I don't offer to help.

GLORIA That's all right, he's got—

ROBERT —I mean, aside from the fact that I'm not interested in seeing it go, I vaguely remember helping you haul all this stuff up three flights of stairs, not that long ago.

VINCENT You didn't have to help.

ROBERT When do I ever have anything better to do than meet someone—I'm afraid the year's been considerably better to me than to you, which I hope you understand isn't saying anything.

GLORIA He's got movers coming half an hour ago.

ROBERT You'd better get a move on.

VINCENT Why? I'm not doing any of it. They're going to come and pack it—

and wrap it—and lift it—and tote it—and set it up again where I want it when I get a place. I do not intend to—

ROBERT —You know what they'll charge for a job like this?

VINCENT —I don't care—I don't intend to get another hernia carrying all that crap down the stairs. I personally am not lifting so much as a saucer. I'm as sick of all this crap as anyone; I'd as soon chuck it out.

GLORIA Vincent is discovering he's wasted his youth; he's thinking of a cross-country trek…

VINCENT I have never said anything about so much as a bus trip to Jersey City. It gets under my skin that we've managed to collect so much crap. Useless, too—possessions. It's "ganglia," dragging me down. It's suffocating. Roots. You know I can't move to another place, because if I could take it to Dallas I wouldn't be living in Dallas, I'd be living here, because I'd be surrounded by the same damn crap that I'd left—or rather brought along. The same damn stuff.

ROBERT And the same you in the middle of it. Are you thinking of moving to Dallas?

VINCENT No.

ROBERT Just asking.

VINCENT All this junk. There's no way out of it.

ROBERT You could give it to the Salvation Army.

VINCENT Well, what I'm not doing is neatly packing it up into little CARE packages. We brought thirteen boxes when we moved in here, with a density unequaled by lead.

ROBERT Seventeen.

VINCENT Gloria could pack the Encyclopedia Britannica into a shoe box. *(Pause.)* And I'm sick of smart ass labels on boxes: "Some old clothes, and old letters, and the stuff out of that middle drawer, plus three old prophylactics that probably won't work, and the corkscrew." *(Pause.)*

ROBERT Do people still use prophylactics?

VINCENT I don't know.

ROBERT Mind if I have some coffee? *(Robert moves to the kitchenette and pours himself a cup of coffee—a habit—he looks rather as if he lives here.)* About you two; I only got one question. I decided one of you has to be impotent.

GLORIA What?

ROBERT I said one of you has got to be impotent. It's the only way to figure it.

GLORIA Well, to begin with, how many girls do you know with that problem?

ROBERT *(To Vincent.)* Oh. Well, then it must be you.

GLORIA Vince is a lot of things, but he isn't impotent—sexually, anyway.

ROBERT So, sterile then.

VINCENT Yeah, well, Robert, it's a sad story. I don't like to tell it actually.

ROBERT *(Sympathetically.)* Oh, hell.

VINCENT Yes, you see I don't talk about it; we try to keep it from people, but I was—well, I was castrated at an early age by a tribe of starving nomad Indians.

ROBERT Well, that explains it.

VINCENT You can't really hold it against them—they only did it for food—

ROBERT Poor devils; but it's sad for you—

VINCENT —Oh, yes—

ROBERT —Being a eunuch like that.

VINCENT Yes, well, I still like to think of myself as a stallion, Robert. *(He turns to the drawing board and begins to dismantle it and the light, etc.)*

GLORIA Why does one of us have to be sterile?

ROBERT Well. I guess you don't have to be—

GLORIA Well that's a comfort.

ROBERT But I was telling a friend of mine—

GLORIA —Who's that?

ROBERT Well, never mind. I have other friends. I have a great many friends. I have friends I haven't even used yet.

GLORIA So OK.

ROBERT I was telling him about you two fighting all the time and he said, just as a matter of course, how many—

VINCENT I thought you said you weren't involved.

ROBERT In what?

VINCENT With marriages breaking up.

ROBERT Well, *I* may not be interested, but *he* was practically falling out of his chair. I mean you don't talk to someone about what you're interested in, you talk about what they're interested in. If I talked about my interests it'd bore him silly.

GLORIA What are your interests?

ROBERT And anyway he said, as a matter of course, how many children do they have?

VINCENT What'd you tell him?

ROBERT I said six and he said "It figures." No, actually, I said none, and he said how long have they been married, and I said about three years, and he said so how come they don't have any kids, and I said I forget which one of you was sterile. He was very sympathetic.

GLORIA I'm sure.

ROBERT Suggested you go to an adoption agency. I told him I'd tell you.

GLORIA Thanks.

ROBERT You think about it though, and he's right. Most women of color marry a white guy, or vice-versa—it's usually vice-versa—wonder why that is—someone should run a poll on that—anyway, the first thing they do is start on a whole litter of young. It was the first thing he thought of.

GLORIA Well, no thanks.

ROBERT It's all in proving you don't give a damn what people think, see.

VINCENT Well, maybe we *really* don't give a damn what people think.

ROBERT Well, it might not be that, but you don't seem to have the normal curiosity—I think they usually have a large family just to see how many different color combinations they can come up with. Like mixing paint.

GLORIA Maybe we don't have that curiosity.

VINCENT Gloria's too busy crusading to have that curiosity.

GLORIA You're damned right!

ROBERT Don't tell me. I'm about as interested in mixed-marriages as I am in mixed-vegetables.

GLORIA It's all right—I'm under fire lately for standing up for what I believe.

VINCENT Or sitting down as it were.

ROBERT Honestly, you take everything so seriously…

GLORIA —Well, it's serious!

ROBERT Okay, it's important to you.

GLORIA I didn't say important to me. It's important to everyone alive—I said I take freedom seriously.

ROBERT When you can get it. *(Quickly.) May it be soon!* Jesus. I was only going to suggest if Vince could work up some of your concern, go along to a couple of rallies—

VINCENT Are you kidding? I've got no guilt feelings. You have to be a masochist to be white and go to those rallies lately.

GLORIA You've got no feelings period.

VINCENT *(Still to Robert.)* When I insult someone I expect him to leave and when someone insults me, I leave.

GLORIA It's those easily insulted puritanical tentacles I admire so—In the history of mankind there hasn't been a more rotten, more disgusting—

VINCENT *(Overlapping a good deal.)*—You obviously aren't familiar enough with the history of mankind to be—

GLORIA —The white people have—

VINCENT —The black people didn't—

GLORIA —The black people at least—

VINCENT —The white people did the—

GLORIA —The black people were—

VINCENT *(Finally overriding her.)*—The black people rotted from screw-worms in the jungle that they didn't have the sense or intuition to cultivate or build—just bringing them to a better climate was their first advancement in fifteen thousand years. And *then* you had to be dragged out of the god-damned *trees!*

GLORIA In the jungle? The black people had empires and temples when you babies were still dirtying up your Alley-Oop underpants! Just don't try to tell me the white man is responsible for one single advancement for the black man. We've had four hundred years of your—

VINCENT —Well, you didn't have enough sense to—

GLORIA —What one thing—one thing, buddy, can you—

VINCENT Well, you didn't know anything. My God, we sent you missionaries.

GLORIA Missionaries?

VINCENT You didn't know what to *do* with them. You *ate* them!

GLORIA You're damned right we ate them!

VINCENT —And laws were passed, you sound like nothing—

GLORIA —Laws and laws your laws and your lawmakers, Old Tom Jefferson with his involuted sentences and calligraphy and his—

VINCENT —Tom Jefferson didn't—

GLORIA —Had slaves on his own Virginny plantation. All men equal, all White men are created equal, maybe—

VINCENT —Screw Tom Jefferson, for Christsake.

GLORIA You screw Tom Jefferson.

VINCENT As far as Tom Jefferson was concerned anyone out of the ruling elite was some kind of schmuck or something—

GLORIA —And you can pass it off as easily as that. Tom Jefferson is a symbol of everything—

(Robert has looked on—from one to the other—in speechless amazement. Finally he finds his tongue.)

ROBERT (Overlapping Vincent.) Hey, hey, hey, hey! What the devil is going on, anyway?

(Beat. They look at him.)

ROBERT Are you really fighting over Thomas Jefferson? Jesus.

GLORIA Yeah, well, Jefferson drew up the plans and Vince over here is still hammering in the nails.

VINCENT Gloria's on one of her White Man Is A Cancerous Growth and Should Be Cauterized kicks.

GLORIA Well, baby, you haven't said anything yet to make me—

VINCENT —If you think hate is as powerful a tool as—

GLORIA I don't think remember, I'm just an ignorant jungle flower.

VINCENT You can say that again, Baby.

ROBERT "The gingham dog and the calico cat, side by side on the table sat. 'Twas half past twelve and what do you think, not one or t'other had slept a wink."

(Barbara enters behind them, smiling and tapping on the door.)

GLORIA *(Turning on him, overlapping some.)* Oh, shut up, you shit head!
(Barbara could be either a very good-looking girl, second best in the class—or a triumph over disadvantages with make-up, dress and hair style. In either case, she is not really stupid, nor all that naive, nor all that innocent. She has had a fairly good high school education in Kentucky.)

BARBARA The door was open downstairs so I didn't ring or…*(She has been in New York not long enough to lose the accent—an accent not altogether pleasant, as a Southern accent sometimes is, more nasal, hard. After an uncomfortable adjustment:)*

VINCENT Hello, Barbara.

BARBARA *(Attempting gaiety.)* Hi, Vincent, Gloria.

GLORIA Barbara!

BARBARA What a charming apartment. I haven't been up here before.

GLORIA No.

BARBARA Vince said he was picking up his things and I offered to help—anything I can do.

GLORIA Well, that's mighty damn—good of you, Barbara. I'm sure he can use the extra hand.

VINCENT Robert, uh…

ROBERT I've got to be running. I've got to take these over to the cafe.

GLORIA What is it?

ROBERT Oh, it's locks, door locks. Like for the rest room. We have to keep replacing the locks on the rest room door. It seems one of the basic laws of behavior is that no man believes someone has beaten him to the john.

VINCENT *(To Barbara.)* Robert works for a cafe—coffee house. He's a kitchen boy general janitor.

BARBARA How do you do?

ROBERT Pleased to meet you I'm sure.

BARBARA You work in a coffee house?

VINCENT He robs them blind.

ROBERT Cinderella had the pantry, I get the john. Scrubbing graffiti. It's not so bad. You can't get philosophic about it though, or you're dead—like the Writing on the Walls—you just have to keep telling yourself it's graffiti. Grrrrr. It's graffiti! *(Rubs it off.)* Grrrr. I wipe it off one week and the next week some joker has put it right back up again. Their art work actually isn't bad at all. A little optimistic maybe, but not really bad at all except when it comes to foreshortening—

VINCENT Robert—

ROBERT I gotta split; I'll not be long.

BARBARA Nice meeting you, Bobby.

ROBERT Bobby. Fine. So long, Gloria—Vincent—Babs. *(He exits, closing the door behind him.)*

BARBARA *(To Gloria.)* I actually didn't know whether you'd be here.

GLORIA Well, you see I live here. It's pretty much of a mess right now. *(Gloria straightens the apartment, almost compulsively.)*

BARBARA Well of course you're packing and everything.

VINCENT I'm going down now. I have to go next door and get some boxes for the stereo. Damn. I should've asked Robert if he had any.

BARBARA Who's Robert?

VINCENT You just met him.

BARBARA Oh *that* Robert. I don't know as I thought too much of him.

VINCENT Well, Robert may seem a little fresh at first, but he's a nice noise to have around sometimes—he puts up with a lot of crap.

GLORIA He puts up with us.

BARBARA Oh, he seemed nice enough. He's got a sense of humor. I'd just have to get to know him.

GLORIA He's a good guru.

VINCENT *(Quickly.)* Gloria—uh.

BARBARA What's a gu…?

VINCENT I'll bring you back some boxes and you can pack up some books or anything you want. I don't want to take it all.

GLORIA That's the last thing in the world I want and you know it.

BARBARA Well, I think you should have it all, Gloria. Isn't that customary?

GLORIA I don't give a damn what's customary.

BARBARA But Vincent is the one who works, you shouldn't be expected to—

GLORIA —I work too, or will very shortly.

BARBARA Well, yes, but—

GLORIA It was decided before you got here, Barbara; please just stay out, it's settled.

BARBARA Yes, but it's not right, really, Vincent. What do you want if anything?

VINCENT All of it, if that's the way she wants it—everything—every last ashtray.

GLORIA Good. You bought it.

VINCENT I didn't necessarily buy it. Who's to say who bought it? Who bought the pepper mill for instance? Who knows?

GLORIA It was a gift from Hal.

VINCENT Well—

GLORIA Please!—

VINCENT Well, how can you say it's mine?

GLORIA —Take it!

VINCENT And the bed—you picked it out, bought it—I didn't see it till it was here.

GLORIA Take it!

VINCENT I don't know why you have to—

GLORIA Don't! Don't! Don't do this. Take the bed. Take it all. Please!

VINCENT Well, I will.

GLORIA Well, good.

VINCENT (To Barbara.) I'm going down to get the boxes. I suppose you can gather up the clothes I have in the closet. And there's a suitcase right there. And the stuff in the medicine cabinet. Okay?

BARBARA Fine.

VINCENT I'll be right back, then.

GLORIA God damn! Just get gone, Vincent. For godsake just get what you want to take today and just get gone.

VINCENT Don't worry. (He exits, closing the door—not slamming it—but firmly.) (Gloria turns and closes the window. The noise from the street that we have grown used to stops abruptly. She sighs and says to herself:)

GLORIA Jesus god, I should've taken Robert up on that Miltown.

BARBARA (Concentrating too hard.) Who's Robert? Oh. Oh yes. What closet are Vincent's things in?

GLORIA They're not. They're in the suitcase by the door. They have been for three days, if he'd troubled to ask. You can clean out the medicine cabinet if you find anything in it.

BARBARA Oh. Well, OK. Where should I put it?

GLORIA What?

BARBARA Well, the things…

GLORIA See if there's room in the suitcase, I suppose.

BARBARA Fine.

GLORIA Would you mind closing the door, Barbara? I'd like to make a phone call.

BARBARA Oh, no, not al all. (She goes into the bathroom, leaving the door open.)

GLORIA (Dials a number at the phone. To herself:) Dumb broad. Deaf, dumb, and blind. (Pause.) Hello, Rachel? Gloria. Yeah. God, no. (The bathroom door shuts. To herself:) Dumb bitch. Hum? No, Vince's sister is over—no, he's here too. Look, baby, what? Is your offer still good? Yeah, he's going to be at some Uptown "Y" or something. "Convenient to work," could you vomit? (Pause.) Good, it'll only be a couple of days or so, till I can find a place. Well, around; it doesn't have to be much. Swell—No, he's taking the works. I said that from the beginning. Well, you're on the outside, it's different from here. You need anything special? No, probably not till tomorrow. No, it's Sunday. Friday—Saturday—yeah, it's Sunday tomorrow. Thanks, you hear? Well, yeah, but—fine. Bye bye.

BARBARA (Coming out of the bathroom instantly.) Is this Vincent's razor?

GLORIA (Looks at her a moment.) Uh. Yes; it's beat up. I don't know if he wants it.

BARBARA You never know. And is this your *Kings Men* or his?

GLORIA No, I don't think—no, that's Vincent's.

BARBARA It's almost gone actually.

GLORIA Well, you'd best pack it anyway. Your mother gave it to him for Christmas and I'm sure it has sentimental value.

BARBARA *(Sets the suitcase on the sofa, opens it.)* Oh. Well, it must have been some time ago, because I know she hasn't sent him anything in three years. Jesus, his ties are getting all wrinkled. *(Fusses a bit with them, tucks them back. Wandering to the window, wanting to talk.)* What a nice view. *(No reaction.)* Gloria? I know it isn't any of my business...

GLORIA What isn't?

BARBARA You and Vincent. But I don't understand why you didn't try to work something out. I mean, I know you fight, but you don't fight any worse than anyone else.

GLORIA Better, usually.

BARBARA I just really don't know why. You have a lot of friends, don't you?

GLORIA Umh.

BARBARA Well, don't you? Have a lot of friends?

GLORIA Oh, we have friends by the barrel load. His friends and my friends. Group one and group two.

BARBARA I just wonder what you'll do.

GLORIA I've worked; and I like working—Vince didn't want me working so I quit and now I can go back.

BARBARA Did you enjoy it?

GLORIA Yes. It was interesting, very rewarding work. Yes.

BARBARA You worked in grade schools—as a social worker, huh?

GLORIA A psychologist.

BARBARA That seems so funny, little kids like that talking to a psychiatrist. Do they lie down on a sofa and all?

GLORIA No, not usually.

BARBARA I don't know why they'd need it, what it'd be for.

GLORIA For their health—you've heard of antibodies? They're in vaccines you inject into the bloodstream to kill toxins. Well, a child psychologist is a kind of anti-mother.

BARBARA Do you think Vince has changed much. *(Pause.)* 'Cause I keep telling him he's changed.

GLORIA Since when?

BARBARA I don't know. Since he came up here—since you've known him?

GLORIA I don't know, I didn't *see* him the first year I knew him, he had a beard.

BARBARA A beard?

GLORIA You knew he had a beard.

BARBARA When did he?

GLORIA The whole first year, or nearly, that we were married. It was lighter than his hair—In the sun it was red; orangeish.

BARBARA He never told us he'd grown a beard.

GLORIA Well, I guess when he first came up here he went very native; those Bible-belters usually overdo it a little. And he's stopped playing basketball so he's getting a paunch. Is that what you mean? Changed?

BARBARA He played ball in New York? Where? I didn't know that.

GLORIA Across the street from where we lived there were about six basketball courts and Vince used to be out there every hour he wasn't working. Even when it got cold they'd be out there.

BARBARA He still has a practice hoop on the garage door.

GLORIA Well he got enough practice here.

BARBARA He used to be the scrappiest player on our team.

GLORIA Yeah, well he's pretty scrappy all right. I could look across and keep an eye on him; he was the one with the beard.

BARBARA Where was that?

GLORIA Barbara, I haven't got—

BARBARA No, really, he didn't write or anything so we didn't—

GLORIA The first year we were married we had a place up over the Waverly Theatre on Sixth Avenue. A door or two from the theatre. Close enough so when we'd go to bed early the damn marquee light used to shine in the window. We could of stuck our heads out the window and talked to the man putting up the new bill. And across the street is where they used to play basketball.

BARBARA Was it nice?

GLORIA I don't know, Barbara, I didn't play with them.

BARBARA I mean where you lived?

GLORIA It was all right; if you happen to like anarchy.

BARBARA I can't imagine Vince with a beard.

GLORIA Well he shaved it off quick enough when he went to work uptown. When we were living at the hutch he worked with a small company that designed store fronts and that was hardly what he was looking for.

BARBARA I don't imagine. What was the hutch?

GLORIA *(Closed.)* Where'd you hear that?

BARBARA You just said it.

GLORIA *(She considers a second, then as perfunctorily as possible.)* That's what they called the place where we lived. One of the black guys Vince played ball with, was up from Georgia, used to raise rabbits and he called the place the rabbit hutch because you can't imagine how cramped it got with eight or ten basketball players packed in there eating spaghetti.

BARBARA *(Sensing Gloria's change and embarrassed by it, doesn't know quite what to say. Awkwardly.)* But then you moved over here. With all this space.

GLORIA *(Indifferently.)* Thompson Street for six months and then here. Dragging all this stuff along both places. Rocks, books and all. Vince has had them since he was in grade school I think.

BARBARA I don't remember them. And then, I suppose you just began—not seeing eye-to-eye on a few things.

GLORIA I suppose you could say that.

BARBARA Like on what?

GLORIA Name something.

BARBARA I just wondered if you had thought it out—like have you talked at all with your folks, like with your mother?

GLORIA Uhm.

BARBARA Well, maybe that sounds corny, but I'll bet you haven't, have you? Even being this far away and all, I still write pages to the folks. Every week.

GLORIA Well, my mother isn't speaking to me lately.

BARBARA Why not?

GLORIA She's a segregationist.

BARBARA Oh. Well, it hadn't hit me like that. Well, I suppose it's natural either way. Mothers and fathers aren't ever pleased with anything their kids do, no matter what, are they? I'll bet she won't be any happier, though, with you separating, will she?

GLORIA I hadn't really thought about it. I've only talked to Mother about four times since I started school seven years ago, and I doubt if she would have much to say about a separation either way.

BARBARA That's terrible. Really it is. I wish you could know the times at home I've defended Vincent. It would surprise you, I'll bet.

GLORIA I'll bet.

BARBARA Even before I met you I said if Vincent wants to marry someone of a different race—

GLORIA —Oh god—

BARBARA —Well, then he knows what he's doing. He'll be a lot happier with her.

GLORIA You'll look a pretty fool now, won't you?

BARBARA Oh, I suppose, but they're outside, really. *(Sitting on the sofa, pulling her legs up cuddly.)* Do you know what I first—

GLORIA Barbara, Barbara, Barbara, before you get all snug and cuddly there— I've got a lot to do and I don't want to be rude, but I just don't feel like a chat. To be perfectly frank I've never liked you and I can't pretend to—

BARBARA Oh, I don't blame you, actually. I've known you didn't like me really. But I've always liked you. A lot. I didn't want to chat or anything. I just—

GLORIA I just don't care to talk about my private life with you.

BARBARA I'm not interested in your and Vincent's sex life—

GLORIA —Oh, my God—

BARBARA —Anyway, I'm sure that it was probably just as normal as anyone. I just wanted you to know that I'm sorry you and Vincent are divorcing like this.

(Gloria looks up sharply.)

BARBARA I still feel that if you had talked about it, you wouldn't have to be, is all.

GLORIA Vince and I have spent the whole day *avoiding* talking about it and I think that's best. The thought of a girl-to-girl chat nauseates me.

BARBARA *(Exiting to the bathroom, quite cool.)* I know why you don't like me— and I don't think it's fair, really.

GLORIA *(To herself in the second she is gone.)* Phony white tramp.

BARBARA *(Reentering, a few articles in her hand.)* You feel that I'm Southern. Because I speak the way I do; you feel I'm just a typical Southerner.

GLORIA Barbara, I don't think of you as typically anything—exactly.

BARBARA Yes you do, you think I sound like a hillbilly and you're right. I can tell I don't talk as well as you, that I don't sound like people in New York. Are these his?

GLORIA Yes. Barbara, in you a hillbilly accent is charming. In my brother, or one of my sisters, it would be a sure sign of stupidity. You can be vapid and dumb and wide-eyed as all hell but if Cynthia or Nora looked wide-eyed it would be comical. They have to practically *squint!* It's a joke.

BARBARA Well, they joke about hillbillies, too. I don't think it's so damn charming. And you're wrong about people laughing at the way Negroes talk. I haven't heard a good colored-people joke in two years—And on TV the only people who can put on a dumb accent anymore are Negroes.

GLORIA Yes. Well, we've earned the privilege.

BARBARA Is Cynthia and Nora the names of your sisters? I didn't know you had more than one sister, Gloria.

GLORIA I have four sisters and two brothers living.

BARBARA I didn't know that. How old are they?

GLORIA I don't know. I haven't seen them in a long time; Cynthia's fourteen; Nora's eight or nine.

BARBARA Why did you say "living?"

GLORIA One brother died at birth and a sister died in infancy.

BARBARA Oh. I didn't know that.

GLORIA Well, you asked—

BARBARA I didn't—

GLORIA —It's an occupational hazard of being a poor Harlem black. You shouldn't trouble yourself with it—

BARBARA —Well, not just black—

GLORIA —It's something the "outside" shouldn't and doesn't trouble itself with. What did you say?

BARBARA I said, not just black. Not just the poor Harlem black. Back home— our home, near Louisville—they aren't city slum or black, they're just poor. But they have baby after baby dying like flies. They have—every shack along the road has a screaming dirty, skinny mess of kids on the porch, and a grave plot alongside the house with four or five markers. It's no different.

GLORIA It's a great deal different, when it's your own sister dead on the bed in front of you, my dear.

BARBARA You don't think about other people, Gloria, you never once do; and you're very smart, actually, about other things—

GLORIA —When every apartment is wall-to-wall screaming and filth, every pore of the rotting building you live in is death, you don't consider other people's misery, Barbara. I *lived* in misery.

BARBARA Well, so did millions of other people. *Worse.* Not me, although it wasn't much better. It's not so crowded in Harlem as it is in Indonesia. In Indonesia people, millions of people, are living on just one bowl of—

GLORIA —Fuck Indonesia! *(Beat.)* Fuck the Indonesians. What the hell are the Indonesians to me?

BARBARA Well, I'm not saying you didn't. We sound like a contest of who knows the worst conditions. I didn't want to start something like that. I just came here to help Vincent.

GLORIA Well, everything is between Vince and me; I didn't intend to go into my dingy family heritage for you.

BARBARA I didn't know you had a brother and sister that died.

GLORIA Well, now that you do, I'm sure you won't let it trouble you, any.

BARBARA Of course it will. Maybe I can think that that helps to explain how you feel about—

GLORIA It doesn't explain anything about me!

BARBARA It's you're so—I honestly don't know! You tell me all that like you were *proud* of your sister dying and *proud* of—

GLORIA *I am! Proud! I am proud!*
     (Vincent re-enters simultaneously with Gloria's line, carrying the boxes for the turntable and amplifier. Sweetly, simply in front of Vincent, Barbara replies:)

BARBARA Well, then, I don't understand that at all.

GLORIA *(From Barbara's changed reaction, notices Vincent.)* Your sister is an imbecile.

BARBARA *(Peeved.)* Gloria was telling me how proud she was of her family's lack of—or rather—her—their, her family's poorness, or the family's—

GLORIA Poverty is the word you're struggling for. She matched me poverty for poverty.

VINCENT *(Goes to the bookcase, disconnecting the amplifier.)* Don't fight, children.

BARBARA Nobody's fighting.

VINCENT Just sing, "Jesus loves the little children of the world."

GLORIA I don't know it.

VINCENT Red and yellow, black and white.

BARBARA *(Sings the first few notes of the Sunday School Song, supersonically high.)* Red and yellow, black and... *(She trails off under Gloria's stare.)*

GLORIA They sound like jelly beans.

VINCENT Well, Jesus loves the little jelly beans, too, Gloria.

BARBARA Can I help? I've just not done anything at all: Gloria had the clothes packed.

VINCENT Did you?

GLORIA Thursday.

BARBARA Gloria has been telling me about her family. It was nice.

GLORIA *Nice?*

BARBARA *(Jumps slightly.)* Well, I mean that we were getting on so well. *(She has wandered to the tube of drawings.)* Is this something from work?

VINCENT What? Yes. It's just some drawings.

BARBARA Can I look? I'll put them right back. *(Takes one out.)* Oh, it's so complicated. It's not what I thought at all... Is this an apartment building?

GLORIA It's a crematorium.

BARBARA A what?

VINCENT It's a section of an apartment building, put it back now.

BARBARA No, I'm interested; all those little rooms.

GLORIA Infinitesimal. Well, forget it.

BARBARA *(Looking up.)* What?

GLORIA I said it's the hanging gardens of Babylon.

BARBARA This is marvelous, Vincent.

GLORIA You tell her to put those up before I remember what I said. Now, I'm not fooling.

VINCENT Yeah, Sister, roll it up and tuck it back in there, OK? You'll get them messed up.

BARBARA Okay. It's marvelous. How come you got the drawing board at home? Do you have to work much at night?

GLORIA Oh, yes. They don't measure quality where he works—they weigh it by the pound.

VINCENT Richter, Richter and Thatcher have a good deal of detail work that I can't get to at the office. I haven't worked much at home, lately.

BARBARA They must be very pleased with you to give you so much to do.

GLORIA Oh, they just love him to death. Richter, Richter and Trickedher represent his place in society. He's devoted to them—to the exclusion of everything else.

VINCENT Gloria is a crusader for permanent slums.

GLORIA That's a lie.

VINCENT Rather than doing something to help, she talks; about "conditions." Should conditions improve, she'd have nothing to talk about, and talk is all Gloria knows. Ergo: Gloria is a crusader for permanent slums.

GLORIA That's a goddamn lie and you know it. I'd advise you to just quit now.

VINCENT *(To Barbara.)* I'm working with a company that is trying to get a contract to build—

GLORIA *(Overlapping.)*—To build uninhabitable brick ovens. Hi-rise slums. You don't prevent slums or clear them, you *elevate* them thirty stories.

VINCENT *(Continuing calmly.)* That is trying to get a contract to build a multi-housing unit to replace slum conditions.

GLORIA Via graft and lobbying and bribery and—

BARBARA Well, I would think that you'd be very proud of Vincent trying to do good at his job, instead of criticizing him.

GLORIA Vincent's job has nothing to do with good. Were Vincent's job anything at all good, I would cheer. Vince is trying to do *well* at his job, which is another thing altogether.

BARBARA Well, I'd think you'd be proud, I know I am. Vince is.

GLORIA I dunno; Vincent, are you proud?

VINCENT I think I work as hard as anyone with what I'm allowed to—

GLORIA But are you *proud?*

VINCENT I work hard at my job.

GLORIA But are you proud?

VINCENT I do what I do well!

GLORIA You proud, Vince?

VINCENT Damn hard! Nobody's ever altogether happy with what they're doing, but at least I know that I'll be put on more interesting work as soon as this particular project is over.

BARBARA *(Slight pause.)* You are proud, though, aren't you?

VINCENT Yes! I wish I could do more, but I'm proud of the *way* I work, my competence.

GLORIA His competence at work. The fact that the work they require of him is incompetent totally escapes him. And loyal. To the company.

VINCENT Yes, my dear, and loyal to the company. Anything else?

GLORIA Your witness. Barbara.

(Vincent exits to the bedroom shutting the door.)

BARBARA I just don't see anything to argue about if you ask me. Vince and I were brought up to believe if you have a job to do, you should do it and do it well. The best you can. Now I just don't know *what* you were brought up to believe—

GLORIA —Well, I haven't time to tell you, Barbara.

BARBARA *(An edge.)* You believe in bitching, as near as I can see. Just bitch at everything and everyone, every minute of the live-long night and day, and that's living a good life.

GLORIA You're closer than you'd think.

BARBARA I know you claim to be a very religious person, but that's not very darned religious as far as I can see.

GLORIA Well, Barbara, there are religions and religions and we won't discuss how far you can see.

BARBARA Vince is an architect and if I was you I'd be very proud of him.

GLORIA At best your brother is a draftsman.

BARBARA *(Yelling, Vincent comes out carrying the clock and a few other items.)* Vince! Are you an architect or a draftsman?

VINCENT It doesn't matter, Barbara. Either one.

BARBARA What's a draftsman? Is he an engineer? What does he do?

VINCENT My job is to draw up their specifications—draw plans, blueprints, and also I do a *good deal* of original work of my own; and I draft the plans for that as well.

BARBARA So you're an architect too.

VINCENT Yes. I'm an architect. Don't labor it.

GLORIA Right, absolutely right, and I'm Anna Freud.

VINCENT I work in a very specialized, a very narrow, qualified, exacting area.

GLORIA Genocide!

VINCENT Okay, now, goddamnit.

GLORIA Instant tenement. Add ashes and stir.

VINCENT We're trying to provide decent housing for people who quite frankly don't deserve it. They haven't the sense or ambition to know they live in slums.

GLORIA Oh they know!

VINCENT It's good housing, shelter they can afford.

GLORIA It's a vast brick ghetto, no different from the conditions they live in now and you know it, and it's poisoned you.

BARBARA Who's it for?

GLORIA For all the starving families in good old Brownsville.

VINCENT One vast pile of filth. The worst black ghetto in New York, probably. The highest crime rate, the highest childbirth rate, the highest child-death rate, the lowest mentality—

GLORIA *(Tortured.)* Right, right, right, Kids' I.Q.'s measured when they're six years old are ten points higher than the same kids measured when they're eleven years old. We used to think that was impossible.

BARBARA *(Incredulously. She's heard one word of the above.)* They're *black?* You mean to tell me they're *black?*

GLORIA As Coley's ass.

BARBARA They're black and you're against Vincent for trying to help them? You're against that.

VINCENT Come on now, Barbara, don't get excited.

BARBARA It was your black sister who died that you were screaming to me about a minute ago. You were screaming about the slums and saying how terribly you lived. You don't want it?

GLORIA None of us want it.

BARBARA Well, I guess not. Well, then don't give it to them. I guess not. It's not good enough, I suppose. I've never heard of anything like it!

VINCENT Barbara!

BARBARA No, now. She may think she's bright but that's just the stupidest thing I've ever heard. That's just the stupidest thing—*well, stick* in your rotting shanties and shake your head about leaving them.

GLORIA Barbara, it's no better. It's high and clean and sterile and barren and *does nothing.* Those crummy, cramped, inadequate, little apartments. "Units" they call them. It breeds the same thing. You can't elevate the floor, you have to elevate the spirit. It's a vapid gesture, like all the others we've had. Reading the plans for that project is like being given the physical dimensions of hell and Rancer, Dancer and Prancer are trying to designate that a philanthropic enterprise. And Vince is a loyal and proud part of it.

BARBARA Is that why you're separating?

GLORIA No—yes—no. It's enough, but no, not at all. Call it heart failure.

BARBARA I don't see how it can be bad if it's better. What is the name of the company, Vince?

GLORIA Maker, Raper and Ditcher.

VINCENT Richter, Richter and Thatcher.

GLORIA And if they and all the other companies had their way, all the slums in the world—would become a vast sea of sterile, cramped buildings like that. One on top of the other on top of the other. Because there's money in it. Everyone would live in a building like that, in a row of close buildings like that, in a city of buildings like that, in a country of dead buildings like that, like Vince's, in a world of nothing else! Now would *you* like that?

BARBARA *(Fast building exchange.)* It wouldn't be like that.

GLORIA Would you like that?

VINCENT Come on.

GLORIA Living there? Objectively!

BARBARA Where? I don't know where?

GLORIA Think for once. Would you like that?

BARBARA It's only for improvement, isn't it? Of slum areas?

GLORIA Would you like that? For all whites?

VINCENT Stop it!

BARBARA It isn't going to be like that.

GLORIA Would you like it if it was?

BARBARA Of course not! No!

GLORIA Would you like that for you? *Think!*

BARBARA What?

GLORIA Units? For you and your family and your kids?

BARBARA No!

GLORIA You wouldn't live there?

BARBARA No!

VINCENT Come off it!

GLORIA In Vincent's house?

BARBARA No, no!

GLORIA Well, neither will I, sister!

BARBARA *(Continuing almost in one rush.)* No, no, no, it isn't like that! You hateful bitch, it isn't like that. You're hateful and I'm glad you're broken up, and I knew you would, because at night I *prayed* you would, because you're no different from any other black, and I don't care *who* you try to be like. You're a hateful, vindictive, militant bitch! You think you're smart, but you're *nothing!* And you know it, too. You know you do.
(Vincent has his arm around her or she would run out. He sits her down on the arm of the soft.)

VINCENT Sit down, it's all right.

GLORIA I only wanted to show you once that you could think. You don't have to defend it just because Vince is a part of it, and I don't either.

BARBARA Think! Think! That isn't thinking. I've *never* been talked to like that. By anybody.

GLORIA You probably—

VINCENT —Knock it off, Gloria.

BARBARA I'm OK now. I just want to know who she thinks she—

VINCENT No, she's had her little purge. *(To Gloria.)* Your hate break. Now you can come down.

BARBARA I'm OK.

VINCENT You take these, OK? *(The suitcase and a deflated basketball.)*

BARBARA And go on? Is that all?

VINCENT I'll bring the rest. You go on. I don't want you around her anymore.

BARBARA Okay.

VINCENT You can just sit in the car; I'll come down in a minute or two.

BARBARA You hurry and finish.

VINCENT Go on.

(Barbara goes to the door, she opens it, but looks at Gloria for a moment. Gloria looks up finally.)

GLORIA Goodbye, Barbara.

BARBARA I meant what I said, I want you to know that—I've never liked you; not for a minute.

VINCENT Barbara!

BARBARA Vince knows that. I've never been talked to like that. By anyone. Not even by my own father. And I've never liked you.

GLORIA I never thought you did. The whites taught me duplicity, I know it backwards.

BARBARA I think you're just like all other Negroes.

GLORIA Well I try.

VINCENT Go on, Barbara.

BARBARA No, I want to say this. I don't feel sorry for you at all. I'd like to just tear you apart.

GLORIA But you're too much a lady.

BARBARA I'm not strong enough or I would try. All you've proved is that you're jealous of Vincent's work, and you don't seem to understand that everyone isn't as shiftless and lazy as you are. I just want to scream, *yes,* I'm white. Ha, ha, ha. I'm white and you're black and I'm just as happy as hell about it.

VINCENT *(Firmly.)* Go on, now damnit.

BARBARA I'm sorry, Vincent, I'll see you downstairs. I said I wouldn't say anything, but you can't be friendly with her. *(She exits.)*

GLORIA *(Brief pause.)* That girl is an education. God, you come from an ugly family.

VINCENT *(Is boiling mad, does not want to show it. He will say anything.)* I won't be here long to bother you. You better go through those books at least and see what you want.

GLORIA Box 'em up, I don't want them.

VINCENT You can't have read them all.

GLORIA Your benevolence overwhelms me. If I want a book, I'll read it at the library. I'll take my clothes and that's all.

VINCENT You can have whatever you want. You paid for the bed.

GLORIA You can say that again. No, thanks. That's all been settled.

VINCENT Well, I'm not taking the television set. I gave it to you—it was a birthday present. I'm not taking it back. *(Beat.)* Where the hell are those movers? I don't know why you had to light in on her.

GLORIA Who's that?

VINCENT Barbara, you know who! I don't know what the hell you think you got out of that.

GLORIA Your sister is an idiot.

VINCENT Barbara is not a genius, no. She never claimed to be; I've never said she was bright. But there's no reason to attack her. I remember her as pretty bright when we were living together back home. I was pretty surprised to discover she wasn't. Things can be different from what you remembered. But she's my sister and we used to have some great times at home.

GLORIA Uhm. I'll bet.

VINCENT You have a second-class mind.

GLORIA Well, you have a third-class sister.

VINCENT I don't know what you think you got out of attacking her.

GLORIA I think in the back of that mind she might remember that she wouldn't want to live in your house.

VINCENT And you'll remember she wouldn't want to live in yours.

GLORIA I can't help the way you people were raised.

VINCENT She wanted to know why we were separating. She couldn't understand it.

GLORIA Well, you tell her your story. I don't care what she thinks.

VINCENT She wasn't that far off in saying it's because you've grown into a callous bitch.

GLORIA Whatever you want to tell her, just don't practice on me.

VINCENT She said all along that it wouldn't work; she said so when we were married. My family did and so did yours—we can finally make them both happy.

GLORIA Who ever thought we'd be the cause of so much happiness? At least what they won't know is our breaking up didn't have anything the hell to do with color.

VINCENT Not directly.

GLORIA Not directly or indirectly. A thousand things else, maybe.

VINCENT Indirectly. As a matter of fact—directly. It had to do with the change in you—and that had only to do with, as you so delicately put it, with "color." Our separation—

GLORIA —If you'd look at yourself honestly, just once and ask what...

VINCENT —Our separation came about because I married an all right girl who was a bit of a nut and a bit vulgar, and a bit smart, and in one year she was a goddamned crusader, for Christsake. She started finding people who—I should say started *searching* for people who just couldn't tolerate her. You hadn't even thought about it before.

GLORIA Oh baby, you can't help but think about that and only that twenty-four hours day. When you see it all day, you begin to breathe it and that's all there *is*. Like *air!*

VINCENT You say that now, but you didn't say it at the hutch. No, you might have noticed people eyeing us, looking at us sideways, but you never let it bother you—

GLORIA —Yeah?

VINCENT And after we moved, you took this subtle shift to the way-out left, this red-shift to the rear. Anymore you walk down the street you're not a person, you're a living spring, coiled for counterattack. You joined *CORE* and *SORE* and *POOR* and *MORE* and God knows what other equal rights group; every excuse to hate and fight. And fight for what? For the right to fight, I think—

GLORIA Right. You're dead right!

VINCENT I swear to God I don't know what the hell you're fighting for. You used to be a human being, but in the last two years you've become a "black;" a professional Negro, and I didn't marry a black.

GLORIA Like hell you didn't. If you didn't know it; I'm telling you now.

VINCENT No, sweetheart. The girl I married thought all people were equal and you—the girl now—you, Gloria—have managed to convince yourself that you're not equal at all. And frankly I'm inclined to agree with you.

GLORIA Good. Good. Because equal to you is nothing. Equal to you is sub-human. If you've suddenly noticed you don't consider me your equal I'm glad you finally realized it.

VINCENT If I ever had any racist feelings—

GLORIA Oh, crap.

VINCENT —Then I didn't know about it. But I can't imagine anyone in this world more prejudiced against the black than I am now. And two years ago, I swear to god I didn't feel like that.

GLORIA Maybe you just hadn't met any.

VINCENT Well, if that's what it takes, I met a few. I had known people who loved, lately you've joined some kind of brotherhood and it's got nothing to do with love at all. It's so easy, this newfound antagonism.

GLORIA New?—New?

VINCENT *(Over.)* It's the easiest thing going. Sister said you were lazy and she hit the nail right on the head. Every damn one of you and your easy, prig-gy liberals with you—

GLORIA Not with me, baby!

VINCENT With you! Crying hate. Mistrust.

GLORIA Not by a long shot. Janet is my people? Piss she is.

VINCENT It's the easiest thing in the world.

GLORIA Ronald with that fuzzy blond mop out to *here* is my people...

VINCENT I know because I found it without even trying.

GLORIA They may be scared enough to preach equality while their guilt lasts but, baby, if they're not black they're not any of them my people and don't you confuse the two.

VINCENT Hate, it's right under the first thought. On top of the first thought.

GLORIA Well, how can you expect anything else, considering the conditions blacks live in today?

VINCENT How long have they been there? In their ghettos?

GLORIA You tell me!

VINCENT And have they had the initiative to organize one rational group, one power, one voice to demand their rights? In any way other than street fights? Riots?

GLORIA I'm not concerned with your views on the situation.

VINCENT Vindictiveness?

GLORIA You just pack and go and we'll all live easier.

VINCENT Hate equals hate and it's never netted anything else.

GLORIA You're learning that, are you?

VINCENT Yes, I'm learning that!

GLORIA Well, baby, you walked me up that great white path to security and the Great Society. Taught me how to knuckle under to protect what you thought was your groin, your position—that bulge in your pants is your money belt.

VINCENT Aw, for Christsake—

GLORIA Well, I don't need security, baby, and the boy in the hutch, may he rest in peace, because he died there—he wouldn't have needed it either. You—whoever you are—can get packed up and go on.

VINCENT Yeah, he died there and she died there and why or how the two of *us* ever got together, I can't imagine.

GLORIA Go on down to your sister.

VINCENT I got away from Kentucky because people here—I thought, anyway—were open. They could comprehend something outside themselves, respond. They had scope. I wasn't sick of small Southern towns; I was sick of small people—ambitions—hopes—small hopelessness even. And my friends here were great. I had a place to flop and a place to eat and I met you and it was wonderful. You probably shocked the hell out of me and I loved it. Because you were freedom to me, Gloria. I'd known people could be free—the way people were meant to live, I just hadn't lived that way. It was great reading Millay and Pound and meeting E.E. Cummings in that stupid drug store every week—you talking about your kids at school and all their problems—I loved helping you and you seemed to love helping me. Planning for something better for people, sure, but I wanted us to be a part of it, too.

GLORIA Well, that's always the first mistake.

VINCENT We can't help everyone else and leave ourselves out. We had a house, the hutch, it was only a beginning, I wanted to think…Only that.

GLORIA Yeah, but a beginning of *what* though? You're not blind, damnit.

VINCENT You can't live like that forever. You don't have to tell me I died there; you don't know how much. It was great but I guess it couldn't stand the transplantation.

GLORIA I guess not. All it comes down to, after all, is—

VINCENT Is, yeah, I've learned you can live through anything. You can see everything die and come out alive. Empty as a —*(A vague gesture "Something.")*—but alive.

GLORIA I'm sure you'll find that when you trot back uptown some nice, slightly unwashed, white liberalette will cure you of that soon enough.

VINCENT No, you'll be happy to know that capacity I haven't got. You've done fine.

GLORIA Oh, she'll cleanse your brown little heart and make it breathe again.

VINCENT You really don't know—how can I tell you, make you understand, what you've managed to accomplish; what you've done to me?

GLORIA I know what you've become, and I didn't have anything to do with it. A company man; a heartless pile of—

VINCENT —After the knifing and twisting of life with you, my capacity to care for anyone has gone, Gloria. Rotted. Simple radiation poisoning has set in.

GLORIA You are what you are.

VINCENT —I will never have the stomach to get near—near another human being, living soul again. I loathe everything I used to admire. I loathe people for every foul—triple-tongued, political, hypocritical word they say. I don't hear what anyone says to me anymore, only their motives for saying it. What they want from me!

GLORIA Your people maybe—not—

VINCENT And I loathe "your people" with every grain of strength I have. After hearing you scream civil rights for three years, I loathe every group, faction, congregation, complexion that ever existed. Automatically.

GLORIA Well, that's just too—

VINCENT I used to—back home, there weren't many blacks in my town but I felt of them as wronged equals. Like the Jews. We never had a Jew in town and I never know there was such a thing as a Jew. And when I moved here and heard the popular mythology, my heart unquestioningly went out to another classified people. An oppressed and pre-judged people. And then I started meeting friends of mine who talked endlessly of bargains; who asked what I was making before what I was doing. They couldn't understand that they were living and supporting the same image they fought—

GLORIA You should listen to you sometimes.—

VINCENT —And I kept saying "It isn't true—the mythology is a lie—it's in me for seeing it. They're no more clannish than Greeks or Chinese or Armenians." And yet all my experience showed me that Simon said, "how much does it cost?" That's what Simon says: "You can buy it for less." Simon says, "What's in it for me?" "Hoard!"—

GLORIA —What do you say, Vince?

VINCENT —And Rastus says: "Eat shit, baby! Get out of the way. Repay!"—

GLORIA I don't know your Rastus!

VINCENT —"Repay me for the wrong your fathers did my fathers." Rastus says with a madness that comes from years of inborn stupidity and narrow-mindedness—

GLORIA —Rastus is white—

VINCENT Rastus says: "Retribution!" I loathe their pompous boasting—their telling you the sexual myth is a sexual myth, and then using it as naturally as a fox uses cunning to get what they can of their *petty* desires.—

GLORIA Oh, look around for—

VINCENT And Gloria, goddamn you, I loathe you. I loathe the look of you, and the oily feel of you and the bitter ear-wax taste, the sour orange-rind smell of you. You disgust me in every way—your strength and muscle and firm round stomach disgust me, Gloria, and your single-narrow-mindedness. I loathe you because you made me hate. Everything else. And everyone else. You destroy. It's all you know. And you've not got a goddamned thing to rebuild with. Not even hope and not energy and not love. Certainly not love! Not in one of you. For all your popularized warmth! Not even love! *(He sinks down, drained, sitting on the footlocker.)*

GLORIA *(She looks at him a moment, then walks a step or two unsteadily to the chair and sits, unrelaxed, with great control, disbelief, barely audible. Finally.)* I used to pray, I really did, that first year at the hutch when I loved you, that we'd have children. I said this—when it began, when we had to move up—only at first, really—this could be saved with a child. Like Robert said; a combination half you, half me. And I pictured him—sometimes a boy, sometimes a girl—he was light as you sometimes, and dark as me or darker, with all kinds of funny hair problems that I had to contend with. And he was the reason, he was what it all meant—and he was always very, very bright. Sometimes dark as chocolate or light as coffee, or a beautiful caramel, and as beaming as any of the laughing Spanish kids you see running all over the street. I patterned him after the Spanish kids you see running all over the street. And sometimes he was cinnamon and when he was, he smelled of cinnamon when I hugged him and he was always equal parts you and me and that's why I loved—him and— *(Losing control.)* wanted him. Because he was the love of the hutch *embodied.* And now the—thought—the thought of that child curdles me and I, oh, I, oh Lord, I only thank the benevolent God for being wiser than me, *(Violently.)* because if a son existed now, I swear I'd bash his brains against the goddamned radiator! You used—to be—and all the while—I was saying make this white flesh melt into this black—and something new! Come from this—and saying YES to you, oh God, it curdles me! And thank God! In his gracious wisdom! And I and I don't care a damn if you loathe me, and if you loathe my people, and I don't give one tinker's damn if you loathe everyone and yourself to boot, and if you've lost your *faith,* and your *heart,* and *hope* and *love…*

VINCENT *(Picks the things up.)* I'm going…

GLORIA *(Wildly.)*…and your humor, and your goddamned *balls.* I just don't care a goddamn about you. I'll never think of you after this except to thank God in his wisdom for saving me from killing my child! I want a child now, yes, more than ever. And by God, I'll have one—with a man— a black man like me—and my son will be so black he's blue!

(Vincent goes out the door. She follows him to the door yelling after him.)

GLORIA Black as the night. By god he'll be *black as the night!!*

ROBERT *(Off.)* Gloria? Gloria? Gloria, what's wrong?

GLORIA *(Turning into the apartment.)* I can't talk—

ROBERT *(Appearing at the door.)* What's *wrong? Gloria?* What was he saying to you?

GLORIA *(Trying to mask hysteria.)* I'm getting out of here. Nothing. Go on back.

ROBERT *(Coming into the room.)* You hurt? Did he hit you, what?

GLORIA It had to come—his stupid sister here—I'm going back—I am—I know that. Back *home,* I can't take this. *(She has a small red phone book, looking through it.)* I don't even remember their number. I haven't talked to—I haven't even called.

ROBERT I thought you weren't speaking to them. Or they disowned you or something.

GLORIA I haven't in two—three—nearly three years. I haven't been home for seven, nearly. But I can't stay on here. *(Dialing.)* I was going to stay with Rachel, but I won't; I can't stay down here. I don't care to stay with these *people* down here, any longer. Answer! *(Catching her breath.)* Oh, God. *(On the phone almost without a pause to listen.)* Hello? Mom? Hello?— This is Gloria, is this Cynthia? What?—is that you, Nora?—Little Nora?— What? This is Gloria, Nora. Is Mama there?—Nora? I can't hear you, baby, for the noise—can you—can you turn the radio, Nora? *(To*

Robert.) I guess she went to turn it off. Hello? She did. *(Back to the phone.)* Hello, Nora. It's been two years.—Honey? I'm coming home, up there—where—what?—Honey, I can't understand you baby. *(Her speech should get slightly Southern, not much.)* What?—speak—get farther from the mouthpiece—where's Mama? At the "market?" Are you saying? Is she visiting? I'm nervous baby, I'm sorry—a neighbor's? What? She's visiting a—Nora—*Nora!* I'm—I can't understand a word you're saying, baby.

ROBERT Speak slower.

GLORIA *(Automatically slower.)* Where's Mama? What?—Nora, she's *where?* Ba-ba-baby? She's where?—WHERE? Say it again. Nora—I'm coming home to live with you—would you—would you like that?—Would?—I can't *understand you!* Speak…*clearly.* What?—What?—*(Beginning to be totally incoherent, she can hardly speak, struggling to understand her sister.)* What?—no, I *can't*—ah, ah, I don't want—be—so—…*(Long pause. She holds the receiver with both hands. Long pause. She puts the phone on the receiver.)* I—can't understand you. *(Pause.)* I can't understand a word she was saying. I couldn't understand. What have you done to her? What have you done to *all of them?* Why have—*how could you allow this?* (She takes the phone and pulls it, as though ripping it out of the wall, the cord pulls from its staples half-way around the room, but remains on the wire.)*

ROBERT *(She isn't facing him. Has totally forgotten him.)* Maybe she was just excited when she heard—

GLORIA *(Whirling.)* Get out of here! Get out of here!

ROBERT I don't want to upset—

GLORIA GET OUT! ON! OUT! GO!! GO!!

(Robert exits.)

GLORIA *(To the phone.)* I can't understand you. *(To no one. To the walls.)* What have you DONE TO THEM? *(Hold a beat. She remains motionless.)*

CURTAIN

ACT TWO

Five thirty AM, Sunday. The apartment is dark except for the blue light from the television facing up in the center of the room. The very vaguest light at the window, not enough to shed any light into the room. A warm slit of light under the front, from the hall.

A long pause. The door buzzer sounds several times. There is a stirring in the bedroom.

All furniture and pictures, curtains, shades, bookcases, everything has been removed from the room. Dimly on the walls you can see where pictures, etc., have hung. The only things remaining in the room are a few dishes and a pan or two, cups etc., in the kitchenette area. A table lamp is near the door on the floor—a new one, and the TV.

GLORIA *(Off stage, coughs, coming through the open bedroom door. She enters the living room, goes into the bathroom. The bathroom lights go on, light from the room cuts across the stage. The buzzer sounds again. She is dressed in slippers and a dark violet robe, she should look attractive, though disheveled. She turns on the lamp. Finally buzzes the bell.)* Son-of-a-bitch! All right now. Son-of-a-bitch. *(Sleepy and very tired. Exhausted. The act should be played very, very slowly. Distantly. Long wandering pauses. After the first few minutes almost the slightest movement should make a statement. She wanders a few steps from the buzzer. Coughs again, turns off the TV. The buzzer sounds again, she returns to it. Holding it down, trying to focus, looking around the room. She does not release the buzzer.)* Christ. Get it? There. Get it? *(Pause, holding it down.)* Think fast. *(Now she releases the button.)* Jesus. *(She walks to the bedroom, slams the door, goes to the kitchenette, turns on the light, takes a pan, puts on some water. After a moment there is a knuckle rapping at the door.)* Open it, it isn't locked. You've got the damn key.

VINCENT *(Enters. Slowly, doesn't look up. Turning the knob back and forth.)* I think I lost the key.

GLORIA *(Without looking up.)* Or threw it away.

VINCENT Or something. *(He fusses a bit with the door latch. Just glancing up.)* This door is stuck, or something.

GLORIA You said nine o'clock. It must be five in the morning or after. *(Both speak in exhausted, drained voices. Whispering.)*

VINCENT I said about nine. *(Pause.)*

GLORIA By no stretch of the imagination is it about nine. *(Pause.)*

VINCENT *(Walks around some. They look at each other very little.)* Man, is this place empty. *(Brief pause.)* They get everything packed all right?

GLORIA They came and I left. I didn't stay to see. I suppose so, it's all gone. *(Pause.)*

VINCENT Stephen said it filled his basement. He's a nice guy. *(Pause.)* It won't be long. He said you left word you were keeping the bed, which is a good idea. I wanted you to keep...you bought it. *(Pause.)* There's a lot of other things, actually, that you—

GLORIA —That's all I wanted. I told him to tell you I decided to stay over a few days—I was going to go to Rachel's, and then I was going to go— well, a number of places, but I decided I might stay on here. *(Pause.)*

VINCENT You wouldn't find a better place. *(Pause.)* It doesn't look like much right now. Anything else you decide you—

GLORIA —I don't think so. *(Pause.)*

VINCENT Well, you know...*(Pause.)*

GLORIA I don't think so. I kept some pans, some dishes. Things like that. I'd already packed them, I had to dig around a little.

VINCENT *(Looking around.)* The place looks cold, huh? Maybe it's just cold *out*. These sterile buildings, God. Spacious, though. *(Pause.)* Who would have thought we had all this space?

GLORIA Yeah. *(Pause.)* You want coffee? I put water on. *(Brief pause.)*

VINCENT I suppose. *(Pause.)*
(Gloria makes a cup of instant coffee for him, one for herself.)

GLORIA Are you drunk?

VINCENT Yes. A little. I had a few drinks.

GLORIA Black or with cream?

VINCENT What'd you mean, black or with cream?
(Beat. She adds cream.)

VINCENT Jesus. *(Beat.)*

GLORIA There's no sugar.

VINCENT Christ. Forget it then. Forget it then, that's OK.

GLORIA You want powdered sugar? There's powdered sugar.

VINCENT Fine. Powdered sugar; brown; confectioner's; honey; saccharine; maple syrup if you've got it. I don't care. *(Pause.)* Why are we whispering? *(Clears his throat. In a normal voice.)* Your neighbors won't know you're home. God that echoes. Empty room.

GLORIA Shhhhh. Come on; someone's—sleeping. *(Half-beat.)*

VINCENT Yeah, well, everyone in the building's—everyone else in *town* is asleep. You should see the streets. You'd think they'd be a few stealthy burglars slipping about. *(Brief pause.)* Well, occasionally a wobbly old drunk. Saw a guy trying to walk straight down the sidewalk; he kept listing to the right, you know? Eyes front, walking kinna half-crab, right off the curb, diagonally across the street, and up onto the other sidewalk and into the side of a building before he finally fell over backwards. Still eyes font. Got very excited, like he *knew* that building was going to hit him. Took quite a fall, too. *(Pause.)* Well, I figure if a building's got your number on it. *(Pause.)*

GLORIA Coffee.

(He takes it off the counter, walks toward the window.)

VINCENT Swell. *(Sips it.)* God, that's hot.

GLORIA Shhh.

VINCENT Is that dawn? Yes, I think that's dawning. Who would have thought it would just go right on? Some nerve the universe, huh? *(Pause.)*

GLORIA Yeah.

VINCENT Who's asleep…?

GLORIA It's a guy. You don't know him.

VINCENT Sure. *(Pause.)*

GLORIA Neither do I, as far as that goes.

VINCENT But you've *known* him.

GLORIA No.

VINCENT Biblically, I mean. *(Brief pause.)*

GLORIA That's neither here nor there.

VINCENT Well, who is he? Let us not be secretive. *(Beat.)*

GLORIA It doesn't—

VINCENT —Not that it matters. Outside of simple Kentucky curiosity. *(Pause.)*

GLORIA I don't remember his name. He told me. After you left the movers came and I went out—

VINCENT For some fresh air.

GLORIA Because I didn't necessarily care to see the "ganglia" packed, and crated, and whatever. *(Beat.)* And I went to a movie, and talked to Rachel for a while, and we went over to the Surf for the evening and sat and drank and she left and he came over—

VINCENT *(With a nod to the bedroom.)*—Him—

GLORIA —He came over and he seemed—strong and stupid and we left and walked this way, and he came up. *(Beat.)*

VINCENT For a nightcap. As it were. *(Pause.)*

GLORIA Yes.

VINCENT *(Loudly.)* Well, and why not; God knows you're on your own.

GLORIA Don't be loud; I don't necessarily want him to wake up. Besides he has to get some sleep.

VINCENT He's resting. I can understand that. *(Slight pause.)*

GLORIA He has to get up this morning at six-thirty. He didn't get to bed before three. I assume he has to get up, he set the alarm for six-thirty. I nearly fainted. *(Pause.)*

VINCENT You kept the clock.

GLORIA I bought one.

VINCENT You could have had it. *(Pause.)* Well, what's he like?

GLORIA Go wake him up and ask him. What does he *look* like? He's tall, thin. He is as nearly as I know supremely stupid. *(Beat.)*

VINCENT Which is a relief.

GLORIA You'll never know—!

VINCENT —Oh, I know! *(Pause.)*

GLORIA I don't know what he looks like, just now. I don't remember his face; he struck me as attractive at the time, I suppose.

VINCENT Which time was that? *(Long pause.)* Well, is he colored, or white, or what? *(Very long pause.)*

GLORIA *(She laughs quietly to herself, Vince joins her without knowing exactly why.)* We don't know anything about anyone until we know what they are. God, you could describe someone down to their most egocentric characteristic, and you still would have no idea what they're really like until you know that they're Irish, for instance—or Scottish. Then you think, "Oh, yeah, yeah." Got him pegged. Or Greek, or Italian. Suddenly you know what to expect of them.

VINCENT Yeah, and?

GLORIA Well, and nothing, but it makes you wonder. He's Spanish.

VINCENT This one? Spanish? Jesus.

GLORIA His principal attraction seemed to be that he didn't speak a word of English. So I say he's stupid, he may be a physicist for all I know. But I can't understand it, so it sounds stupid to me. And then he knows the same eight or ten unbelievably profane words in English that I know in Spanish.

VINCENT Yes, I know them, too.

GLORIA And he used them for terms of endearment, which is a shock, believe me. *(Pause.)* So we didn't even try to talk at the bar; we just sat around. It was quite a relief. Smiled a lot.

VINCENT Yeah. You assume he meant them for terms of endearment. *(Pause.)*

GLORIA Why did you come back, Vincent? *(Pause.)*

VINCENT I talked to Robert on the phone. It must have rung for ten minutes.

GLORIA He said. Or rather he didn't say, he left a note. *(Pause.)*

VINCENT God, was he brief. Yes. No. I said, are the movers there? Yes. Are they about through? No. Is Gloria there? No. How'd you get in? The movers are here.

GLORIA Well, I kicked him out. He was getting on my nerves.

VINCENT What'd you give him back his tea or something?

GLORIA No. *(Long pause.)*

VINCENT Maybe I should come back some other time. If you're going to be here I'll know where to reach you; or I can phone or something. *(Pause.)*

GLORIA I'd just as soon you didn't, Vince. I'd as soon not see you if it's all the same.

VINCENT Well, goddamnit, I can't talk to you with some trick in the next room, sleeping it off. Whatta you think I am? In my bed, yet—or your bed—my old bed. *(Pause.)* That sounds like a song. *(Tries a note or two.)* "My old…" *(Pause.)*

GLORIA I don't know why you came up here, I told them to say that I was staying on; I meant if there was anything you had to see me about. Anything urgent. *(Brief pause.)*

VINCENT I don't suppose there's anything you want to say? *(Pause.)*

GLORIA I don't know. *(Pause.)* No. I just want to begin something different; something else. I want to just be able to start out with nothing and see where I can go this time.

VINCENT I wondered.

GLORIA I'm just not up to a post mortem, I guess. No, I don't have anything to say—no.

VINCENT *(With some humor.)* Well, I thought we could shake hands or something and go away at least not fighting.

GLORIA *(Some humor.)* "Don't go away mad?"

VINCENT I just thought we should say—ah, I don't know. Needless to say I've thought about it all evening— *(Pause.)* They say it's good to have everything out in the open. Well, that's a lot of horseshit; I—or maybe it isn't. Maybe with the air cleared… *(Pause.)* "We have to think about the kids?"—"Who's going to support your mother?" Hell, we don't even have a joint bank account to settle. I'll have the insurance changed over, or whatever you have to do to insurance. I'll have my company's I.B.M. machine contact the insurance company's I.B.M. machine. I guess that's all—it's all been said and done, etcetera.

GLORIA I'd think so by now.

VINCENT Or it hasn't really. *(Pause.)*

GLORIA Well, this afternoon for a while I wondered and I decided we both know what wasn't said—so it's all right to just drop it there.

VINCENT I suppose. How come you decided to stay on? *(Long pause.)*

GLORIA I wasn't going to. I thought for a while that I'd go back uptown. I called Mama—it was only an impulse really. *(Pause.)* My youngest sister, Nora, answered the phone and I'm afraid it's been a while. You said you used to think of Barbara as very bright. I used to think Nora was a wonderful, very proper little lady. She's living a mile away in some other country. I couldn't understand a thing she was saying. Not a word—she was trying to tell me Mama was at the store or—I don't know which. I tried to yank the phone out but it didn't work. It never does.

(Vincent laughs quietly.)

GLORIA Those stupid things never work like they do in the movies. You might know. Anyway, it was upsetting. That's why I went out when your truckers came up. And one of the reasons I didn't want to sleep by myself. Jose or Prado—

VINCENT —Or whatever—

GLORIA Yeah. Well, people should be able to comfort one another, God knows.

VINCENT And I suppose he did. Well, that's good.

GLORIA Not so much; not that it matters. *(Pause.)*

VINCENT Oh, well…

GLORIA What? *(Pause.)*

VINCENT I don't suppose I'll be back up—or rather down—I don't know that many people down here. I won't have much reason to come downtown.

GLORIA You'll be busy at work anyway.

VINCENT *(A little defensive.)* Yes. Don't start that. Lay off that, please. Just lay off; I know, I know, but there it is. *(Pause.)*

GLORIA *(With humor.)* Well, for once I wasn't thinking what your work was, just that you'd be busy with it.

VINCENT Well, *I* was. Thinking about it. Most of the afternoon; I tried to explain to…*(Falls silent.)*

GLORIA Barbara?

VINCENT Yes, well, Barbara understands my point of view better than I do. I should have had her explain it to me, I'd have been better off. They—Southerners—have this gimmick, this knack for not understanding something outside of what they accept as right—I don't know, it's this facility they have. You just dial into things that you decide are all right. Everything else doesn't exist. I mean whole countries—whole centuries don't exist for that girl. Whole problems, if they are problems. It's a facility of the South. *(Pause.)* A human facility, I guess; not just there. *(Pause.)* I got in the room all right. If you can call it a room.

GLORIA Good. You won't be there long?

VINCENT No, I'll find a place. That room drives you to finding a place. YMCA. I think they're taking undue advantage of my Christianity. Twenty four-fifty a week for a closet. That's Christian? And you should see it.

GLORIA Not likely.

VINCENT *(It is much easier to talk about anything else.)* Well, it's something else. You could fit eight of them—ten of them in this room. They've got some spray paint now that's not one color but about six. Sorta speckledy-spackledy; covers the whole room. Sink, walls, ceiling, floor, bedstead, door— even nails on the wall. Everything. You feel like you're in a time chamber. No up, no down. It doesn't look like paint at all; you know what it looks like? It looks like bird dung. Pigeon droppings. I'm living in a renovated chicken coop. At best you feel that about five painters must have locked themselves in the room all with a bucket of paint each and had one hell of a fight. *(Pause.)* One window. Looks out onto the air shaft and the tenth floor john. *(Beat.)* Which is something else, too, by the way. *(Pause.)*

GLORIA But you call it home. *(Pause.)*

VINCENT Temporarily. *(Beat.)* Everything is scaled-down to wonderland size. Even the soap; you wouldn't believe it. *(Pause.)* You open a tiny drawer— which is a very complicated procedure because it's been painted shut— and there's Gideon's Bible. You know something about Gideon? For all his benevolence? He was cheap. You should see that paper he uses.

GLORIA I'm tired, Vince.

VINCENT I'll leave; that's OK.

GLORIA No, that's all right; I just don't think you came up here to tell me about the "Y." *(Pause.)*

VINCENT Well. Yes. I suppose I did, I must have, I can't think of anything else.

GLORIA What'd you do this evening?

VINCENT Nothing. Talked to Barbara a while; she's matriculating in a school for airline stewardesses this spring. I said I thought that suited her perfectly; she was complimented, of course. Talked to Stephen about all the junk in his basement; told him I'd get it out by next week. Saw my room. Left my room, and walked around thinking about absolutely nothing. I guess that's something. I was told somewhere that it's impossible to think of nothing, but it isn't. Your mind can go absolutely blank. I assume you had some revelation. You're one up on me if you did.

GLORIA No. Well, not today. A couple of months ago.

VINCENT Oh, well; months ago. Months ago I got at least one revelation a day. My daily revelation, I called it. One-a-day revelations.

GLORIA You said I had or our marriage had stunted your capacity to care any—

VINCENT —Oh please: don't bring up anything I said this afternoon.

GLORIA I guess not.

VINCENT We weren't that far apart, what we wanted. *(Pause. Uncomfortably.)* God, there's such—I can't imagine talking to you like this.—Like we'd never known each other before. If I'd had known we'd be so goddamned clumsy I don't think I'd have bothered. Maybe it's that guy in there—I don't think so. *(Pause.)* It's a hell of a thing to tell yourself, "Well, fellow, you've made a real hash of your life—or out of three years of it anyway—Maybe your whole life."

GLORIA I'm hip.

VINCENT Well, I'll go home.

GLORIA You want another coffee? *(Slight pause.)*
(He is looking distractedly out the window. It is light enough outside now to cast some light into the room. The room is not dark.)

VINCENT Huh? No, I have a taste in my mouth you wouldn't believe. *(Pause.)* Well, one more. For the road. Quick one. *(Pause.)* I'm glad you're going to stay on. *(Looks out window. Without much interest.)* Well, I'll be damned: "Neither sleet nor snow nor dismal dawnings…" *(Pause.)*

GLORIA *(Looking up.)* Who is it?

VINCENT The Fabled Milkman. Cherrydale Farms. I wonder if cows are really all that goddamned contented. *(Rubs his fingertips across the sill.)* Jesus, you cleaned this off; there's a film of dust over it already. What a dirty goddamned city. *(Holds up his hand.)*
(Gloria is across the room at the kitchen area.)

VINCENT Look at that. *(Pause.)*

GLORIA It's New Jersey.

VINCENT *(Looking out the window.)* He could turn his lights off. *(Pause.)*

GLORIA It's late, Vincent. I haven't been to bed yet. *(She isn't looking at him. Pause.)*

VINCENT *(Still looking out the window, rather delighted by the coincidence.)* He did.

GLORIA Good.

VINCENT The zinc rusted all over the windowsill.

GLORIA Is that what that is?

VINCENT It's got iron traces in it; probably moisture got to it here and it oxidized. Not much. God, this room looks—oh, well, everything does. Jesus.

GLORIA You should see it from down there without the drapes. *(Pause.)*

VINCENT I imagine. *(Very long pause.)*

GLORIA I used to notice windows. I used to walk down streets like over on Eighth Avenue, where there's a good building and then an old slum building right next to it. And every once in a while some especially dilapidated looking apartment; grimy as hell, you know, with the old plastic window curtains tied up in a knot and rotting old stained windowshades…look like maps—Some really Harlemesque apartment; and I'd think—God, that people have to live in places like that. And without really realizing it; sometimes someone would be leaning out. Or while I was looking up I'd see, sometimes, just passing by, looking up, someone would pass the window, or lean out, or they'd be moving around up there. And if they happened to be white I automatically stopped worrying about them. I suddenly lost all empathy—right in the middle of the pain. I didn't dislike them, but right in the middle of my fantasy some old bald-headed Italian in a filthy undershirt would lean out of the window, or some big busted old mama with her dress pinned up in front, and I'd start thinking about a pair of shoes I wanted to get, or home, or maybe some meeting somewhere. I didn't really know I did it, until I caught myself once. There was a black guy and a white guy, kids playing out somewhere and I was feeling sorry for the black boy—how he was dressed so poorly. And the other one got up—and he had this sore on his head—I don't know; he had blond hair and a sort of bowlcut and his pants leg was ripped up to about his knee—I guess it was, anyway, his knee was all scraped up. And I realized that I was searching the black boy for some injury. Desperately, almost, hoping he'd be *lame* or something. And I started thinking back and I hadn't always been like that. With the kids at school—but, they were such individuals to me. And I tried to help all of them. Probably because I was very happy then, all very secure, when we were living over the theatre there, and nothing much threatened me.

(Vincent laughs, lowly, doesn't turn around. She doesn't look up. Pause before she goes on.)

GLORIA And I said, well, baby, we look after ourselves, nobody else does—looks after us, someone had better. I can manage to make that sound humane. But a black who was the least bit sympathetic never escaped me. Beady-eyed, eagle-eyed old Gloria. And then—it wasn't long ago either, I was—Now, God knows, I can take care of myself. You and I know I'll stop and listen to the pitch of any bum; if nothing else, just out of curiosity. It wasn't late at night. Or dark. And I wasn't in a hurry. I don't remember the circumstances; just that I crossed the street. There was this kind of typical black bum; looking like I was his godmother or something, coming at me: Saint Gloria. Not drunk—visibly—just probably hungry, and for all I know now going to ask me how to get to Columbus Circle or somewhere. Eight feet away from him, I thought: Oh, I just can't take it—I looked both ways, and crossed the street as neatly, as you please, never looked back; never gave him a second thought till I was home. And then I thought, well, sweetheart, it's spreading. Pretty soon, sister, a crippled little black girl could be pulling at your skirts for old Glory, and old Glory'd not even look down. *(Brushing someone aside disdainfully.)* Step aside. *(Pause.)* You crawled into your company and I crawled into a cocoon. You tucked up into your company and I tucked up into a shell.

VINCENT Or something. *(Pause.)*

GLORIA Yeah, or something.

VINCENT I should quit working there.

GLORIA All I was saying, really, is that I've got no room to talk about you. If I took stock of myself, I'd probably find I had no inventory.

VINCENT It's no way to set up shop.

GLORIA Um. Your coffee's over here growing skin.

VINCENT Um.

GLORIA (Towards the window.) It's getting morning—if you can call it that. What a dismal goddamn day. I haven't been to sleep yet.

VINCENT Yeah, me either.

GLORIA (Looking out the window.) It's just—I *am* a member of a race. A deeply wounded mess of people, and for once somebody—in my lifetime—I know I'll see the end of an era that suppresses a race. Oh, it's been so incredibly long, and it seems so goddamn impossible; and you see people like Barbara, I don't mean her, but people like her, who have such a strong foundation and don't even know they have it, and you see it in your own people, too—and it seems so impossible. And you look for a reason, all the time, for a reason—because if there isn't any reason it's just all too goddamn sad or tiring.

VINCENT Um. (Beat.)

GLORIA Why don't you go up to your room and leave me feeling sorry for myself?

VINCENT You're not feeling sorry for yourself.

GLORIA (A little loud.) Don't tell me who the hell I'm feeling sorry for. We didn't used to be callous.

VINCENT Sure.

GLORIA (A little loud.) Well, damnit, we didn't.

VINCENT You're going to wake up your spick trick. (Pause.)

GLORIA Don't use those words, Vince. (Pause.)

VINCENT I didn't mean…

GLORIA I know, but God—Oh, I sound like a school teacher, it wasn't his fault he wasn't comforting.

VINCENT You should get a job; a job is very comforting. You have your job to do. Your niche. And you do your job and guard your niche, and life is very simple. You have only your responsibility—to your company, which is synonymous with yourself, you believe. And any outside responsibility (Pause.) is only a threat.

GLORIA It wasn't exactly like that.

VINCENT Even if it was I don't know how to change now. And *you* believed in a people. "A Peoples." That's the trouble; we talk of a group of people as a "Peoples." A race—maybe if we'd never had the word we wouldn't have noticed.

GLORIA Maybe if we'd have been *blind*, we wouldn't have noticed. *(Pause.)* I wish some goddamn little green people—they're always talking about in the science fiction magazines—would descend from Mars and try to move in on us. Unite this goddamn, messed-up country and world, in some kind of constructive effort. *(Pause.)*

VINCENT *(This exchange all kind of slow, flat and sad.)* Poor little green people.

GLORIA Bastards.

VINCENT Try to move in.

GLORIA Green bastards.

VINCENT Kill our men, rape our women.

GLORIA Kill our women, rape our men.

VINCENT Take our jobs.

GLORIA Try to get in our schools...

VINCENT We got nothing against race; we got red and black—

GLORIA —Red and yellow, black and white.

VINCENT Red and yellow, black and white going to school together, but those little greens are over-sexed, stupid, they got pointed heads. *(Very long pause.)*

GLORIA Fat chance. *(Pause.)*

VINCENT Or something like that. *(Pause.)*

GLORIA Poor little greens.

VINCENT I don't suppose I will quit though; not right now.

GLORIA Work?

VINCENT Well, it's experience—Maybe some day I'll tell them what they're doing and they'll fire me.

GLORIA Then you wouldn't have a job.

VINCENT How about that?

GLORIA Don't be poor, Vince, they'd as soon exploit you as anybody. Nobody loves a poor American.

VINCENT What are you going to do?

GLORIA I think I'll get on at the Monroe School, I'm pretty sure.

VINCENT I meant...

GLORIA I can't think about it; it's too draining. It requires all one's energy. That's the only bad thing about it—you can't do anything else. What time is it?

VINCENT Quarter to six.

GLORIA Forty-five minutes. 'Till the alarm.

VINCENT I'm fast, too.

GLORIA Jesus, I'm tired. *(Pause.)*

VINCENT *(Very long pause.)* I wanted us to have children too. I had the same picture of him that you did, actually.

GLORIA Well, what we don't want is to talk about private little things like that. Warming little intimacies aren't for us.

VINCENT No.

GLORIA I don't want to feel that maybe there's something there when I know there isn't.

VINCENT No. Still…

GLORIA I'd like to just—blow it off altogether.

VINCENT Sure.

GLORIA Maybe for you and maybe for me, but not for us. Not any more. We've spent three arduous years finding that out.

VINCENT Two years.

GLORIA I'll buy that; the first year we didn't learn a thing.

VINCENT *(With humor.)* Maybe we learned everything the first year and forgot it the next two. Then we started getting principles—they take a lot of maintenance. It wasn't the same. When I think back, I can't believe it.

GLORIA Uhm.

VINCENT Well, keep in touch. *(Very long pause.)*
(She shakes her head finally, slowly.)

GLORIA I really don't see any reason. *(Pause.)*

VINCENT Well, whatever you want, either way.

GLORIA *(A bit more energy.)* I mean, if I get run down by a truck, they'll contact you—you've got my insurance policy.

VINCENT *(Laughs.)* I'll get it changed. There's time for all that jazz. Well, I'm sober now anyway.

GLORIA *(A bit more energy.)* I want to get an apartment started, get some things in here, I guess.

VINCENT I have to get a place, too.

GLORIA Sometimes I think this place will be fine and sometimes I want to move into a very small furnished room. If I wasn't totally ingrown already now would be an ideal time to retire into myself.
(Vincent laughs, just lowly.)

VINCENT I'll go on; you know where to reach me.

GLORIA You keep saying I know where, I don't know why.

VINCENT Well, if something comes up. *(Long pause. He finishes the coffee in a gulp.)* God, that's cold as a bitch.

GLORIA I'm glad you came by.

VINCENT I'm sober now anyway.

GLORIA Do you have to go to work?

VINCENT It's Sunday.

GLORIA Right, right. Get some sleep.

VINCENT You too, Crawl in with your hot pepper in there.

GLORIA Well, it seemed like a good idea.

VINCENT I'm glad I came over; I didn't know I was going to really; I was in the Village, wandering around. Habit, I suppose.

GLORIA *(Smiles.)* Uhm. *(Pause.)* I'm glad you came back; it's better this way. I guess.

VINCENT I'm sober now, anyway. *(He touches her arm briefly.)* Well, I'll see you. Or I won't see you, as it were. I wish you luck.

GLORIA You too, Vincent.

VINCENT *(Rapidly, briskly now.)* Oh, well, Jesus Christ; goodbye, good luck and God bless, I guess. Okay?

GLORIA *(Walking him to the door.)* Okay. Goodbye to you; good luck, Vince. *(Vincent stands beside her at the open door for a moment then exits briskly. Gloria closes the door.)*

GLORIA Poor little greens. *(Goes to the stove. Lights a cigarette. Turns off the over-head light. Puts the two cups into the sink. Runs a little water. Turns off the lamp by the door. The room is quite light now. A very grey, morning dim-light slants into the room. She looks at the front door. Pauses. Wanders to the window, looking out into the street. Takes a drag on the cigarette. Crosses her arms. Leans against the window sill.)* What a goddamned dismal day. *(The only movement in the room is the smoke from Gloria's cigarette. Silence. A full thirty second pause, please. Nothing moves. Gloria continues looking blankly out the window. Curtain.)*

END OF PLAY

Lemon Sky

For Jim and John

INTRODUCTION

Any introduction to this play should begin with Alan's first line: "I've been trying to tell this story, to get it down, for a long time, for a number of years, seven years at least—closer to ten."

And I had. This is my most nakedly autobiographical play. I had the story, after all, it happened, but I couldn't get it down. I wrote the scene between Alan and Jerry, typed on yellow paper, sometime about 1959. The play suddenly happened nine years later. I was working on *Serenading Louie*, which was turning into a bear. I carried the Louie notebook all over Europe. I couldn't work there. I corrected the proofs of *Rimers*, wrote about one page of a libretto for *Summer and Smoke*, gaped at Europe for six months, hung out with the LaMama Troupe, and came back with *Louie* still an inchoate mess.

I've had my share of miraculous experiences and one of them was the genesis of this play. I had told the story to all my friends, it didn't help, I couldn't write it. I'm a terrible pest to my friends, talking about my work, making them read scenes, sometimes aloud to me, everyone always knows what I'm working on. So everyone knew *Serenading Louie* was the story of two troubled marriages. I was at some bar/restaurant, an actor was regaling about ten of us with horror stories of his ex-girlfriend. He was very angry and very entertaining. Everyone at the table, probably including the actor, knew I was taking notes. He was just too good. When I got home that night I stretched out in a hot tub (not a hot-tub, just a regular tub with hot water) and tried to remember how his harangue began. I felt if I could remember his first words, I could write the whole speech. I closed my eyes, trying to concentrate, but instead of the actor's voice, a voice I had never heard before, said Alan's first speech of *Lemon Sky*: "I've been trying to tell this story, to get it down, for a long time..." I opened my eyes and said, What the hell was that? Then I realized, Oh, sure, that's one way *Lemon Sky* could begin, but that's not what I want for that play at all. I don't want it narrated. I'd always imagined *Lemon Sky* as a straightforward, realistic, old-fashioned play. I closed my eyes again and tried to remember that guy in the restaurant. Alan said, "I've been trying to tell this story..." And he went on...and on! For almost two minutes! All the way past Doug's "Hugged me! Hugged me, by God!" I was stunned. We like to talk about characters speaking to us, sometimes I say I just take dictation, but this was ridiculous. Nothing like this had ever happened before. I got out of the tub, wrapped a towel around me, and went in to the typewriter. All right, so this isn't the way I'd imagined the play; it won't hurt to write that down and see if it leads to anything.

The first act flew. I couldn't type fast enough. Words were spelled approximately, abbreviated, when I got to the Alan/Jerry scene I wrote, "That scene on yellow paper goes here," hoping I could still find it among my stuff. I got up from the typewriter about ten the next morning, still undressed, and called Marshall. "I just finished the first act," I said. *"Serenading Louie?"* "No. *Lemon Sky.*"

A couple of days later I started act two. It took about a week. Then I stared at the damn thing for another week. I knew everything that would happen in the short act three. I was just reluctant to go there. After a week I said, Well, how long can it take to write fifteen minutes? It took about forty-five. Claris Nelson and Marshall came over to read the completed play while I finished the last act. They sat on the sofa, sharing the only copy. I typed the third act out coldly, not allowing myself to get involved in the drama. I slipped the finished pages into their hands while they read, went into the kitchen, filled a pan with water for instant coffee, turned on the gas, turned off the gas, went into my bedroom, shut the door, and cried my eyes out. Certainly the only time anything like that had happened. I fell asleep and awoke hours later to a note of congratulations they had left.

The play went so fast I never got in the title. I decided I didn't mind, there's enough landscape in the thing. But just for the record: one week a heavy fog hung over the lemon groves; at the end of the week the fog lifted and it rained. The rain scented everything it touched with the fragrance of lemon blossoms. That was a good deal more pleasant than the aftermath of the fire in act three. A fog formed in the hills after the fire, hung there for days, then moved back west over the city. The smell of stale burned wood permeated every corner of the house, seeping into every piece of clothing. The sofa stank for a month.

I never looked back on this one, I wrote it and The Devil take the hindmost. Whatever that means. I never wondered if my father or stepmother or brothers had read it. Then one day Jim (Jerry) wrote me. It was my first contact with him since I had left fifteen years earlier. He said he and John (Jack) had loved reading the play because they had remembered little of that time, and had never really known what happened. It had been this hole in their past. And my father had read it too. He said, Yeah, that's about right.

PRODUCTION

Lemon Sky was first presented on March 26, 1970 by Neal DuBrock at the Buffalo Studio Arena Theatre, Buffalo, New York, with the following cast:

ALAN . . . . Christopher Walken
DOUGLAS . . . . Charles Durning
RONNIE. . . . . Bonnie Bartlett
PENNY . . . . Kathryn Baumann
CAROL . . . . Lee McCain
JERRY . . . . Shawn McGill
JACK . . . . Frank Martinez III

The production was directed by Warren Enters, and designed by Stephen J. Hendrickson. Lighting was designed by David Zierk.

The Buffalo Studio Arena Theatre production (with Steven Paul and Willie Rook as Jerry and Jack) was subsequently presented at the Playhouse Theatre, New York City, on May 17, 1970, produced by Haila Stoddard, Mark Wright, Duane Wilder and Neal DuBrock. A staged reading of a working version of the play was given in the summer of 1968 at the Eugene O'Neill Theatre Foundation, Waterford, Connecticut.

CHARACTERS

ALAN, twenty-nine now, seventeen when he went to California
DOUGLAS, his father
RONNIE, his father's wife
PENNY AND CAROL, both seventeen, wards of the state living with Douglas' family
JERRY AND JACK, Douglas' and Ronnie's children, Alan's paternal brothers, twelve and eight

SCENE

1970 and the late 1950s.

One of the thousands of homes in the suburbs of San Diego, California. This one is in El Cajon, a city surrounded by low mountains. The home is more indicated than represented realistically: there is a back yard with redwood fences separating it from the neighbors, a low sloping roofline against a broad expanse of sky (which is never yellow); there are no walls, but indicated division of rooms: a kitchen with a breakfast nook, refrigerator, stove, cabinets, etc.; the living room, carpeted, need only have a sofa and TV for furnishings; Alan's bedroom, upstage, and a garage with photographic printing equipment.

There is furniture in an area of the yard and a garden against the redwood fence. The kitchen and an area indicating the bathroom may have tiled floors, a patio can be surfaced in redwood or concrete or flagstone. The stage area should be very open and free. Sometimes the characters move down "halls" and into "rooms" and sometimes they cut across the entire stage paying no attention to the room divisions.

There is no green in set or costume; celadon, sage, anything else, but nothing green.

The lights move from area to area, defining our focus as well as the time of day and condition, and as many scenes as possible are bathed in a bright cloudless sunlight.

LEMON SKY

ACT ONE

The stage is dark and undefined. All the characters are on stage—standing far upstage just barely lighted—we should "feel" they are there without actually seeing them.

ALAN *(Comes forward from the darkness. He is twenty-nine now. Thin and light, though not blond. Enthusiastic and pensive. He speaks rapidly and at times— when talking with the other characters—with a marked Midwestern accent. A little too preoccupied to begin a play, he enters a pool of light downstage and speaks to the audience.)* I've been trying to tell this story, to get it down, for a long time, for a number of years, seven years at least—closer to ten. I've had the title, I've had some of the scenes a dozen times, a dozen different ways, different starts. The times I've told it to friends as something I wanted to do I've come home and tried to get it down—get to work on it—but the characters, the people ignored the damned story and talked about whatever they darn well pleased and wouldn't have any part of what I wanted them to say. They sat down to coffee or some damn thing. The trouble was I wanted not to be the big deal, the hero, because I wasn't. No one was. Or how do I know who was? If it happened this way or that, who knows? But dad—my dad— *(Quickly.)* If it's all autobiographical, so, I'm sorry, there it is; what can I tell you—But how can I write about dad? Tell him. I knew him, lived with him, in San Diego, for six months. *(Quickly.)* I always say I lived in California for two years because it sounds more romantic. Bumming around the beach a couple of years, on the coast, it sounds great. Six months is like you didn't fit in. Like why bother. Like restlessness. The title because—I don't know—it had something to do with the state. California. I mean, the nut fringe; first Brown, then Reagan and—who knows what they'll come up— *(Breaking off, returning to the thought above.)* But finally I said, so if you're a hero; if you can't admit that you weren't, if you've got to make a—if you can't admit that you were really as big a bastard as everybody else—If you can't admit that, then for God's sake let it stay! And the fact that you can't will say more about you than if you could. Leave it be! My father, what do I know about him. If he's nothing, I mean *But nothing!* Then the fact that he comes off the short end of the stick shows something. From that you know that there's *more* there. You know? Leave it! Do it. Straight. Get it down, let it get down and let it tell itself and *Mirror,* by what you couldn't say—what was really there.

DOUGLAS *(Still in the shadows upstage, we can not see him clearly. With great emotion.)* Hugged me! Hugged me by God! By God you can't! No matter what anybody anywhere says—

ALAN *(Finishing the sentence, as if recalling a quote.)* —You can't separate a kid from his father.

DOUGLAS *(Just a bit more visible.)* Even after—after this long a time. Even after this—time!

ALAN Oh, God—

RONNIE *(Faintly answering Doug, they begin to be visible.)* I know, I know, Doug.

ALAN *(Over.)* —What could I do? I got off the bus. I have a splitting headache from the altitude; from going over the Rockies. And then down to sea-level—like a drop of ten thousand feet. Two and half days on a scenic-cruising *Greyhound* with faulty air-conditioning.

RONNIE A migraine, he said, tension—

DOUGLAS Well, yes, tension…

ALAN *(Overlapping.)* Finally I had to go to a doctor after three days. I could hardly talk. He said it was tension, the change in environment, just needed acclimatization and aspirin. Maybe it was—all I know is it started while I was in the Rockies or in Arizona: I woke up and my head was splitting. Like I wanted to die, there, forget it. And with this headache—the bus pulled in and I—there's only one guy standing there. A very distinguished looking man, I think, my God, he's so handsome, he's so good looking, so young. In this dude suit. White dinner jacket—sport jacket, but white. Wool. Sun shining. *(Sunlight beams around them.)* And I said…Dad? *(Douglas reaches out, Alan flies into his arms, quickly, then retreats.)* I mean what could I do? Shake his hand? But it was *right.* I felt it was right. *(Then with immediate irritation.)* No, mother hadn't said anything against him—or at least what she said I was willing to forget. All the way back in the goddamned car—

DOUGLAS *(Douglas is a strong, grey-templed man, forty-five. Oddly romantic, childish and dogmatic with great energy. Though considerably heavier than Alan he is no taller and there is a marked physical resemblance between the two. Douglas wears a white wool sport jacket and grey slacks, after he goes to work and comes back we never see him dressed in any but work or sport shirts again.)* Now, I know, she must have told you things about me and she's a good woman—

ALAN *(To the audience. Cutting in.)* I just wanted him not to feel bad—and not to think mother had said anything. *(To Douglas.)* Really.

DOUGLAS Hell, I wanted you out here years ago.

ALAN Sure, you don't have to think about it, dad. Really. I don't hold anything against you. *(To the audience.)* I almost wished it hadn't come. For a minute. It was *pain*ful! His explanations! That was over, years ago—finished.

DOUGLAS I know, but I had to say it.

ALAN You don't have to think about it, dad. Really, I don't.

DOUGLAS *(Loosening up.)* She's a good woman. But with a man like me—Al, she was at me day and night with suspicions and limitations; I couldn't breathe. All that—she didn't let a guy breathe.

ALAN *(Distantly.)* I understand, really.

DOUGLAS Ronnie is different, a different kind of woman. She *lives.* You'll love her.

ALAN I'm anxious to meet her. *(Half to the audience, half to Douglas.)* And I have two brothers—half-brothers—I've only seen once, I hardly know them. Not at all.

DOUGLAS You'll see them asleep—or tomorrow. I've got to go back for the second half of the day.

ALAN *(To the audience.)* He worked at an aircraft factory. Nights. The swing shift.

DOUGLAS It pays better, not much, but it helps. You have the daytime to yourself, you work six hours instead of seven. I like to get out. You have some decent time to yourself. I just want you to understand.

RONNIE *(Coming forward a step, extending her hand. She is small, attractive, blond of perhaps 38 with a good deal of taste and poise.)* I was working in the garden—

ALAN *(To the audience suddenly.)* If it was staged…I mean she knew dad was coming to get me. He called to see if the bus was on time. He said he had waited only eight minutes—

DOUGLAS —Bulova—

ALAN —so she—

DOUGLAS —Never wrong.

ALAN —Knew I'd be in at that time. What do you do? You meet a kid. Seventeen. Just out of high school, your step-son, you've never seen before…What are you going to be doing? What*ever* it is will make *some* kind of impression. You borrow a white sport coat to meet the kid, and you put on a pair of those thick big white gloves, with dirt—from the *ground* dirt—on them, those white work gloves with blue elastic wrists, big thick things—for *men,* and— *(Framing it.)* You are discovered in a garden hat so the California sun doesn't burn you and so you won't frown.

RONNIE *(Coming forward a step.)* I was working in the garden, pruning.

ALAN *(To the audience.)* Rose garden. The roses.

RONNIE *(Showing him around the yard.)* There's the Bird of Paradise, it's never going to bloom. I got it because it's Jack's favorite. The only flower he likes.

ALAN *(Suddenly, wanting to hug them.)* Jack! Jack! Little Jack!

RONNIE Probably because it's very futuristic. "Space man" or "Jungle man."

ALAN *(Back to framing the scene.)* —Pruning the roses; I hear the car drive into the driveway and the gate open at the side of the house; I turn around; I come across the back yard smiling.

RONNIE *(Coming to him, taking off a glove, extending her hand.)* Welcome, Alan. Welcome. Hello.

ALAN I take off a glove and extend my soft hand…

RONNIE I was working in the garden. Pruning.

ALAN The roses. And a hand shake; *(To the audience.)* and Dad looks on beaming. *Beaming.* "You'll—

DOUGLAS —You'll—

ALAN —"Love"—

DOUGLAS —love—

ALAN —"her."

DOUGLAS her.

ALAN Blond hair. She looks like Blondie in the funnies; but she—you do love her. She's *worried* and *planned* and—

RONNIE *(Cutting in.)* Do you smoke? You want a cigarette?

ALAN *(To the audience.)* And of course you smoke but you didn't know if you should and—

DOUGLAS —A beer.

ALAN Yes, thanks, I didn't know—

DOUGLAS Sure, take it, drink up. Hell, Carol drinks and worse I think. You don't have to go on binges.

ALAN I don't, no…

DOUGLAS Ronnie smokes sometimes. About one a month.

RONNIE Not that much even.

ALAN *(To Ronnie and Douglas, with a marked Midwestern accent.)* I've got this incredible headache, it's just the altitude. How high are we?

DOUGLAS I don't know.

ALAN Coming through the mountains…

RONNIE You want some coffee?

DOUGLAS Ronnie makes the best damn coffee in—

(They move into the breakfast area—Alan sitting, Douglas leaning against the stove.)

ALAN Good. *(Laughs, overwhelmed, nervous.)* Good, yes… *(To the audience, happy—without accent.)* What do I say? Because I didn't *plan*. Because I didn't have a setting—it wasn't my home I was coming into—it *would be* mine, but I couldn't sit at the breakfast nook and pull up the ashtray and serve coffee out of the good cups like it was every day and lean against the stove and talk about work…

RONNIE You look as I expected.

ALAN *(When speaking with them, with the accent.)* You look—do too, look like what I expected.

DOUGLAS I've got to get along.

ALAN How come?

RONNIE Doug's on the night shift, so he has days off.

DOUGLAS I still have to get in half a day.

ALAN Good.

DOUGLAS I told them if the bus was on time I'd make it in; if you'd have been late I'd have taken off.

ALAN *(He has stood. Very joyously, throwing out his arms. Wildly.)* Where are they all!? Where is it? *(Looking around, as though at the surrounding landscape.)* A breakfast nook and out the kitchen window all the back yards are private with redwood fences around them. Higher than your head. And mountains all around. Out the living room window—Mt. Capitan…

DOUGLAS The big one—with the bald head, that's Mt. Capitan.

RONNIE *(Suddenly, quietly but urgently.)* Alan, Mt. McGinty is on fire, the whole sky, wake up, it's incredible…

DOUGLAS *(Overlapping.)* —With the brush, Mt. McGinty. And the blue one in the distance,—

ALAN —Mt. Otay—

DOUGLAS Behind that, Jerry would—

ALAN *(Quickly to the audience.)* —My other brother.

DOUGLAS —Know that one, he knows them all. *(Turning to look out the kitchen "window."*) El Cajon Mountain, Cowles Mountain and Mount Helix.

ALAN ...Out the kitchen window, with a spotlighted cross on top and expensive homes, but very expensive homes—built along the road that helixes up to the cross.

RONNIE They turn the lights off at midnight.

ALAN And the whole mountain disappears.

DOUGLAS You can see it for miles.

RONNIE We're surrounded.

DOUGLAS Behind Mount Helix is La Mesa, the city of La Mesa, over on the other side, we can drive over there; Lemon Grove, they're all about the same. La Mesa, Grossmont may be a little more exclusive—a little more expensive.

ALAN On the way here from downtown.

RONNIE How do you like the traffic? Is that some drive?

ALAN Yeah, that's something else, isn't it? I've never seen traffic like you've got here. I don't know if I'll want to drive or not.

DOUGLAS Sure you will; you get used to it.

ALAN But on the way out we must have passed a hundred houses that were going up. Half-constructed.

DOUGLAS Across from the college they're building three hundred houses. Ranch types. A whole suburb, one guy. *(Almost to the audience.)* A whole city: shopping centers, two theaters, one regular and a drive-in, three hundred houses. Big, ranch-type houses.

RONNIE There's supposed to be four hundred new residents in California every day.

ALAN Every day.

DOUGLAS It's a big state, Al; it really is. Four hundred.

RONNIE Every day.

DOUGLAS Don't let anybody tell you the gold rush is over out here, boy.

ALAN I guess not.

DOUGLAS Guys are making a killing out here.

ALAN And the climate I suppose—

DOUGLAS *(A brief concession.)* —March is a mess. Late March into April—it rains, but that's about it for the whole year. And it's a little cooler, but outside of that—

ALAN I don't suppose you get any—

RONNIE *(Both are shaking their heads, seriously not ironically.)* No, no snow—

DOUGLAS —Very little; up in the mountains—

RONNIE —It seldom even freezes. Up in the mountains. The Lagunas and higher. We drive up or else the boys would never have seen snow. Of course you don't see it falling which is half the treat. It falls during the night. It'll snow a foot and then thaw within two days.

ALAN A foot? Overnight?

RONNIE A lot more, sometimes.

ALAN That's going-to-hell snowin'.

DOUGLAS Alan, you'll love it. It's heaven. I mean it's really heaven. You'll love it here.

RONNIE We hope you do.

DOUGLAS You will! Hell! By God, anybody who wouldn't sumpins wrong with 'em er sumpin, huh?

ALAN I think there'd have to be. I do already. We were coming through New Mexico and I didn't believe it…the air-conditioning wasn't working. Of course who needs it in Nebraska. But by the time we get to El Centro—it's burning hot. Your first stop in California: El Centro. What do you do your first stop in California? You buy a glass of orange juice. Never. Whatever you do buy orange juice at the Greyhound bus station in El Centro, California. Yeahhh! God awful. The worst. The worst single paper cup of orange juice I've ever had in my life. *(To the audience by now, as well as them.)* It's not native in El Centro. Oranges can't grow there. Gila monsters you could buy. Navajo blankets, moccasins—turquoise ear rings, Apache tears you can buy. That's it. Of course, even getting to El Centro is a nightmare. You know California, you've seen the pictures: palm trees, sunsets, swimming pools, oceans and mountain springs? The first five hours—five and a half—you are treated to the world's most barren desolation. The Mojave Desert. Telephone poles are stuck in a big hunk of asphalt to hold them upright. The asphalt is boiling. You think: this is California! Oh, wow, who does the public relations on this place! *(Back to them, exaggerating.)* It's a hundred and five degrees! It's March! I want you to know March and it's a hundred and five. In Nebraska it's forty-seven and it's a warm day when I left.

RONNIE I know, I remember.

DOUGLAS She worked there.

ALAN *(To the audience, rather a different mood, straight, low, no accent.)* What I've heard about Ronnie is dad met her and dated her—he was still married, sometime during that time, he was still married to mother.

DOUGLAS In Lincoln. Private secretary to the attorney of the state. State Attorney, same difference, huh?

ALAN *(Continuing.)* And maybe they came out here together, maybe not. He said he'd send for us—mother and me. He ran off, out to here. OK. She never blamed him.

RONNIE A wonderful man, and an interesting job.

ALAN You take shorthand and all that then?

RONNIE Oh, yes. I want to forget it; it's like riding a bicycle, you can't. They let the secretaries run the country I think. From my experience.

ALAN Probably they do.

DOUGLAS I've got to get along.

ALAN How come?

RONNIE Doug's on the night shift, so he has days off.

DOUGLAS So I can get in half a day yet.

ALAN Good.

DOUGLAS You darn-betcha.

ALAN Yeah. *(Laughs.)*

DOUGLAS *(Very sober. Embarrassingly straight and serious.)* I can't tell you how much I've wanted you here.

RONNIE *(Sober.)* He has, Alan.

DOUGLAS I've tried. I wrote once or twice, but your mother thought I was trying to kidnap you or some damn thing. She wouldn't let you come.

RONNIE He cried. It's the only time I've ever seen—

ALAN *(To the audience—cutting it off.)* —He said he had to go; he worked on the night shift, he could get in half a day yet. That it was great having me here. Finally. He'd dreamed about it.

RONNIE *(They have moved from the kitchen. Showing him around.* That's going to be your room—

ALAN Great.

DOUGLAS *(Returning to previous. Sober.)* So bad. I can't tell you.

ALAN *(Sober.)* I'm glad to be here. I am.

RONNIE —The patio, it will go here; you've seen the garden. The living room, the TV—it's in the cabinet, I can't stand a naked eye staring at me. We almost never watch it. Doug watches the fights and the ball games in the afternoons.

ALAN That's right, I can watch the games.

DOUGLAS *(Showing him around.)* That's the dark room.

ALAN Wow. I didn't know that.

DOUGLAS The mounted picture there, the second one, I won an award on last year. It's taken actually with a red filter looking straight into the sun like that—it's called "Sun Spot"—that's the sun here and the reflection here; the way the sun hits the water. It's a bitch of a shot to make because of the glare. The reflection; you have to use a filter, have to know what you're doing. *(Slapping the table.)* That's a professional enlarger; that's as good as they make them.

RONNIE Doug went through a woodworking phase about five years ago so we have a table saw and a lathe and all of that. He'll build the patio this summer.

DOUGLAS Not by myself I won't. Not now that I have help.

ALAN Right. I'd love to.

RONNIE Dad's workroom you've seen.

ALAN Do you develop your own film?

DOUGLAS Develop, print, enlarge to any size, all in the same room…the whole works. It's not difficult, it's goddamned exacting, everything's timed pretty close; you have to know what the hell you're doing.

RONNIE *(Pointing out.)* Mount Helix with the cross; and Mount Otay, isn't that god-awful? Over there—nearly in Mexico.

ALAN All around. It's beautiful.

DOUGLAS You'll love it.

ALAN *(Enthralled.)* I do. I do. I do.

DOUGLAS *(Suddenly serious. Man-to-man.)* Carol…Now, I want you to know, don't be embarrassed. We have these two girls living here.

(The girls can be seen dimly in the distance.)

ALAN You wrote me, I know.

DOUGLAS Well, Alan, they're wards of the state. They've had terrible lives, you don't know—

ALAN —maybe I—

DOUGLAS —Just terrible, you don't know. Penny's father left her, her mother died, she's lived with one bad foster home after another. They're happy here. The woman said we were one of the best homes in San Diego County. They live here like it's their home.

RONNIE They really do.

DOUGLAS They've been here—Penny a year, Carol a year now and half. It's their home and we all get along like a family.

RONNIE You'll have Carol's room and she can sleep with—

DOUGLAS And Carol…Her mother and father both died when she was too young to remember it—

RONNIE She does though.

DOUGLAS She says she doesn't. Penny's good. She gets along fine. Carol. I want to talk to you man to man. Alan, Carol is a whore. She's promiscuous. She came here bragging she'd slept with six sailors in one night once.

RONNIE Seven, but one more or less.

(Alan laughs.)

DOUGLAS She has a boyfriend now, she's trying to straighten out. Hell, she was on pills, she was on God knows what. Things I hadn't even heard of.

RONNIE But she dates this guy regularly now; he's a darn nice guy. You'll meet him.

DOUGLAS You have to treat her like, think of her like a sister. We can't have you—

ALAN OK, I won't.

DOUGLAS It's important.

ALAN How can you keep them? They must cost…

DOUGLAS Well, the state sends us sixty dollars a month toward their board—

RONNIE It's not as much as they eat even. But we make a home for them.

ALAN *(Joyous.)* Where are they! Penny! Carol! Jerry! Jack! Jerry's twelve and is a little me. A little blond me only fatter. A little. Jack's a brush ape. A—a— renegade. Jerry and I look a little alike, Jack takes after Ronnie, except for his eyes. Penny's a dope. She's great. But she's a dope. Carol's gorgeous!

RONNIE Not really, she's attractive. Striking. She could be a model. She has that kind of figure. Beautiful skin.

DOUGLAS Not really, though, she knows how to fix herself up is all. She's a come-on. She's not got a personality. She's neurotic. She's had a terrible life, Alan, you don't know. *(Suddenly messing his hair.)* Fella! devil! *(To the audience, hugging Alan's head against him. Proudly.)* I mean he was my kid. He looked like me. More than Jerry ever thought about. When I was his age I was skinny like that. I had to work out— *(To Alan.)* I could never gain weight. But God…!

RONNIE —When we were married—

DOUGLAS I put on weight the first week. It's the air. You will too. And Ronnie's a good cook.

ALAN Good.

RONNIE Which reminds me are you hungry?

DOUGLAS *(Seriously.)* They've gone out, we wanted them to, so we could meet you. Get to know each other a little first. We told them they'd see you in the morning. One more day won't matter—you'll be here a while. Penny'll be in. She went to the movie with Rose, I imagine.

RONNIE Rose, you've got to meet. She's unbelievable. Are you sure you can't eat?

ALAN Really. *(To the audience.)* I've got this incredible headache; a migraine, only I don't know it and I've not had one since—three days it lasted—all through that first day and night. It can't go on like this of course, there'll be a scene soon. Dad had to go to work, he could get in half a day— night—yet. He always called it day…the working day.

DOUGLAS I want you to go down there. You can get a job; if you're going to be going to school. It costs, you know.

ALAN I wanted to work somewhere, to pay my way—

DOUGLAS I wish to God we could—

RONNIE Afford to pay your way—

DOUGLAS Alan, we can't; we just can't. I want to, but we can't that much. We'll help, sure, all we can…

ALAN No, I want to. I said I would.

DOUGLAS Hell, it's healthy. Everybody out at State is working part-time anyway. Earn their keep. We'll have to get you a car, won't we? You drive?

ALAN Yeah, fairly well.

DOUGLAS Get you a little Austin or one of those. What'd you think?

ALAN *(To audience and them.)* What can I say, I think it's great…

DOUGLAS We'll go over and look; you gotta have it to get you to school, doncha? I'm not going to squire you in, you don't want to have to take a bus every morning. Huh?

ALAN *(To audience.)* There'll be a scene. Those who are confused will say thank God, something to watch, maybe everyone will stop flying around. *(Douglas stands a moment watching, then turns with a proud smile and exits.)*

RONNIE I guess you'll want to get some sleep soon.

ALAN Before too long. I couldn't sleep on the bus. I almost broke my neck.

RONNIE You want to go right now?

ALAN No, no.

RONNIE Whenever you're ready.

ALAN Could I have another coffee?

RONNIE *(She pours another coffee.)* He's talked about you so much. I didn't know about you at all when we were married. He told me the first night; it was quite a shock. I didn't even know he had been married. He cried. He said he wanted to bring you out here and I wanted you too. But your mother—and she was right, don't you think?

ALAN Yes. *(To audience.)* What could…?

RONNIE It's better this way. You're not torn apart, half in one place and half in another. He missed you so much. That's why he wanted to have another kid right away. You're not shocked or embarrassed or anything, me speaking with you frankly?

ALAN No, God, no; it's a relief…

RONNIE Good. I've looked forward so to knowing you. Doug's mother gives us pretty regular reports about you.

ALAN She does?

RONNIE Oh, sure. That's why we asked you out. She said you were out of high school; she thought it was about time you saw some of the country—and that you and Doug got reacquainted.

ALAN She knew I wanted to go on to school.

RONNIE What are you going to study?

ALAN You know, I don't have any idea. Liberal Arts—I don't know.

RONNIE There's time. We'll take you up to San Diego State so you can get registered; it's a beautiful campus. Don't decide for a while…Jack has a birthday party coming up—his eighth. Two dozen local hellions: you'll want to escape from that, I imagine. Maybe you can take Jerry to a movie or something. He considers himself much too adult for that crowd.

ALAN Our course—he's eleven.

RONNIE No, please. Twelve. And a half: he stretches it a little; he was born Christmas Day. You knew that.

ALAN Yes. But that's all. *(To the audience, a marked contrast as he drops the accent.)* I'd seen them; just once, five years ago, Jack was three, Jerry seven. Dad and the kids came to town and it was arranged that if a friend of Mother's went along we'd all go to the zoo in Omaha, and we had a picnic which I remember as the most horrible experience of my younger life. Everyone worried about how I was going to react and me not knowing what was happening. Just I didn't want any of it and I couldn't get it through my head how any of these people could be related to me. And I was freezing to death, which is all I really remember: it was November and all the animals had their winter coats and were ugly anyway.

RONNIE *(Standing, whispering—stage whisper.)* You want to see them? *(They walk to between the boys' beds.)*

ALAN *(Same whisper.)* Don't wake…

RONNIE No, you'll meet them in the morning. Jerry. He has asthma and snores like a tank. Of course Jack could sleep through anything.

ALAN *(Whisper.)* He's cute.

RONNIE *(Whisper.)* Well, of course he's cute. He looks like me. He's the hairy one. He takes that from my brother; look at those arms. He has hair like that all over him.

ALAN *(Whisper—to the audience.)* Blond, like a white, a little white orangutan or something. *(Penny comes in the front entrance, walks to the refrigerator door, opens it, and stands in front of it. Penny is nearly eighteen, she is slow and dull moving and almost heartbreakingly unattractive.)*

RONNIE *(Hearing the noise.)* That's Penny.

ALAN *(Beginning in whisper and changing into regular voice as they move out of the boys' area.)* Penny, on whom the plot will pivot, such as it is. On Penny and a photograph taken my first day in California and my first day at the ocean. First ocean, the Pacific. Real salt, I almost hadn't believed it. I had to go taste it to be sure. Jerry on one side, me in the middle, Jack on the other. A picture of the three grandchildren to send to my grandmother.

RONNIE Doug's mother wrote back she said she couldn't believe it. That wasn't Alan between those two kids that was Doug when he was seventeen.

ALAN Really?

RONNIE Oh, now he's very distinguished, very proud of the mustache and the greying temples.

ALAN *(To the audience.)* He had borrowed the jacket from a friend, but he liked it; it suited him. And it did. So he bought it from the guy.

PENNY *(They come to her. Still with the refrigerator door open.)* Pleased to meet you. I've heard a lot about you.

ALAN *(To the audience.)* And I feel like I should bow. *(To Penny.)* They didn't know a thing. It was all conjecture.

RONNIE Penny's a science major and very serious about it.

PENNY Well, I'm not that serious about—

ALAN What do you want to do with—

PENNY Oh, well, I'll probably teach. *(Dead pause.)* I like kids. I guess.

ALAN I couldn't be a teacher if they paid me and I understand they don't.

PENNY California's not bad. They pay well here.

ALAN I guess I've heard that.

RONNIE Do you want something to eat?

PENNY *(Closing the refrigerator door.)* No. I've got to go to bed.

RONNIE Did you see Rose?

PENNY Uhm. She's given up politics, she's learning to play the guitar. *(Alan laughs.)*

RONNIE Penny dates the best looking boy at the college.

PENNY *(Pause.)* He really is. *(Shrug.)*

RONNIE He's a tennis pro.

PENNY Not pro.

RONNIE Well, not pro, but he will be.

PENNY He was in the Olympics.

ALAN They play tennis in the Olympics?

PENNY Oh, sure. Or maybe it was skiing, because he skis. His dad's got a lodge in Colorado. Carol and I are—Carol and me—damn—Carol and I!—are both going with millionaires—Not really but they have a lot of money. Phil drives a Pontiac convertible—it's so beautiful I feel stupid driving around in it—especially the way he drives.

RONNIE Why, how does he drive?

PENNY I don't know. Conspicuously. I mean the top's never up unless it's raining. Even in the middle of winter. I've had a cold since I've known him. Do you mind if I go on to bed?

ALAN No, if you're sleepy.

PENNY 'Cause I am.

ALAN I can see you tomorrow.

PENNY Goodnight, Alan. Ronnie. Is Carol in yet?

RONNIE No. God knows, she's out with Sonny.

PENNY Goodnight. *(Exits to bedroom.)*

ALAN And that's all of Penny that night. That first night. That was it. But more, there's more.

RONNIE I want to tell you about Carol. It's terrible.

ALAN *(To audience.)* Now this is funny…I sat there sober faced and believed every word.

RONNIE *(To the audience.)* Well, I had to tell him something, right? I mean the girl is a whore. Let's face it, she's a nice kid but she's sick. With Sonny, Sonny is religious—that much is true.

ALAN *(He leans against the counter and watches, smiling, listening to a favorite family joke.)* Go on, go on…

RONNIE *(To audience.)* Well, I didn't know if he'd believe it or not; what do I know? He's seventeen, my boys are twelve and eight. But if I didn't say something that first night then Carol would have him seduced by the next afternoon. So I told him she had this incurable "disease." That wasn't painful. But it was an impossible disgrace. I said they were trying to cure it but it was only fifty-fifty.

ALAN Trichinosis.

RONNIE Well, I couldn't think of a medical-sounding name that I thought I could remember. When did you know?

ALAN Not for years. You can lie to me, I'll believe anything.

RONNIE Of course I didn't know if he'd buy it or not.

ALAN I said trichinosis was something you get from eating pork.

RONNIE *(Seriously, to him.)* Well, *one* kind.

ALAN She said this was a different kind, it was similar, but much worse.

RONNIE *(Seriously to him.)* And very rare. *(To audience.)* I thought with all those sailors he might believe she could have gotten anything. And it doesn't show up on the boy. But he passes…

ALAN *(To her.)* He's a carrier.

RONNIE Right. And he passes it on to the next girl, who might be someone he likes very much, Alan. And respects. And—

ALAN And I bought that.

RONNIE *(To audience.)* And I said she wasn't sleeping with Sonny, which was true as far as any of us knew.

CAROL *(From the shadows.)* It was true.

RONNIE *(Reassuringly to her, quickly.)* No, we knew. Anyway I described it dreadfully. All the symptoms.

ALAN *(To audience.)* And all the time I have this pounding headache, I'm practically fainting from.

RONNIE Well, who would know? You didn't show it.

ALAN *(Audience and her.)* I have this smile plastered on my kisser, and this look of concern. I didn't care if this girl had last stage syphilis. I was dying there in the middle of the kitchen my first night.

RONNIE Anyway I made poor Carol sound like a very unattractive sleeping arrangement.

CAROL And of course I was going balmy because I thought why isn't anything working with this guy. Why isn't he turning on to me? How should I know he thinks I'm Typhoid Mary—I'm coming on like the Army and Navy Band with about sixty colors flying and this cat's outrunning ostriches in the other direction. I changed toothpaste. I did, I changed my toothpaste. Twice.

RONNIE *(Suddenly very sober.)* Doug used to talk about you.

ALAN I was only five.

RONNIE I know, he loves children. Sometimes I think Doug should have had a girl. He'd have been a better father to them. You should see him with the neighbor girls. He really loves them. *(Long pause.)*

ALAN *(To the audience.)* I didn't tell her that I had had a sister. I thought about it, but I didn't say anything. That's what I was thinking about—a lot that first night.

RONNIE No, you didn't.

ALAN *(Audience.)* I'd had a sister who was born dead, it would have been dad's only daughter. Dad—was out every night until God knows what hours. He would come in with lipstick all over his shirt and mother was pregnant, and he'd swear it was someone's sister and mother would check his story and the guy wouldn't even have a sister—like he didn't even bother to make the story convincing and then he'd rage at her for not believing him and spying behind his back. That's what he meant by "after him." Snooping at his heels all the time. So mother got her labor pains one night when he was out and she was walking the floor, this was eight months along only. And she called a friend of dad's to ask if he knew where dad was—this guy's name was Carl. So Carl and his wife drove mother to the hospital and the baby was born dead. Still-born. Mom said she didn't much care at the time. It wasn't even buried—they don't—they consider it never lived. *(Pause.)* I don't know. I know Carl beat the shit out of dad and right after that dad left. So if Ronnie thought he was guilty, about leaving *me*—or wanted another *son*—probably not.

RONNIE He wasn't going with me.

ALAN Even if he was you didn't know.

RONNIE It was a full year after that that we…

ALAN *(Removed, uninterested.)* He'd been in California a year—He'd met Ronnie, but he came back afterwards and dated her; that's when they went together a year, after he'd already left. She said. I didn't ask dad. It doesn't matter. Anyway, that's what I was thinking; or rather trying not to think that night. And trying to not blame him. *(Pause.)* She would have been four years younger than me.

RONNIE Thirteen.

ALAN Well. What time is it? It must be after midnight.

RONNIE Are you kidding, it's one-thirty or after. We talked for three hours straight.

ALAN Briefing me on the neighborhood. Ronnie was the neighborhood confessor. Since she didn't give a wild flying damn what anyone did and didn't gossip she got all the juiciest stories.

RONNIE It's always been like that.

ALAN And I liked you very much. Which is no mean trick for a stepmother.

RONNIE And you told me about Doug being in jail.

ALAN How did I—

RONNIE We were just talking about anything, and you asked—

ALAN *(With an accent.)* Is dad still interested in drawing and painting? Grandma's attic is full of stuff he did.

RONNIE The paintings of boats and all the airplanes? I think he's always been crazy about airplanes—no, he doesn't do that anymore.

ALAN I used to go up and look at them every time I went there.

RONNIE Well...he builds things...and you saw all the photographic equipment. I think he must have stopped painting when he was a teenager.

ALAN Yes, I think mother said he did them when he was in jail.

RONNIE *(Beat.)* When he was where?

ALAN Didn't you know that? I wouldn't want to...

RONNIE No, it's OK, what?

ALAN Well, he was in on a—not a robbery, but a burglary of a house with some guys when he was sixteen—and went not actually to a jail, but to a reform school for a year—And that's when he did those—It was a long time ago, I guess it isn't anything necessarily that he should have told you.

RONNIE Or that you should have been told for that matter—

ALAN I'm sorry, I wouldn't have—

RONNIE No, it doesn't matter. I asked you— *(To the audience.)* And he was so damned honest—I could have clubbed him.

ALAN *(To the audience.)* I was. I was.

RONNIE You want to go to bed, don't you?

ALAN I think so.

RONNIE It's after two.

ALAN I'm falling on my face.

RONNIE Go on to bed, it's all right.

ALAN Are you going to wait up for dad?

RONNIE No, no, he doesn't expect you to wait up. You won't need more covers than that.

ALAN No, not here. *(He laughs, sits on the bed and tucks under.)*

RONNIE Goodnight, Alan.

ALAN I'll see you tomorrow.

RONNIE I won't wake you; Doug gets up early; he never sleeps more than four or five hours.

ALAN Good Lord.

RONNIE I know, don't worry, we'll let you sleep. Tomorrow anyway. Everyone keeps his own hours.

(Carol approaches the front door.)

ALAN Right.

RONNIE *(Turning to the front, leaving him.)* Speaking of which.

CAROL *(Entering. Carol is nearly 18, tall, very thin and smashingly attractive and quite a wreck.)* I know, it's late, I wasn't watching. Where's Alan, did he come?

RONNIE Yes, he came.

CAROL Doug here?

RONNIE He went on to work.

CAROL Went to *work?* Well, of course, he went to work, Carol, what'd you think, he'd stayed here with his son? How's Alan?

RONNIE Very nice. But that isn't the subject.

CAROL Oh, Christ, Ronnie, don't start!

RONNIE It's two o'clock.

CAROL *(Looks at her watch, puts it to her ear, shakes her arm during speech.)* It isn't any—well, my watch's stopped. Damn.

RONNIE You know I don't care, but they ask.

CAROL We've been sitting out in front for over an hour, didn't you hear us drive up, I thought I saw you at the window.

RONNIE Carol, I don't care.

CAROL Well, neither do I. He was so sweet.

RONNIE I like Sonny.

CAROL We talked— *(Partly to audience.)* Sonny's dad has a ranch in Texas— over twenty thousand acres, which he says is small—That's probably larger than Rhode Island. And they raise Herefords and houses and oil and have about half the money in the country and investments everywhere. His mom and dad are paralyzed over what's going on in Cuba, apparently they own it.

RONNIE Anyway, be that as it may, I've a vivid imagination but it fails me when I try to conjure up what you do until—

CAROL *(Cutting in violently.)* Oh, Ronnie, would you stop it! Just stop it, already! No he doesn't lay me, no, never, not once, look at my hands for God's sake! You think I can stand it? *(Exposing her hands, which are bloody on the palms.)*

RONNIE Good god, what's wrong with—

CAROL —Well, it isn't stigmata, you can count on that. Sonny is Catholic with a vengeance and I've never thought I could be in love with anyone. There it is! *(Rather to the audience.)* Carol's problem, never thought she could cut it and I am—very much in love with a Rich Texan Catholic and he has land, lots of land and principles that I never even knew were principles. And I used to take "downs," but pills are wrong, of course, so I promised him I wouldn't take them any more. No, we no longer live in a yellow submarine, we live on a Red Perch. And he makes out so damn beautifully and I can't ask *him* and I can't be "bad," his word, not mine, and I can't calm down with the pills and I claw my *hands,* the palms of my hands apart. *(Totally breaking off—disgusted with herself.)* Well, shit, Carol, there's no sense in causing a war about it, I cut them down yesterday, I'll cut them off tonight. But that won't help, because I'll bite my lip or something else if I can't get a hold of something to take to calm my damned frazzled—

RONNIE Carol, I'm very lenient and I know you can wrap me around your little finger; I know you've had to do that in order to get anything—

CAROL —Don't make excuses for me for God's—

RONNIE —Carol, I want to say something. I know you want to stay here for the next eight or whatever months until you're eighteen, and I want you here, but if I see one pill, one of your tranquilizers, I'll report it. It's something I can't tolerate. I have two young sons here and I can't risk them taking something by mistake…

CAROL *(Overlapping.)* You don't have to tell me that. Do you think Sonny would stand for it? He's a lot better police dog than—a LOT better police dog than you, believe me—

RONNIE There've been two different cases in the last year of kids being poisoned by taking their mother's barbiturates or someone's who had left them around the house. If I know you're taking them I'll feel obliged to tell Sonny as well as the welfare…

CAROL *(Screaming.)* You don't have to tell anybody any goddamned thing! Because I PROMISED him, you know what that MEANS? *(Regains her control, holding her hands.)* That I didn't need them.

RONNIE Does your hand hurt?

CAROL Yes, they hurt like fire.

RONNIE Let me put something—

CAROL Oh, I'll do it; you're supposed to be bawling me out. You *can't*, Ronnie. I can get out of anything, I'm a master.

RONNIE You're also a mess.

CAROL You're telling me.

RONNIE Let me put something on them.

CAROL *(Hotly.)* No, dammit; you're not going to stain me up with iodine, thanks.

RONNIE I'll put some salve on them, not iodine.

CAROL They're not that bad, really. I'll do it. Are you waiting up for Doug?

RONNIE No. He'll be in.

CAROL Alan's in my room?

RONNIE For tonight. We'll arrange something.

CAROL Just let me flop somewhere.

RONNIE Put something on your hands, that salve.

CAROL Okay. Goodnight.

RONNIE Carol. Don't. *(Pause.)* Don't stay out this late. They want you in by twelve.

CAROL I won't, Ronnie. You're great. I'm sorry, I won't. *(Kisses her on the cheek.)*

RONNIE *(To the audience.)* She will, and I can't blame her, of course. He's the only thing she's got—Sonny. She's on probation with the state and us and Sonny too.

CAROL So, I'm used to it. Don't make me out a martyr. I hate it. Besides I can do it better. I haven't even got started on my mom and dad and poor upbringing and what a rotten life I've had. Besides I'm a nymphomaniac—coupled with a for-all-practical-purposes—eunuch—in the shape of a Greek God.

RONNIE Which isn't necessary with you but it doesn't hurt anything.

CAROL It hurts. It hurts. Everything. All over. Goodnight. *(She goes off to the girls' bedroom.)*

(Ronnie stands a moment, then goes off to her bedroom. The stage is empty a few seconds then Douglas enters, goes to the kitchen, opens a can of beer— takes a hunk of cheese, looks into the girls' bedroom, then Alan's and exits into his bedroom as the lights fade to a deep midnight blue. All is quiet for a beat then a very slow dawn. At a nice bright sunshine the lights hold. Jerry stirs in his bed and sits up suddenly. Jumps up and sneaks down to Alan's room. Creeps in and shakes him gently.)

JERRY Alan? *(Sits on the side of the bed, waits.)* Alan? Are you awake?

ALAN *(Stirring.)* Huh? *(The scene is whispered.)*

JERRY Good morning.

ALAN Good morning. Is it morning?

JERRY Almost.

ALAN Do you always get up this early?

JERRY I woke up.

ALAN It isn't daylight yet, is it?

JERRY Oh, yeah—*(Starts to window to pull the shades up.)* It's Sunday, it's real bright out…

ALAN NO! I believe you—that's OK. Are you *(Smiling, focusing on him now.)* Jerry or Jack?

JERRY Don't you know?

ALAN Yes. You're Jerry.

JERRY Jack's asleep.

ALAN And let's see, you would be twelve and a half, right?

JERRY Right. I'll be thirteen…

ALAN Christmas Day.

JERRY Right. What's the matter with your head?

ALAN I don't know; only it's splitting wide open. It has been all night—ever since we crossed New Mexico. I think it has something to do with the altitude. Are we at sea level?

JERRY No, one thousand three hundred eighty feet. That's Mount Helix.

ALAN How do you know, are you studying geography?

JERRY No, there's a sign on the highway. Do you want some aspirin?

ALAN Where's the highway?

JERRY About two blocks from here.

ALAN Oh. Do you have any, do you think?

JERRY What?

ALAN Aspirin?

JERRY Oh, I thought you meant highways, did I have any highways—

ALAN —No, aspirin—

JERRY —I'll get you one.

ALAN Could you? Bring me three if you have plenty.

JERRY *(Has run out—returns.)* You shouldn't take more than one.

ALAN Huh? Oh, it's OK, honey, I always take three. Two doesn't do any good and four makes me sick.

JERRY OK. *(As water runs.)*

ALAN *(Calling.)* What time is it, Jerry?

JERRY It's seven o'clock already.

ALAN *(Flops down in bed.)* Oh, God. Jerry, I didn't get to bed till three or something.

JERRY *(Re-entering.)* Do adults need eight hours sleep?

ALAN *(Between aspirins.)* Eight or ten.

JERRY Dad says he can't sleep but four hours. He says you shouldn't.

ALAN Then why do I feel like this?

JERRY Did you ride the *Greyhound?*

ALAN Yeah.

JERRY You know, I like you! *(Hugs him enthusiastically.)* I didn't know if I would or not, but you're nice. How come you didn't come to live with us a long time ago?

ALAN You don't remember visiting me and the zoo? In Omaha?

JERRY No. Mom's told me though. It seems weird having a new brother and already he's as big as dad. You should have been living with us when we had the farm.

ALAN Did you have a farm?

JERRY Your head still hurt?

ALAN Yeah.

JERRY *(After a pause.)* Jack and me called it a farm, but we just had a big open lot with a bunch of trees.

ALAN An orchard?

JERRY Kinna—we had some orange trees and a plum tree and a fig tree...

ALAN You had orange trees?

JERRY Oh, sure.

ALAN I've never seen them growing before.

JERRY We used to have oranges all the time. Me and Jack used to make orangeade and sell it only nobody ever bought it because they had more oranges than we did. Dad bought it and we drank it.

ALAN *(After a pause.)* Oh, God. I like you too. *(Squeezes him. To audience.)* So I didn't sleep, I guess. Not much, that first night. And the last thing I wanted to do, or thought of doing...

DOUGLAS *(Entering.)* We'll just drive in, you make your application, it'll take about ten minutes time and we can drive over and take a peek at the ocean you haven't seen.

ALAN *(To audience and them, following Douglas into the kitchen for coffee.)* The personnel manager at Ryan Aeronautical hated me on sight with no love lost.

DOUGLAS Aw, that son of a bitch, all that brass, ball-breaking office flunkies. That's all they are, Alan, ignore him, don't give him the time of day.

ALAN Do we have to go today? I can hardly see.

DOUGLAS He's going on a month's vacation tomorrow. They can process you while he's gone, you won't start working for a month.

CAROL Buy now pay later.

ALAN Maybe I should do something else; grocery clerk or something.

DOUGLAS Well, what do you want, boy, it's up to you, do you want to make enough to go to school or do you want to go to the movies? We'll all go, we'll go on to the beach later.

ALAN No, it didn't take long, he said we'd have two divisions of engineering personnel; temporary and full-time. I said I would much prefer the former and he said there was a greater possibility of being hired in the *latter,* and that was that. So providing I'm not lying about never having joined the communist party or something I'll be set. I'll start in a month or so.

DOUGLAS As soon as he's back.

ALAN At the Aeronautical Engineering Training Center—riveting school.

PENNY How can you manage full-time work and full-time school?

DOUGLAS So he'll go part-time to school until he can get on temporary at the plant.

ALAN No, no.

DOUGLAS Well, I say if you can cut both full-time, why not? Now if you're serious about working down there, they have a scholarship program. You can go into electrodynamics or something like that and they'll pay the bill, all the way—

ALAN It's my second term, I don't know what I want yet.

DOUGLAS Well, don't be negative, give it a fair shake. Just objectively what's happening in the world—they're putting rockets into space—they got hydrogen bombs and cobalt bombs, atomic submarines—they bounce signals off Mars and Venus and every other goddamned thing.

ALAN I know.

DOUGLAS Physicists are looking at the sunspots and predicting the weather— Every field. All of them, what you need—

ALAN I don't know anything—

DOUGLAS —is physics, by God.

CAROL That sounds like a good book.

(Alan laughs.)

DOUGLAS Well you can joke around—I just want you to think about it. All I'm saying is if I was a kid now it wouldn't take me three minutes—three seconds to make up my mind—Engineering, Electrodynamics, you just have to open your eyes.

ALAN And of course the head is worse—But the ocean! I've lived 800 miles from it all my life!

RONNIE *(Coming into the kitchen with Jack.)* I wish you would, but only if you want to.

ALAN No, I like you very— *(To audience.)* I'm embarrassed and I've no idea how to tell her. *(To Ronnie.)* I'll call you Ronnie, like dad does, I couldn't! I like you very much! You know! *(Grabbing Jack and wooling his hair.)* And you! Brush ape! Nut! Huh? This is the other one. Jack. Can you see

his arms? He's covered all over with white hair. He's our little white orangutan. He's had straight A's since the day he was born.

JACK Yes.

ALAN And he's a smart ass—I mean aleck.

JACK Yes.

ALAN Yes.

JACK What's an aleck?

ALAN I don't know, but you're one— *(To audience.)* Don't you wish you had a
smart answer for all those simpleminded great questions he asks? Like an
aleck is a Something or Other Without its Whatchicallit and you're going
to be one if you keep asking—Oh, Jack! Jack Jack. He's so bright the
teachers think it's unhealthy. Go go go go. *(Jack and Jerry go, running off.)*
I won't! I promise I won't *(To Ronnie.)* and you can't either—

RONNIE OK, OK, I won't—

ALAN —I won't tell you a lot of juvenile anecdotes but I want—I want to
bronze the little bastards and sit them up on the mantelpiece. One! Just
one I'll tell while they're gone, one quick one—I want to get badly, badly
drunk and distribute a wallet-full of slobbered-on and bent-up photographs all along the bar—and say notice his hair, notice that one's toes,
look at those teeth. Just one little anecdote that Ronnie told me—when
Jerry was five they all went up in an airplane—big thrill for Jerry who
used to watch airplanes take off by the hour when they lived by the air-
port. So they're all in the plane, Jerry's on Ronnie's lap and after they've
been off the ground for a few minutes he squirms around and whispers
excitedly in Ronnie's ear: "when do we start getting small?"

DOUGLAS *(In the darkroom. Red lights on. Projector light on.)* That's *on* now.
Two three four five. *(Projector off.)*

ALAN *(Walking to the darkroom.)* How can you tell when to turn if off?

DOUGLAS You have to know what you want—the less you expose it the lighter
it is, the more you expose it the darker. You burn it in.

ALAN When did you take this?

DOUGLAS Couple a months ago.

ALAN And you're just now getting around to printing them?

DOUGLAS Aw, I got no time. Wow! look at that, I tell you, boy, mmmm. Don't
crowd, now, just don't crowd.
(Alan laughs.)

DOUGLAS Is she a piece? Huh? Look at those boobs, hummf. I tell you.

ALAN She isn't the least bit over-doing it, you don't think?

DOUGLAS What do you talk, with a butt like that?

ALAN That's what I was looking at.

DOUGLAS Can't miss that, huh? That's too broad for you—Hell, you got a lot to get a hold on there. Oh yeah.

RONNIE *(To audience. The lights brighten.)* Well, Mrs. Collins said she wouldn't let her husband out to take pictures of bare-assed girls in the woods over her dead body and I made the mistake of saying it kept Doug off the streets.

CAROL *(To Alan.)* So she hasn't spoken to Ronnie since.

RONNIE Really. Well, how was I to know her husband spent half his time on Delmarco Street.

ALAN I take it that's the…

CAROL Right.

ALAN And now she's not speaking to you. *(Half to the audience, then fully.)* San Diego is just like every other small town just under a thousand population. And California. Californians. They're insane—well you've seen the movies they make out here, they have no idea at all what people are like—well, it's not their fault; they've got nothing to go on—they're working in the dark. They're mad. They are. The shoes they wear, when they wear shoes, the clothes they wear when they wear clothes. This place is impossible. Nobody walks. Nobody walks. Anywhere. Two blocks—if the old man has the car you don't go. You drive to a movie and they're all drive-ins, the food is all drive-ins; mini-hamburgers and cherry malts. The traffic is seventy miles an hour bumpertobumper going into town, six lanes abreast. The supermarkets. They're mad. They take up blocks. They're open 24 hours and they're packed jammed full with—four in the morning, they're buying watermelon and lettuce and a ham and a gallon of Gallo port and they've got the kids and the babies and the shopping cart and the portable radio and the whole family—the sandals flopping. They're nuts! They live on the beach. They all cook outside and eat outside and sleep outside—and of course it's a beautiful outside to do it in. The downtown San Diego is white day and night with sailors and those big fluffy moths and seagulls and pigeons and sand and I've finally seen the ocean. All of us, we had to beg dad to take a picture of us. He's not taken a picture of the kids, Ronnie said, in almost two years.

RONNIE He's got a hundred tons of cheesecake.

ALAN All lined up, the three of us.

RONNIE Doug's mother wrote today and said that that wasn't Alan, that was Doug when he was seventeen.

DOUGLAS I told you! What'd I say!

RONNIE That was Douglas when he was seventeen.

DOUGLAS I said it was! By God! You can't—No matter what anybody anywhere says!…Wait till we get you flying by in a flashy MG. I tell you, sir-e-bob!

ALAN MG?

DOUGLAS Or Porsche or Austin, one of those babies.

ALAN Blue.

DOUGLAS Red, hell, red. Man, what do you talk?

ALAN Purple. Compromise.

DOUGLAS Huh?

> (*Ronnie and Alan laugh.*)

ALAN It's beautiful. It is. I always wanted a big old family like this, it's just great. And it's not going to last…

CAROL (*Holding a bottle of pills, takes one, with a glass of water.*) Well, that ought to take the hair off!

ALAN (*To the audience.*) Of course we're immediately in a conspiracy.

PENNY What are they, dope?

CAROL Oh, yell it out, Penny, and get us all kicked outta here—Dope. Good God. You know that paint that little boys spray on little model airplanes?

PENNY Yes. OK, I know.

CAROL —smells like ether, it could kill you if you breathe too deeply?

PENNY —I said yes—

CAROL —Well, that's dope. Dope. They're a very innocent sounding p-i-l-l called Mellaril. One of the seven wonder drugs, and you're going to ask what it does: well, it does wonders.

PENNY Are they strong?

CAROL They're stronger than I am. (*Messing with Alan's hair.*) What do you think, Douglas?

PENNY It's called a duck's tail.

DOUGLAS What, you want a duck's ass on the back of your head? (*With humor.*) You want it all swirled around like that you look like—I don't know what—like some of those high-school punks, or Penny's—whatsit…

CAROL You don't like it? Doug, you're square, you can't get around it.

DOUGLAS What the hell are you talking? He looks like a drugstore cowboy.

CAROL Doug, you don't know your ass.

DOUGLAS (*Too sharply.*) Who you telling about ass?

PENNY Phil even wears his hair like—

DOUGLAS (*Enormous.*) Miss innocence, we just won't talk about the way your boyfriends…do anything, huh? *Huh?*

ALAN (*A long embarrassed pause, then quickly.*) Dad combs his hair straight back and has since the day he was born and that's the only way to comb your hair. It's been just twenty-four hours. And the head's still beating and it's all too fast. In six months I'll be sleeping in a park in Chicago with a letter in my pocket from Ronnie telling me that Carol is dead. But who would know that now? We're sitting down to eat. Outside. That's California. We're...

RONNIE Shhhhhhh!

(He stops. They listen a split second.)

RONNIE No not, thunder, you feel it?

ALAN No. Yes! I think...

CAROL Shhhhhh!

(They concentrate.)

ALAN Yeah. Good God.

RONNIE You get used to it. It doesn't bother the natives. If it *thunders* they run out into the street and think the world's coming to an end.

ALAN They don't have thunderstorms out here?

RONNIE Almost never. I've heard it thunder maybe four times in twelve years. People nearly died of heart attack; it even scared me the last time.

ALAN Could I have another coffee?

RONNIE Shhhh!

ALAN *(Smiling at it, aside to the audience.)* It feels like—you've felt it in the cities—when a big, loaded, lumbering diesel rolls by outside or if you live near a subway—and the whole building—all the walls—the chair you're sitting in gives a gentle prolonged shudder. That's it. Only there's no truck going by—it just happens of its own accord.

PENNY Shhhhh!

RONNIE There, feel it.

(A beat as they listen between all these lines.)

ALAN *(Smiling.)* Good God.

DOUGLAS See? Isn't that sumpin?

JACK It's silly.

PENNY Did you hear?

CAROL Shhhhhh!

(They all concentrate, smiling slightly, feeling the vibrations.)

RONNIE *(Very gently, slowly, to them, no one changes his position.)* Feel it?

(They continue to smile, tensed, intently concentrating. Five seconds or just over. Slow Curtain)

INTERMISSION

Act Two

Alan, Penny, and Carol outside. Bright sunlight. Carol is in a vivid orange robe over a bathing suit.

ALAN *(To the audience.)* Same song, second verse, as the poet said, couldn't be better but it's gonna be worse. March. April. May. June or July or August. About. Everything goes well enough but it's complicated. It's difficult to leave well enough alone.

CAROL Because "well enough" is an intolerable state to be in. Take it from me.

ALAN I'm home today for a—home. Oh, wow. And it is now. Really is. For a short time. A very short time longer. My last class is at three usually and I go to work from school. Today is Saturday—No school, work, no school, so I can spend some time home before we leave for work at five. Penny and Carol are on vacation…it's summer.

PENNY I still don't know why you started school summer term.

ALAN Because I was very suspicious that if I didn't I wouldn't start at all. Two momentous events have elapsed! Dad has developed an absolute passion for milk. And he's teaching Penny photography.

PENNY Well, not photography. There isn't anything to learn except point and snap. I'm learning developing and printing.

ALAN You like it?

PENNY Sure, it's fascinating. I'm a little sick of seeing that red white and blue bikini in every picture we print.

CAROL Ha!

ALAN Dad's got this bikini he takes along to his sessions with the girls—

CAROL It's pathetic.

ALAN —And the whole session is taken up—apparently, we only see the pictures—with first coaxing her into it and then nearly out of it. She unties it here and pushes it down there—or else she doesn't. Which is even funnier.

PENNY It's awful—it's cotton and tacky and just ugly as it can be.

ALAN *(To Carol.)* I'm surprised he hasn't got you posing for him by now.

CAROL Oh, honey, I'm on to that crap. He squires around those dames down to the beach with that stupid car—

ALAN Chrysler convertible.

CAROL Nothing but big cars in this play—

ALAN Right, which isn't typical—some of the guys build their own so they drive these sorta car-collages.

CAROL But Doug squeals around in this big fat Chrysler, which is perfect, but he doesn't know it. He took a million pictures of me; I'm not photo-genic—He didn't even notice it—it's all in his head—he never notices. Slobbering around "you got nice eyes, you got nice legs, you got nice tits." Hell, I haven't even *got* tits, the creep.

ALAN Probably he wanted you to—

CAROL He wanted in my pants. It was humiliating. When a girl seventeen has to tell a man forty-five to grow up something's wrong. I just found it repellent and I told him.

ALAN Not in those words, I hope.

CAROL Yes, in those words: Doug, grow up, you're repellent. Listen, half the foster fathers I've had have tried to make me. Since I was six. It's not my scene. Men are asses. If they knew what they looked like they'd all march into the sea in a line like lemmicks.

PENNY It isn't lemmicks, it's lemmings.

CAROL You're terrific. I think you're my favorite sister. *(To Alan who laughs.)* You can go to hell too.

ALAN I went to one outing with dad and whatever you do you have got—you have *got* to go to an amateur photographers' meeting with cheese cake models. We went up to Redwood—out in this cactus park with four hun-dred photographers and about forty girls. Ten to one. And they're draping over every fence and adobe wall and bench in the park. I've got this 35mm Leica that dad's lent me. Barely explaining how to work the damn thing and all the guys are frisking around this gal—she's on a Mexican serape—and the guys are practically having heart attacks: "Click-adyclick-adyclickadyclickadyclickady" all around like a plague of locusts and they're all jockeying for the best angle to shoot straight down her breasts, which are pumpkins, and they're giving her: "That's it, honey. Wet your lips, baby. Wet 'em again. Now slack. Just let everything go to hell. Toss your hair. Pout. Pout. Indignant. Hate. More. Hate. Kill. Kill..."

CAROL That's insane.

ALAN And I'm standing there with this damn dumb Leica saying—Oh, I don't know could you just sorta, maybe—smile?

CAROL I know that whole scene.

DOUGLAS *(Entering.)* Hey, Alan, how come you didn't show?

ALAN Huh? Where?

DOUGLAS This guy is impossible, isn't he? Where? I mean this wasn't impor-tant but he'd forget it if it was. *(Giving his head a wrench.)* Is your head on tight? We wouldn't want you losing that.

ALAN Yeah, yeah, I think. What did I forget.

DOUGLAS Club meeting yesterday afternoon. Nothing happened, you can go to them or not, suit yourself.

ALAN *(To the Audience.)* The few times I have gone you couldn't—

DOUGLAS *(Interrupting. Serious afterthought.)* Al—hey!

ALAN Huh?

DOUGLAS Stanley tells me you're not coming to work. Something like three days last week you missed? A while back? What was that?

ALAN *Three* days? No. Maybe two once but not three.

DOUGLAS What the hell's so important? The days I don't drive you in you're just not showing up? I have to squire you in?

ALAN I have been.

DOUGLAS He says you're a good worker—*(Half to the audience.)* He's a good worker, he picks things up, but you can't—

ALAN Listen, I still do more in three days than the other guys—

DOUGLAS They're getting their five days' pay and you're—

ALAN You should watch the shop steward sometime. Oh, wow. I thought your department sat around on their retired duffs—there were guys—

DOUGLAS Retired duffs? *(Mock indignation.)* I'll have you know—I mean a few "Government Jobs" that's very important stuff—

ALAN Right, right— *(To the audience.)* "Government Jobs" is slang for doing something of your own—I went in… *(Back to Douglas.)* …the other day and two different guys were making mailboxes and one guy was repairing his wife's mix-master.

DOUGLAS Well, they're paying you to come to work five days a week, man, that's what—

ALAN They're paying me by the hour. Maybe one week I missed two days because of tests at school I had to cram—

DOUGLAS Well, learn to study—crap—organize yourself, man, you take a job you go, it's a simple thing.

ALAN Dad spoke for me down there and he thinks I'm giving him a bad name taking off—I'm a beatnik.

DOUGLAS They want you there five days a week—they don't give a damn if you sit on your fanny or stand on your head, man they don't care as long as you show up—

ALAN You know that's true, they really don't. You should see those guys— Nobody works. Nobody works. It's amazing! *(Including the audience.)* I could tell you the name of the transportation jets we're building down there and how we're doing it—the entire aircraft industry would collapse tomorrow morning. Would you believe chewing gum? I'm not kidding— there's a little hole, no one's looking, what the hell. I don't miss that much, really.

DOUGLAS You just see that you get whatever it is you have to do done today so we can leave on time. I'm not going to wait around for you…

ALAN *(To the audience.)* So what do you do when you hear that? You decide right there that you're not going, right?

DOUGLAS *(Instantly furious.)* You think it's funny—you want to do it now? Huh?

ALAN Later.

DOUGLAS You want to do it now? We'll do it now. Come on, we'll do it now.

ALAN We'll get to it. Later.

DOUGLAS *(Looks at him a moment then to Penny casually.)* Penny, we're gonna work right after lunch, Okay?

PENNY Whenever.

(Douglas exits.)

PENNY I keep asking him to print up some of his pictures of Grand Canyon or something but it's always those darn girls—girls are so stupid to do that. Oh, I guess they think of a career but, wow, that's so stupid. It's no worse though, I'm always imagining my wedding. Do you do that?

CAROL Do what?

PENNY I can't pass a church some days without going through my whole wedding in it. You know, I'm running out of the door in my wedding dress with my hands over my head, keeping off the rice and trying to wave to everybody at the same time. Sometimes I'm sitting perfectly still and I catch myself tossing my bouquet at someone.

CAROL Who are you thinking about marrying?

PENNY Well—I'm not. I don't want to get married. I'd like to be a scientist just as much. I picture that too.

CAROL Penny has a very rich fantasy life.

PENNY Well, I do. I think it's healthy. I see myself in one of those white lab coats with a bunch of those bubbly tests tubes and coils all around—analyzing blood and making notations—

CAROL Blood? Good God, you have the most morbid goddamn sense of duty.

PENNY Do you like being away from Sonny as much as being with him?

CAROL What?

PENNY Really, it's funny but I think sometimes when I'm with Phil I'd really rather not be, so I could be away from him—*wanting* to be with him. You like Phil, don't you? He's nice, isn't he?

CAROL Do I—I don't know him.

PENNY You went to school with him before he graduated, I didn't. I'll bet he was popular at Grossmont, wasn't he?

CAROL *(Spirited.)* I didn't know him. We didn't run in the same crowd. I thought he was a stuck-up jerk. He's all right. He's nice. He's beautiful. Yes, he was popular. My God, I guess he was. Aren't there any boys at your school?

PENNY I don't go with any of them—

ALAN *(Overlapping some.)* Carol goes to Grossmont, Penny goes to El Cajon.

PENNY My gosh, why don't you like Phil? Good grief. All we can ever talk about is Sonny…I don't even like Texas. I don't know what a Hereford looks like. I'll bet you don't either. *(To Alan.)* She used to talk about all Sonny's beautiful Black Anguses—She didn't know if they were horses or automobiles. *(Beat. To Carol.)* Are you going to marry Sonny?

CAROL I hope to hell. I'm not going to come this far at such unimaginable expense and wind up—and I'm going to invite all my scores and wear white. I can't wait. *(Digging in her purse.)* Goddamnit I brought a bottle of baby oil out here—I'll bet I spend a fortune just from losing—
(Penny hands her the bottle of oil from beside the chaise.)

CAROL Penny, why don't you put on your swim suit? You're going to just bake.

PENNY No, I'm not staying.

CAROL Well, you're driving me nuts out here dressed up like an Eskimo. *(To Alan, handing him the oil.)* Get my back, will you?

ALAN You don't need that stuff.

CAROL I have delicate skin.

ALAN What is that you put over your eyes? Plastic spoons? You know I knew a girl once who went blind from sunbathing with plastic spoons over her eyes? They melted. You're going to be solid brown with white eyelids.

CAROL Would you shut up?

ALAN *(As he rubs Carol's back. To the audience.)* Ronnie about a month ago—I came in moaning that I was failing what? Math, probably—I'm failing math every other day. And she said the term isn't over yet, you've got to have faith. You have to understand she was serious as hell about it. It scared us to death. I really believed it. She said if you have faith the size of a mustard seed you—

CAROL Turn it down, why don't you?

ALAN *(Stopping rubbing her back.)* I'm going to stop because I think you're enjoying this in all the wrong ways. *(To the audience.)* You have to understand I thought I'd probably exposed myself to trichinosis.

CAROL You went in and washed your hands.

ALAN I did not. How many pills today?

CAROL Who counts anymore? Three or four so far and that's pretty far.

PENNY You shouldn't take those and lie in the sun.

CAROL God, the things you're opposed to. You're worse than Sonny sometimes.

PENNY I'm not opposed to them, you just shouldn't. Maybe I should go with Sonny and you go with Phil.

CAROL *(Rapidly strung together.)* *That* does it! I'm going to take a shower.

Penny do you have any bobby pins something has to happen to—don't answer, you don't use them, right? What kind of sister are you anyway? I swear to God. You don't know *any* two-part harmony songs...you don't buy cheap perfumes I can steal, you don't use a brush, you're immoral—always suggesting we swap husbands. What the hell good are you outside of making peanut butter divinity? Jesus H. Christopher I wish I were on the moon. I nearly am.

PENNY Well, why do you take them? You know Ronnie will kick you out if she finds out and Sonny made it a condition.

ALAN He didn't make it a condition, he just said he'd never speak to her again.

CAROL It turns me off. It turns me way, way off.

ALAN It's a kind of Norwegian Fly.

CAROL Icelandic.

ALAN *(Singing.)* "Try Icelandic Fly, gets you there on time..."

CAROL You couldn't possibly have said that, that song didn't come out for ages.

ALAN That's all right, you aren't even alive. You've been dead ten years.
       (They laugh.)

CAROL I would like to thank the theatre for rescuing me from that dreary cupboard in that dreary condition.

PENNY Dank.

ALAN Drear.

CAROL *(Overlapping them.)* I want to—right—thank the drear management for the magic of the theatre which enables me to be continually young and alive and beautiful and current—

PENNY And here.

ALAN Topical.

PENNY God yes, topical.

ALAN We hope.

CAROL *(Biting her lip, sitting down, almost in tears.)* Shit.

ALAN Hey, Carol—come on, it's all right.

CAROL A lot you know, buddy, a lot you know.

ALAN Really—remember those Red Skelton radio programs, and he played the mean widdle kid?

PENNY Yeah, right—

ALAN And he would describe something dreadful that happened to him and start crying I scared me widdle self?

CAROL I don't remember.

ALAN I think you scared you widdle self.

PENNY Sure you remember. On the radio. I remember it.

ALAN Maybe she listened to a different program. Fibber and Molly McGee. *(Beat.)* Don't get maudlin, Carol.

CAROL Locked in your goddamned side show; dragged out to play second fiddle in a three ring— *(Slinging a cigarette all the way off, out the wings, walking away a few steps, furious.)* Fuck!

ALAN *(Calling.)* Come on, come off it, mung head.

PENNY Mung? Wow.

CAROL I hope it burns down the theatre.

PENNY That's the worst kind of head, mung head.

CAROL I'm hip. *(After a deep breath, she regains composure, waves it away.)* OK, I'm back.

ALAN She's back. *(Singing.)*
She's back and she's better than ever before.
Campbell's Pork and Beans.

ALAN, PENNY AND CAROL *(Three part harmony. Quite on the patio, not for the audience.)*
Back and they're better than ever before
Back and they're better than ever before
Back and they're better than ever before
Campbell's Pork and Beans. Hey!
(Jerry and Jack come running in.)

ALAN *(To the audience immediately.)* Most of the radio stations out here are incredible. They're three times as powerful as allowed by the FCC or whoever but the broadcasting towers are all in Mexico so they can get away with anything. They play rock and roll all day and night and commercials commercials, more than you'd ever believe and about half of them are in Spanish so— *(To Jerry and Jack.)* come on. So they go like this:

JERRY *Para refrescarse tome Coca Cola frio.*

ALAN Isn't that great? Well, what's that got to do with the story? Well...nothing, actually, only we feel we should throw in a little local color from time to time.

CAROL *(Announcement.) Local Color!*

PENNY It takes a while for the untutored eye to recognize it but—

CAROL —The color green does not occur in California naturally.

ALAN *(To the audience. Readjustment. Straight.)* Southern California is in the colors of perpetually early autumn: Umber, amber, olive, sienna, ochre, orange; acres and acres of mustard and sage. The colors.

PENNY *(Straight.)* The herbs too.

ALAN And grass dies. It has a season of winter and the weather does not. So instead of grass they plant—a lot of the lawns are planted in dichondra. A little clover-like thing that grows about two inches high and doesn't require mowing and it's very cute but it isn't grass, is it? And it's green the year round.

CAROL Only not green.

ALAN Right. And that bright eye-breaking, bright-sun-shining-through-oak-and-maple-and-elm-onto-bright-green-ferns-and-grass-green does not occur. Of course you could care less. It's something you rather gladly or at least unknowingly forfeit for nearly continual sunshine.

PENNY Weren't we doing a play a while back?

ALAN Right!

(Everyone listening to Ronnie who has entered during the last sentence. Ronnie in mid-sentence. Another time, earlier.)

RONNIE —the size of a mustard seed can move mountains…

PENNY Can you work math?

ALAN Well, I don't seem—

RONNIE *(Very seriously—mock religiously.)* No, now, I'm not kidding. The Bible says you can move mountains and you can. And I have that faith.

PENNY And you can move mountains?

RONNIE It doesn't matter what you three feel, it's my faith that's important. Now, do you see Mount Helix out there?—

ALAN *(As they look.)* Are you kidding?

PENNY Come on—

RONNIE —No, now, we're all going to look away, go on—

PENNY That's sacre—

RONNIE —Look away now, it's a simple demonstration of my faith—

(They turn away from the mountain.)

ALAN Right. Now what?

RONNIE Now. When we turn around again, Mount Helix will be gone. Because I have that faith. Because I know it will be gone. In my heart. Now turn around slowly, and Mount Helix will be gone. Now.

ALAN You. *(They don't believe, but they are a little uncertain.)*

RONNIE *(Turns slowly and gazes off.)* Well…

CAROL What?

RONNIE Just like I thought, there it is. Damn.

ALAN What?

PENNY Don't scare me.

(They laugh.)

RONNIE I must have miscalculated. Look at it.

CAROL Yeah, I think so.

RONNIE I think it's even grown. My faith isn't the size of a mustard seed, it's the size of a poppy seed. And poppy seeds don't move nothing.

CAROL Poppy seed moves the world.

RONNIE That's a different poppy seed.

CAROL *(In starting to get up, drops the bottle of pills, picks it up, nearly falls over. Holding her head and trying to put the bottle into a pocket of the robe.)* Oh, wow.

RONNIE Are you OK? You look like hell.

CAROL *(Nearly floating away, trying to come down a little.)* Hmmm? I'm sorry, I washed my brain and I can't do a thing with it. Where are you? *(She gets the bottle into the pocket, will not look at Ronnie directly.)*

RONNIE What's wrong? Look at me.

CAROL *(Handing the robe to Penny.)* Penny, sweetheart, could you take this in?

RONNIE What's wrong?

    (Penny takes the robe in.)

CAROL No, I'm OK. I ate something, it didn't agree with me.

RONNIE Look up. Is that all?

CAROL Well, it's my *time* as the Victorians would have it. I'm dizzy a little is all. *(She exits.)*

    (Penny has taken the robe away and is back now. Ronnie looks at Alan and Penny a moment. Some tension.)

RONNIE *(Rather to the audience, breaking away.)* Well, once in a while you have to admit you don't understand a thing about what kids are doing with their lives nowadays.

    (All the others enter for lunch.)

PENNY —Because they went all the way to the top of Mount Helix and dragged down this poor palm tree.

RONNIE I told you it wouldn't grow.

ALAN Well how would Jerry and I know that? This poor baby palm was thriving in the garbage heap, we transplanted it into the back yard next to Jack's bird of paradise and the poor little palm died before sundown. With its boots on.

CAROL Boots off, I think.

ALAN Well, whichever is the nobler.

RONNIE I think it's two separate schools of thought.

JERRY Off! "I ain't gonna die, partner with those damn boots on!"

DOUGLAS Jerry, don't say damn in front of your brother, he won't be old enough to say that for fifteen years yet.

JERRY Why not?

RONNIE And you've got a few years to go yourself.

JERRY What should I say?

JACK Say "Hockie."

DOUGLAS That's enough out of you too, no hints from the gallery, peanut.

CAROL He's ladykiller.

JERRY What can I say if I can't say that?

CAROL How racy should it be?

JERRY Pretty racy.

CAROL Well, you should try—

JACK "Hanged."

JERRY Yes! That hanged thing ain't worth the powder it'd take to blow it...

RONNIE No, no.

JACK Danged, Danged.

JERRY All-fired.

RONNIE No—say—I can't think of one—Well, don't use any of them, good grief, there's at least—

JACK Good grief!

RONNIE No, don't say good grief either. There're two hundred thousand acceptable words in the language, you don't have to wallow around in the vernacular at your age.

JERRY I don't know two hundred thousand—

DOUGLAS Well, you better be for learning them.

JERRY How do I know if they're acceptable?

RONNIE OK. You come to me and whisper them in my ear and if they happen not to be acceptable I'll wash your mouth out with soap.

JERRY No.

RONNIE See? I thought not.

(They are leaving.)

RONNIE What do you say?

JACK May we be excused?

RONNIE Yes, you may; don't tear the house down.

(Jack and Jerry exit.)

RONNIE The kids on the block have a bucket brigade of profanity. I think they have a collective mind. One of them learns a new word and everyone on the block knows it in an hour. We had an entire month of "shitfire" last year. I can't imagine where they got that one but they loved it.

CAROL Probably from Douglas.

RONNIE (To Carol.) You aren't supposed to say that.

DOUGLAS They aren't supposed to listen. Hell, I wouldn't want them to be like Alan's college buddies up at State, all potatoes and no meat. They all look like they're made out of unbaked dough. They even talk like it.

ALAN My friends? Whatta you talk? My friends swear like sailors, it's part of the emancipated young adult jargon.

DOUGLAS Well, I'd be surprised if they knew what it meant. We dropped him off the other morning—

ALAN Yeah, yeah, last month sometime you dropped me off.

DOUGLAS Two weeks ago Friday.

ALAN Compromise purple. *(To audience, aside.)* Now, you see, I think that's the funniest line in the play.

DOUGLAS And he introduced Ronnie and me to a few of them. Sasha and Joan and Owen and—don't they ever get out into the sun?

ALAN Into the sun? Are you kidding? Oh, my God—into the sun! I've discovered there's this whole beautiful poetical intellectual coterie that wouldn't be caught dead in the sun. They're nuts but they're great. Kinda like the Castilian Spanish—the whiter you are the brighter you are. They're nuts but you love them for it—a lot of the young kids out at State—

DOUGLAS Young? Young? Young? Them? Oh, man, they're on their pensions. Who are you trying to kid? They're cadavers. Ronnie, you read—Carol, did you see that magazine thing they put out at State?

CAROL No…

ALAN I brought that home, I haven't seen it yet—

DOUGLAS *(Overlapping.)* Well, that's what I'm talking, Ronnie. Right there. I want you to look at it some night and see if it can turn you on.

CAROL What he's saying, Alan, is it doesn't stack up to the garage collection of the complete Early Stanley Gardner—

DOUGLAS —Listen, twit. Unless you've read those books just don't knock them. People are a darn sight more interested in life than in those plants and those creepy ferns and creepy shadows and creepy creeps. Nobody reads that magazine except your creepy college would-be poets. Oh, man, I didn't graduate from high school and I'll bet I can take any of them on in anything except arithmetic, huh?

ALAN Dad and I are both rotten with figures.

DOUGLAS Some kinds of figures.

ALAN Probably you could.

DOUGLAS Yeah, you damn betcha. What do they retain? Huh? History: I'll bet you don't even know the Presidents of the country, your own goddamned country, do you?

ALAN God no. I only know the capitals of the states because I had a jigsaw puzzle.

DOUGLAS And the vice presidents.

ALAN I don't know any of the vice presidents except Truman.

DOUGLAS Well, I don't imagine ten out of the eight thousand of them know them either. Who was Washington's vice president?

ALAN I don't know.

DOUGLAS The first vice president of the United States?

ALAN I said no. I'm stupid.

PENNY Adams.

DOUGLAS Right.

PENNY Only that's it.

DOUGLAS *(Reciting rhythmically.)* Washington-Adams, Adams-Jefferson, Jefferson-Burr, Jefferson-Clinton, Madison-Clinton, Madison-Gerry, Monroe-Tompkins, Adams-Calhoun, Jackson-Calhoun, Jackson-Van Buren, Van Buren-Johnson, Harrison-*Tyler!*

ALAN Hey, that's great. And many more, huh? Tyler of Tippecanoe and Tyler too fame?

DOUGLAS Right…

ALAN Who was Teddy Roosevelt's first vice president?

DOUGLAS *(Beat.)* Cleveland-Stevenson, McKinley-Hobert, McKinley-Roosevelt, Roosevelt and nobody, Roosevelt-*Fairbanks. (Beat—then building.)* Taft-Sherman, Wilson-Marshall, Harding-Coolidge, Coolidge-Dawes, Hoover-Curtis, Roosevelt-Garner, Roosevelt-Wallace, Roosevelt-Truman!

(A very long pause. Silence. Everyone is still.)

JERRY *(Entering with a small postage stamp-sized piece of photograph.)* Look at me, that's terrible. Right across my ear.

RONNIE What?

JERRY My picture. The picture Dad took of us.

RONNIE Doug, you didn't tear that up, did you?

DOUGLAS What? Tear what up?

ALAN I wanted a print of that.

DOUGLAS What? It isn't any good.

RONNIE Your mother loved it; I told you what she said.

DOUGLAS Well, mother, bless her heart, doesn't know much about photography.

ALAN Well, I don't either, but I wanted one.

DOUGLAS No, I tore it up; it was a bad print anyway; it's too light; I'll print it up again.

ALAN You never even intended to.

DOUGLAS *(Quite directly.)* Well, now, how do you know what I intended to do and what the hell I didn't intend to do? Huh?

RONNIE It's the only picture we had of them; you haven't taken a picture of the boys in two years.

DOUGLAS It was a lousy picture, I'll take another one; the light was bad. It was a snapshot for God's sake. Penny, are you going to help me or not, huh?

PENNY Yeah, I will.

JERRY He tore it right across my ear.

ALAN I really wanted it.

DOUGLAS *(Much too loud for the occasion.)* All right now, will you just shut up about the goddamned *picture* now! Now I've *had it! With you!*

(He exits with Penny.)

RONNIE *(Topically.)* Doug and I had a terrible argument about you last night.

ALAN What? Wait a sec—I'm not getting the drift of—

RONNIE *(Going on.)* Actually he argued. He said you should excuse the expression, you hadn't had a "piece of ass" since you'd been here.

ALAN I hadn't what?

DOUGLAS *(To Ronnie as the two are suddenly isolated in the living room.)* You saw that gang of dough-balls he was hanging out with at school.

RONNIE I don't know if he's quite "hanging out" with them.

DOUGLAS Well, I'm not saying *what* he's doing with them, I know what he's not doing. When has he been on a date? Squiring Cookie to the local movie in El Cajon and back twice, what's that supposed to mean?

RONNIE Well you could hardly expect him to go for Cookie—Cookie's hardly the freshest thing on the block—And it's a small block.

DOUGLAS When's he gone out?

RONNIE I don't know, when's he had time? Full-time work, full-time school.

DOUGLAS Oh, time's ass. Summer term, everyone else on vacation, goddamnit, he hangs around the house, he hangs around school, he hasn't had a piece of ass since he's been here.

RONNIE Well, he's been here four or five months, I don't know.

DOUGLAS Well, nothing. He's not getting anything from that gang of dishwater dames at school and if he is he ought to be ashamed of himself. I can tell you that. What's the hell's the matter, hasn't he got a libido?

RONNIE I don't know if you're proud of him for—

DOUGLAS Proud of what?

RONNIE Well, he doesn't drink, he doesn't scoot around on a motorcycle, he's no—

DOUGLAS Well, maybe he should! I told him he could have the car anytime he wanted it, he hasn't asked for it once.

RONNIE Well, whenever are you not using it?

DOUGLAS Plenty is the answer to that, plenty.

RONNIE You also told him you'd get him a new Austin; he hasn't seen that.

DOUGLAS Not on your damn life until he shows some interest. What, am I going to get a car to rust in the driveway? *(Somewhat to the audience.)* Took him out to the damn lot, looked around mildly, came back saying he liked them all and started taking a bus to school, what the hell?

RONNIE Well, I don't want to argue.

ALAN When would I have time?

RONNIE That's what I said, Alan. Still.

ALAN I can't see it's any of his business anyway, good God.

RONNIE I told him he didn't have a detective on your tail, how did he know?

ALAN Tail is funny. Oh, well.

DOUGLAS *(Continuing with Ronnie.)* When I was his age I knew the score all around. I'm not going to break him in like a hunting dog, stick a quail in his mouth and have him spit it out till I can teach him what it is. He isn't stupid. What kind of man doesn't know where the hunt is? Huh? I don't want to tell you! It just isn't living. Life is for living, Ronnie. The Best Is None Too Good.

ALAN *(Rather rapidly.)* I'll bet a hundred times Mom's told me that—Your dad always said the best is none too good, the best is none too good. She used to say I was like him a lot—you're like him a lot—and she was right, damnit, more right every day I live—

DOUGLAS No, by God he isn't—like me! Not on your life he isn't. Maybe I got into trouble and maybe I got with some kids that were a bad influence I don't say I was an angel but I knew where the food was and where my hands were and my mouth and my cock and my belly and if I knew what I had I knew where to put it too. And I had women. I mean real women. Hell, the first woman I had was thirty-five years old and I was a kid fifteen and don't think she didn't teach fast. Hell, I'm younger now than he is. And I grew up in the same goddamned two-bit Nebraskan town he did so don't pull that.

RONNIE I don't think it's at all unusual for a boy of seventeen to be more—

DOUGLAS I don't want to hear it. I'm younger now than he is now. You squeal around a corner with the girl's hair flying out, by God and she's all over you. Wiggling her behind in your lap, by God you pull over to the curb and let 'em have it right there. You pull into a garage. Or a lot, a parking lot. What's he's going to do, take a cheap bottle of booze up to some wet hotel room? What does he know? I never went to one cheap hotel room with a bottle of cheap booze in my life. You think I'm going to sit on those sway-backed mattresses, burn-holes all over the furniture varnish. Glass circles. God knows what laid what there. Out in the damn grass alongside the road under Nature's clean sky with the wind blowing and *stars!* All that smell of lipstick. Hell, the beaches at night are lined up, where's he? Huh? Goddamnit, he's eighteen years old, what's he doing; jerkin' off?

RONNIE Well, tell him, honey, don't tell me—I'm not interested in seducing young girls.

DOUGLAS His mother stunted him. Neutered him. He's humiliating. Just looking at his damned—all right, he's a damn all right looking guy, or could be. There's nothing wrong with him. He's let those two damn phoney girls twist his hair up like a pretzel—all curled up like some kind of rock and roll singer.

RONNIE That's what the girls are going for nowadays, I guess.

DOUGLAS Oh, shit, Ronnie. Nowadays. Hair that long, curled up like that, I can hardly sit at the table with him without throwing up! I'd like to snatch him bald—nowadays; women go for men and that's all! Women go for vitality, vigor, exuberance, strength. Balls for God's sake. What are you talking? Huh?

ALAN You know—

DOUGLAS Huh?

ALAN —dad asked me—

DOUGLAS Aw, hell, go on! *(Exits.)*

ALAN —last night to contribute twenty-five dollars each week to the family fund. To pay my way around here…for room and board. For twelve years he didn't pay a red cent to my welfare and suddenly I'm a drain on the budget. Another mouth to feed. God damn. I found out what the mortgage on the house is—

RONNIE Well, I told you that. It isn't a secret surely.

ALAN A hundred and three dollars a month.

RONNIE For twenty years though.

ALAN Unless you pay it off sooner and you're paying a hundred twenty—which is what the two girls bring in—they just sign over the checks to the mortgage—*actually!*

RONNIE That isn't even what they eat.

ALAN *(To the audience and Ronnie.)* I didn't believe it…And he wants a hundred-plus a month from me as my contribution to the gas and food. I don't feel I should be working for you. Down there for you…All I bargained for was part-time work and full-time college. I'm full-time working and I can't save the money to quit work because you people can't afford to keep me here unless I pay my own way!

RONNIE Don't you think you should pay toward it? Because we can't. We'd like you to know that.

ALAN I didn't think I should pay. I quite frankly didn't think I should pay. I worked down there with noise that would bring down mountains seven hours a day when I could pull myself together after school to go and I didn't really mind if it was doing something. All right we're all of us selfish. If I was using it for tuition and books and school but paying the rent on dad's house!

RONNIE *(Suddenly. Quietly and seriously.)* You're an equal member of the family, Alan. The inheritance will be divided three ways equally between Doug's three kids; you'll get just as much as the kids do.

ALAN *(Thrown.)* What? Well, that's a long time off—what kind of talk. Anyway—

RONNIE I just want you to feel—I want you to know that, Alan. Truly.

DOUGLAS *(From the other side. Quite heatedly and suddenly joining them. He has taken up a lunch pail and a pocket holder for pencils with a red and green badge on it, which he carries in his shirt pocket.)* Stay where? By God when I say come on to work, I mean it. What the hell have—where are you sick?

ALAN All over. I'm not sick—I don't feel like working. I don't feel well. I don't want to go. I have things to do, I don't feel good—well.

DOUGLAS Stanley tells me you're never there five days a week. At least when you're home frisking around all day like today, by God you can go to work. Since when didn't you feel well?

ALAN Since now. What's wrong? What difference does it make?

DOUGLAS Listen here, mister, if school gets in the way then you can quit school. I don't see working getting in the way of school. Are you missing there too? Huh?

ALAN No, not yet.

DOUGLAS You mope around like a sick calf, now it's about time someone put a firecracker under your tail. See if there's any life in you. You and Penny— the whole lot of you. Maybe you should take liver tablets or something.

ALAN *(With some humor.)* Perhaps I should. What's wrong, can't I be sick?

DOUGLAS If I believe it. There's no goddamned reason why you can't go in except you don't want to…By God now, Alan, and I'm serious, I just want to know one thing—

ALAN Why should I? Of what importance is the job down…

DOUGLAS Because I told you to. I said so…I told you to get ready, I wasn't having you make the whole damn carload of us late again. Now are you coming or not?

ALAN No, goddamnit! I'm not. That's what I said. I don't feel well. I've got three chapters to read on—

DOUGLAS *Listen here!* Now, once and for all. I'm not going to say this twice now, this has been coming. Do you want to stay here? Answer me?

ALAN *(Letting down, relaxing.)* Yes, that's what I've been saying. I told you. It's as simple—

DOUGLAS I mean do you want to *stay* here. Live here. In this house?

ALAN *(Quite thrown.)* What? I guess so. Yes, what, yes, of course I do.

DOUGLAS *(Very strongly.)* Then by God if you do you better know this is my home. And I say here. I call the shots here. And what I say goes, mister. And those that don't like it can find a roof over their heads somewhere else. And you better be for learning that fast. Because I don't take any shit. None.

ALAN I know—that—

DOUGLAS None! Mister! Not from you or anybody else, huh? And you better be for learning that fast! *(Exits.)*

ALAN *(Standing where he was. Tries to speak to the audience. Very upset, trying to*

be rational.) I—my whole body—hell, I can't do—was pounding. Well, I hadn't—He left. I—I—Ronnie went down the hall.
(She does.)

ALAN And into—I went out—blindly, turned around and went out into the back yard *(He does.)* and fell down on the ground and bawled like I never remember bawling before or since. Sobbing. I. I *(Fighting for objectivity.)* Now, what was going through my—what was I thinking? Well, of course all the times I had wanted a father and not had one. The times I had wanted to live with dad. The struggle mother had had during the war, working in a garment factory. And before that the little I could remember—of—remember of dad, before. And what I had been told, mom's stories. And my sister who had been born dead while he was out with—whomever it was he was out with. That had always been my picture of him—mom walking the floor, him coming in and her crying—Ronnie was in the house. I was very aware of that. I expected her to come out and talk to me. Something. Ronnie and I were close—friends. If I had left. Then. Where would I have gone? I couldn't consider it. This is where I had come to—right to the edge of the continent. I didn't think about going. I couldn't leave. I didn't know what we had been fighting about. I honestly didn't; not then. Well, neither here nor there. Finally I got up. Aching. And went inside.

RONNIE I knew you went out. I knew you were crying. I didn't look out. I assumed you wanted your privacy. I wasn't going to embarrass you.

ALAN *(A kind of laugh.)* Humf.

RONNIE I just sat. Tried to sort the wash, not to listen, cleaned up the bedroom—Penny had vanished, very unlike her, nobody had seen her all afternoon. Rose finally called at eleven and said she was over there, which was all right, I suppose, at least we knew where she was.

ALAN I went to bed about twelve. Dad came home after work, I heard him in the kitchen making scrambled eggs I suppose or French toast. I almost expected him to come in and apologize. All right, I did expect him to. I don't know for what. I couldn't sleep. I got up and dressed after he'd gone to bed. Actually went to a bar. Deserted bar.

RONNIE And came home drunk as a lord.

ALAN You shouldn't have stayed up.

RONNIE I woke up and wondered where you'd gone.

ALAN The next morning—bright and early Dad's photography club went off to the mountains. And I woke up with a hangover—so we begin and end both with a splitting headache—and Penny came home to leave.

PENNY *(Ending a very long cross during the above to Ronnie.)* Ronnie? Ronnie?

RONNIE What, Pen?

PENNY Could I talk to you alone?

RONNIE How come you stayed with Rose, Penny, you should call when you decide to leave like that, we were worried abo—

PENNY I can't stay here, I love you very much but I'll go live with Rose, I've already asked them and they said it was alright, I didn't tell them why, I wouldn't tell them that—I—

RONNIE What's wrong, Penny? You know you can't live with Rose. Penny, that's stupid?

PENNY With her mother, I can live with her mother. She can take me. Ronnie, yesterday afternoon—with Doug—we were in the darkroom—we were just standing there and—like always, working—and he put his arm around me, and he started talking to me about—talking to me about how I liked to help him and about how good a foster father he'd been to me and what a good relationship we had and he kissed my cheek. I didn't know what to do. I thought of once when I was about fourteen a man tried to put his hand in my lap in a movie once. I felt the same way, and he put his hand up under my shirt on my stomach and tried to turn me around and kiss my mouth—with his mustache on my cheek and I—I just pulled away and got out—went out. *(Beat. Then she catches her breath.)*

RONNIE Well, don't cry, you're OK, aren't you?

PENNY I want to leave here.

RONNIE Well, I don't blame you honey—but you don't have to do that, my God, the sky didn't fall in, Henny Penny.

PENNY What will he do? I can't look him in the face, Ronnie. I'm going to pack now because I don't want to sleep here. You can tell the authorities that I'm still here if you want to and they won't know the difference, they never care anyway. I don't want to tell them why.

RONNIE Oh, Penny, stop being so much. It's all too pathetic. I mean, damn. It's just stupid. *(To the audience.)* I mean, Penny, for God's sake. Look at her. She hasn't a single quality anyone would go for unless you happen to really desire pure virginity in the abstract. I mean, I know her qualities but you couldn't expect Doug to see them.

PENNY Ronnie, I don't want to leave.

RONNIE I said you didn't have to—

PENNY I hate Rose! She's fat and stupid and she talks too much and I hate her boyfriends—they *all* have beards and… *(Now she does cry, and quite loudly, openly.)*

RONNIE All right *do* cry if you want to. Go on. It's absurd. Don't be silly.

JACK *(Entering, Carol just behind.)* What's wrong with Penny?

CAROL *(Entering.)* Come on, buster.

JACK What's wrong?

CAROL Where do you want me to start?

RONNIE Jack, honey, go on outside.

CAROL *(Exits with Jack.)* Come on, loverboy…

PENNY Why did he do that?

RONNIE I don't know. You're not going to leave now, Penny. You don't have to see him if you don't want to. It's only six months, Penny, don't be silly.

PENNY Why did you tell him? You knew what he'd say…You're very bright—Why the hell did you tell him, Ronnie?

RONNIE Penny, I'd always known pretty much what to expect from Doug. I wasn't worried about him being brought up for rape charges by those girls he ogles over, sublimation is a wonderful thing. As long as it works. *(To the audience.)* But to make a creepy pass at Penny. It hadn't entered my mind. What was he trying to prove? *(Back to Penny.)* And you wanted to crawl away and do you think he wouldn't know why? Doug—if the heat gets too hot will just pick up and leave as you—Alan—well know. And I have two kids to think about…I'm sorry, Alan, are you OK?

ALAN It's OK.

RONNIE Now I mean, I wonder.

ALAN It's just as well, really.

DOUGLAS *(Entering.)* Well, we went up into the mountains this morning—you've never seen anything like it. Some of those—

RONNIE If you aren't the most ridiculous, childish oak I've ever seen…!

DOUGLAS Why's that?

RONNIE Penny's in there hysterical; she tells me you made a dumb sloppy pass at her in the garage yesterday afternoon. If you aren't an ass—to begin with for thinking she wouldn't come immediately like a shocked virgin and tell me. Confess to me.

(Douglas stands shocked and silent.)

RONNIE I can't believe you did something like that. I hope you don't delude yourself into thinking she liked it. She wants to leave is what she's think-ing—she wants to go live with Rose—I told her it was stupid. If you don't know better than to upset a girl like that. I swear to God if it's true—you ought to be ashamed of yourself. I know I am for you if you're not. Or I would be, Doug, if it weren't all so laughable.

(Beat. Beat. Douglas continues to look at her. No one moves except Carol and Alan.)

CAROL Well, that ought to be it then.

ALAN I'd think.

CAROL He says no, right?

ALAN As best I recall.

(Curtain)

ACT THREE

Alan comes forward. The stage is rather dark at the beginning, growing slowly and steadily lighter.

RONNIE *(From the darkness, faintly.)* Alan, honey, get up, Mt. McGinty is on fire, the whole sky's…

ALAN The greatest sight while I stayed in California was something that the Californians *do* fear. Their homes—many of them—and many of the nicer ones—range up into the brush and forests in the mountains. In the fall when it's dry—even for here. Bone dry. Dead. Fires light the sky. Mt. McGinty and Otay in the distance burned. The sky was red. The mountains were ochre with dried grass and brush one day and that night streaked with red fire and the next morning black. Houses were destroyed, timber and game and the view. Along about this time a poet—of local fame at school—who had left State a few years earlier—came back for a day or so. I have tried to remember what he wrote, but outside of a firm conviction that he was the most brilliant person I'd ever met, and wrote more perfectly than—Oh, skip it. I can't remember a word, in any case, and that's odd. It was probably more lines about creepy ferns and creepy shadows for creepy creeps. I do know we spoke, that we walked up into the mountains that had burned—around a landscape that looked like the moon. Charred mesquite and ashes six inches deep. The brush some of it—the fire had gone through it so quickly some of the brush stood—like ashes on a cigarette—stood three feet high—the white negative of the brush exactly intact and you touched it and it disintegrated. And into the woods that were saved to commune with what was left of nature. And after three afternoons of walking I skipped two days of school to stay mostly in my room and when I went back the poet had left—he wasn't around. It is of pertinence only as a very ironic coincidence. Ronnie said about Mt. Helix—just like I thought there it is. Who knows what a person is made of? I promise not to tell you if you promise not to tell me. I left Nebraska to come to the promised land because I had to. I left because I had to. This is the state I'm in. California. So much is true here, so much is open; so much is honest and so much is impossible to admit. Even of what I know is there, what I realize is there. In this state.

CAROL It's a good enough state to be in.

ALAN "I want to thank the theatre?" Poor bitch.

CAROL Right. Where else am I? Nowhere.

ALAN You're always here, in my state. With all those possibilities, if only…

CAROL Yes, I knew. "If only" is a good state.

ALAN *(Ironically.)* California.

CAROL Not that it matters—when you look at it from this distance, but that week—the week of the fire—I got engaged to Sonny. We will say briefly that the marriage didn't come off and the following year quite without me giving a damn I became a highway statistic and about as violently as one would have expected. My date for that particular night got rather too drunk and like the idiot he was drove us off—it's funny—it was funny then—shot like a rocket off Inspiration Point.

ALAN And landed in the valley below.

CAROL Hours…Actual hours later.

ALAN And burst into flames.

CAROL *(Pause.)* If you say so.

ALAN Ronnie wrote me—her second and last letter, some time back.

CAROL There should be something enormous I should say—what an opportunity. I was very good that last year. No one knows. I know it doesn't seem like it. But I was so damn good. I'm not saying I'm sorry. Goddamn I hate people who say they're sorry.

ALAN Right.

CAROL Once we were engaged we didn't get along—suffice it to say without ruining the story that something came up with which Sonny violently disagreed and we told each other to fuck off.

ALAN And your date for that particular evening, who drove you over the cliff—

CAROL Was a clod, forget it. I was aware that we were nowhere—I mean nowhere *about* to make the corner ahead. Mountain road. And I stiffened, like I was looking for the brake on my side of the car and not a word, not a scream, saw it all—thought: my God, some driver is going to come along and see the barrier torn up on this curve and be scared to death. Saw it all. In slow motion if you please.

ALAN And Sonny wasn't with you?

CAROL How do you mean? "Wasn't with me?" *(Rather bitter for just a second.)* Well, that shows what you know, doesn't it? No, Sonny was in downtown San Diego, right?

RONNIE Right, or so he said.

CAROL At the time. There. Sonny was somewhere in San Diego or so he said getting drunk and listening to records. At the time. *(Beat.)* Which shows what he knows, doesn't it? You didn't know right away, did you?

ALAN No, some time. Ronnie wrote me. A reply to a request for a loan of money.

CAROL You don't tell me your dreams, Alan, and I won't tell you mine.

ALAN Deal.

CAROL Deal.

RONNIE Doug is an excellent provider, Alan; you can't see it, I know, but he is. And I'm an excellent manager, all considered. And I have Jerry and Jack and they are more important to me than anything in the world. *(Proudly.)* The boys are quite grown, of course, and quite normal and I'm very proud of them. You would be too. Jerry bowls.

ALAN Bowls? Really? Jerry twelve. Jerry fifteen. Jerry twenty-five. Jerry thirty. Thirty-five. Forty. *(Nearly crying, but recovering.)* Jerry, Jerry. And hairy Jack. It's like a cartoon strip and after one artist quits another takes over and you can hardly tell the difference—yet something…Quite normal? I had hoped—eccentric somehow.

DOUGLAS To each his own, I guess.

ALAN Deal.

DOUGLAS Not at all eccentric. Not at all. Just ordinary.

RONNIE In an extraordinary sort of way.

ALAN Deal.

RONNIE You were so drunk that night. I thought you'd faint right on the floor.

PENNY I.

(Everyone turns to her, a pause.)

DOUGLAS Yeah?

PENNY I don't care, one way or the other.

RONNIE You always wanted to be a teacher.

PENNY Not civics. I don't think. I teach civics. I'm not good with them really, you have to be more of a disciplinarian than anything.

ALAN Married, right?

PENNY Oh, yeah. Kids.

CAROL No white coat?

PENNY No rice, really, either.

DOUGLAS So, all those deals, some of 'em get good cards, some of 'em—

CAROL *(Cutting in.)* And some of them get a lousy hand and haven't the nerve to bluff or the sense to fold. Thanks, anyway, Alan. I appreciate it. You know you hardly entered my mind. I had quite a world going for me there.

ALAN People are always entering people's minds at inopportune times. The least I could do—

CAROL *(Singing gently.)* Walk right in, sit right down, daddy, let your hair hang down…

ALAN What are you on?

CAROL I don't even know.

PENNY *(To Ronnie.)* I liked Doug really. I'd never had a father that I remembered.

RONNIE I know, Penny.

PENNY I didn't want to leave.

RONNIE You didn't have to leave, my God, the sky didn't fall in, Henny Penny…

PENNY What will he do? I can't look him in the face, Ronnie.

CAROL God bless us every one.

RONNIE Yes, indeed, Carol.

ALAN Deal. God bless us every one. I must have drunk about—*(Drunk.)* about—about—

RONNIE Come on.

ALAN About a keg of stale beer. I'll bet I really did. You know California beer tastes like slop.

RONNIE Right, no good at all; you shouldn't drink it.

ALAN Now you tell me.

RONNIE Why don't you go off to bed and get some sleep now before you wake up the whole house. Even Carol's in bed already.

ALAN You go on to bed. The bartender kept sitting beers in front of me and he knew I wasn't of age. I should report him for selling beer to a minor. I don't think he even charged me for the last couple, though. Just as soon as I finished there'd be another one there like the Sermon on the Mount. Bread and fishes. He says we have a couple of girls and I said no, thank you, I just want to get very stoned. I haven't been stoned since I left Nebraska—I haven't you know.

RONNIE I know.

ALAN And he said, "Don't get sick it's gonna be a scorcher tomorrow." He was from Kansas. There's no such thing as a Native Californian.

RONNIE I thought you wanted me to go on and now you're talking.

ALAN Did I make any sense?

RONNIE Very little sense.

ALAN I was so dizzy I couldn't even see the room. And—go on…

RONNIE OK: "Go on to bed, it'll be a good day tomorrow."

ALAN And tomorrow came and the Kansan was closer.

PENNY You can tell the authorities that I'm still here if you want to. They never care anyway.

CAROL They never gave a wild flying damn about any of us really. Who cares about anyone?

RONNIE It's impossible to take seriously. Penny? It's an insult to me for one thing which of course Penny couldn't know, but I'd expect you to see that. I swear to God you ought to be ashamed of yourself; I know I am for you if you're not; or I would be if…

DOUGLAS *(Cutting in.)* It's a goddamn!

RONNIE Oh, come on, Doug, so you tried to sneak a quick—

DOUGLAS *(Over her.)* That lying bitch—is what I'm saying. I might want her to feel at home. Can't I put my arm around her and give her a squeeze; goddamnit she's never had a father! Her life—the bitch. Not another night under my house, that bitch if she thinks she can accuse me of—*Alan!* I want to talk to you. Now this isn't something that I want passed around and I don't think you'll—I don't want to see her face here again. No, by God, she can go to Rose, she can go to hell for all I care. She's not spending another night under my roof.

RONNIE Doug, it doesn't matter—of course she can—

DOUGLAS Like hell it doesn't matter. Doesn't matter! You try to show some affection for someone—I didn't touch the tight bitch, I didn't go near her, what's she trying to pull? And by God if you believe it you can go to hell too. I won't have it. I won't have it, by God.

PENNY I didn't want to cause anything—why did you tell him—I'm leaving.

DOUGLAS The whole goddamn bunch of them can clear out for all I care. They can get out now.

ALAN Why did you tell him?

RONNIE I didn't say you did, I said Penny said you did. I think it's funny; there's nothing to get upset about, Good God, Doug.

ALAN Why did you tell him?

DOUGLAS No, by God I never touched her.

RONNIE She says you kissed her on the cheek. She didn't say any more than that.

DOUGLAS Well what the hell's wrong with that, a father kissing a daughter. *If I had!* I'm supposed to be her father, she's never had a family; what the hell would be wrong with that? If I had! Which I didn't by God.

RONNIE It just isn't important.

DOUGLAS Well, something is—Alan!

ALAN What?

DOUGLAS *(Very tense—more intense than shouting.)* This is important—more than that girl—as far as I'm concerned.

ALAN What's wrong? I've not missed work, any if—

DOUGLAS Just let me talk if you will, please now.

RONNIE Nothing is of such importance, Doug—

DOUGLAS *(Overlapping.)* I said Goddamnit I'm going to talk now. Doug is gonna talk for a change now—I might know something!

ALAN *(To the audience.)* He—I don't know. If I had known then what he was thinking perhaps—

DOUGLAS *(Whirling him around, cutting in. Overlapping.)* LOOK AT ME

WHEN I'M *TRYING TO*—Now you've been avoiding, conniving and lying the whole goddamn time, now I'm going to talk.

RONNIE Doug, it isn't necessary to—

DOUGLAS All right now! Penny, you stay goddamnit right there, I'll deal with your lies— *(To Alan.)* Jerry tells me that you and Phil have been sitting out at the cliffs in his sparkling Pontiac. Last night and night before that and night before that.

ALAN With Penny and Phil, yeah. I went into work the following day, I don't know—

DOUGLAS That doesn't interest me! It's your job, brother, you can get fired from it if you goddamn well like—I just want to know if it's true?

ALAN What? Is what true? I don't know what you're getting at, Dad, I haven't any idea what—

DOUGLAS You goddamned *bas*tard, stall for time. You know, don't you?

ALAN Well, I don't see any point in—

DOUGLAS Yes, you are, goddamnit, it all fits—everything fits, suddenly it dawns. Suddenly it dawns. Yeah, and everyone—all your friends at State know it. Well, he has to have—I'm talking about Phil, you know god-damned well what I'm saying—he has to have someone to cover for him, he can't spend *all* his time with the sailors from the queer bars downtown. Everybody else is too wise to fool. Penny wouldn't ask questions—she has to take what she can get and she deserves just what she takes. If she's the coverup of some rich queer she's too stupid to ask questions…I feel sorry for the lying bitch if she's that stupid. But you're not dumb. I thought you had some physical problem maybe, I should have been wise, man! It's sure easy for you—going out with Penny and him, what are you—holding hands behind her back?

ALAN Lie! That's no…

DOUGLAS Then what are you doing?

ALAN What are you saying?

DOUGLAS I'm saying you're through around this house. Not with my kids—not—you're not going to make sissies out of my two boys and you're not going to breathe in my house—not my air anymore!

ALAN That's a lie—how can you say that with Penny here—she knows bet-ter—and Jerry…

DOUGLAS Penny knows goddamn well it's true. Look at her. Ask her if he's once tried to lay her or even thought about it. Hell, ask Carol, Carol knows it and Ronnie knows it and every other goddamned person in the county knows it and you do too. He's famous. Everybody's so goddamned afraid to hurt, disillusion little Penny's feelings—so they let her live in a dream world. He must be laughing himself silly. Hell, he must spit on her. He knows a good thing when he sees it.

ALAN Ask Carol—

(But Carol is already shaking her head, better not ask me.)

ALAN Well, if it's *true* what do you mean saying it? What do you mean by saying that?

DOUGLAS *(This intense, not loud.)* Not in my house.

ALAN He never touched me. I don't know why you can't leave my sex interests alone or to myself.

DOUGLAS I intend to protect my own. I'm not having it. Now, I can't take this.

ALAN What do you mean? What are you doing?

DOUGLAS I'm telling you to go back to where you came from—we don't need you here. It's been disturbance since you came. Now, you take your little imitation leather suitcase in there and your record player and everything you've *touched* in this goddamned house and pack them back up into a little—

ALAN No! By God. Damn you! I'm going to say one thing! You're lying and I don't know why! But you are and you know you are! I'm no good at this—

DOUGLAS Well, if you think I am…

ALAN You see! That's all I know. What you are not! You're Not! You're nothing! You think the best is none too good and you don't have any idea at all about the best! You'll never see it! And all your lies prove it!

DOUGLAS Get out. That's all I want from you, mister, that's all. That's all. That's all—just go on. Out. That's all.

ALAN *Mur-der-er! (Sobbing.)* MURDERER! I had a sister and you killed her. Killed your own daughter trying to be a man—Whoring and if that's what you want me to be like and Jerry to be like and all of us, then I may have the satisfaction—

DOUGLAS *(Slaps him sharply across the face.)* That's a lie! That's a Lie!

ALAN NO! You killed her! As well as if you had beat her to death…Jerry's sister and Jack's sister and my sister! You drove my mother insane with your whores and you're so proud of it! And you've come out here with her. And you're never going to forget it!

DOUGLAS That's a goddamn lie. She never.

ALAN She was born a bloody dead mass! Not even human—thrown to the trash to burn and you did it! You know it!

DOUGLAS *(Injured—quietly.)* How can…you have no idea. What that did to me. No idea. You'll never know as long as you live—you couldn't—you'll never—by God—have a kid to know what it's like—Now you get your things in there—and you get out of here—in half an hour. I don't care where you go. You just get out of my sight now!

(Penny has left just before Alan's line "Murderer." She goes down the hall. She walks to the door of the bedroom and takes Carol's orange robe, under her arm and to the bathroom. At the door of the bathroom Carol reaches her. She tries to close the door but Carol blocks it. They struggle with the bottle of pills. Carol's line comes now.)

CAROL No, Penny!

PENNY No, let me—stop—stop—stop!

CAROL *(At the same time.)* The hell do you think you're doing goddamnit— Give THEM TO ME!

(Penny screams. Carol is still struggling with her. The pills fly from the bottle across the floor scattering all around them. Some are in Penny's hand. Penny and Carol both go to their knees, Carol trying to hold Penny's hands away from her mouth—Penny trying to stuff the pills into her mouth. Struggling.)

CAROL Stop it, Penny. Stop it…Stop it—give them to me, what are you trying to do?

PENNY *(At the same time.)* No, don't—get away, CAROL, get away—No, Let me! Carol, don't.

RONNIE *(Reaches them.)* Penny—Stop it—Did she take any?

CAROL I don't think so.

(Jack enters.)

PENNY Please, please, let me!

(Ronnie gets a strong hold on Penny—Jack picks up several of the pills.)

CAROL Jack, stay away, go out! Don't touch those!

RONNIE Jack, put those back—throw them down. Every one. Now!

(He does.)

RONNIE What are they?

CAROL I don't know.

RONNIE What are they?

CAROL Just never mind—it isn't important—they're aspirin.

RONNIE *What are they, Carol?*

CAROL I said never mind, it doesn't matter, Penny, baby, come on, honey—

RONNIE I said goddamnit you tell me what they are!

CAROL *(Screaming.)* They're Mellaril, Mellaril, dope! What the goddamn hell do you think they are—and I don't give a shit what…

(Ronnie slaps her across the face—Carol immediately slaps her back. Douglas arrives, slings Carol halfway across the stage.)

DOUGLAS Take them! Take them! All! Take them every goddamn one!

RONNIE It's all right. Carol, take care of her.

CAROL I'm sorry. Let her take care of herself.

PENNY I'm OK. *(She turns to go.)* Leave me alone. All of you just don't touch me!

(Ronnie reaches toward her.)

PENNY Don't touch me!

(Ronnie turns, Alan follows her. Douglas begins to pick up the pills.)

ALAN Ronnie, Ronnie.

RONNIE *(Interrupting.)* I didn't know you had had a sister who had been born dead, Alan. I'm very sorry. I don't know what to say.

ALAN All—I shouldn't have said anything. I have—I don't know what to do, Ron, he's—nothing he said is true—I can't leave you and Jack and—what am I supposed to do? What am I...?

RONNIE I think you'd better go. *(She walks away, toward her room.)*

DOUGLAS *(Finishing picking up the pills. Going to her as she leaves Alan.)* Ron—Ronnie.

RONNIE Doug, I don't want to talk to you—I want to lie down. Where's Jerry?

DOUGLAS He's outside.

RONNIE I just want to lie down.

DOUGLAS Ron—Ronnie, baby—what could I do?

RONNIE Nothing, Doug. It's all right.

DOUGLAS Everything's going to be all right.

JACK *(Going to Alan.)* Do you have to go?

ALAN Yeah, I will.

DOUGLAS Really. Forget it. It'll all be over. We're better off, Ronnie.

RONNIE I'm sure, Doug, I don't want to think about it.

DOUGLAS *(Turning, looking to him.)* Alan? Alan, I want you to know—All those years...

ALAN I know, dad.

(Douglas and Alan are very far apart. Jack beside Alan, Douglas by Ronnie, Jerry alone outside. Penny and Carol together near their room.)

PENNY Oh, God, Carol.

CAROL It's all right, baby. Nothing matters.

JACK I don't want you to leave; you just got here.

ALAN It's OK, baby...

JACK Really, don't.

(It begins to grow dark again.)

ALAN Baby, it's good to remember that someone said that...

DOUGLAS *(Calling as though across time.)* All those years. I wanted to help. What was I supposed to do? Alan?

(It continues to grow dark.)

JACK Please. Take me with you then.

ALAN Baby, I will. Really, don't worry. You're eight years old and a little white orangutan.

JACK Really, though, let me go with you, Alan, can I?

ALAN You will, Jack, I promise.

(Only the faintest light remains on Alan and Jack—Jack turns to go in, leaving Alan alone in the spot.)

DOUGLAS Hugged me, by God. By God you can't—

PENNY Pleased to meet you, I've heard a lot about you.

DOUGLAS No matter what anybody anywhere says, you can't separate a kid from his father.

JERRY Alan? Are you awake?

PENNY Good night.

JERRY Good morning.

CAROL *(Their voices tumble over each other.)* Thanks anyway, Alan; I had quite a little world going for me. Walk right in, sit right down— *(Continues to end.)*

JERRY *(Cued by Carol's "Alan.")* We had orange trees and plum trees and a fig tree.

RONNIE *(Cued by "orange trees.")* If you have the faith the size of a mustard seed you can move mountains.

(On "Faith," Alan laughs to himself.)

DOUGLAS *(Cued by "size.")* I know she must have told you things about me.

PENNY *(Cued by "told.")* I'll probably teach, I like kids.

RONNIE *(Cued by "teach.")* Welcome, Alan. Welcome, Hello!

ALAN *(Crying out.)* LIGHTS!

(The stage lights bounce up bright and full, everyone is still. Alan turns and walks out. They follow, urgently whispering. Douglas is the only voice we hear clearly.)

DOUGLAS I just want you to understand, Alan.

Alan.

Alan.

Alan.

(The stage has returned to darkness before Alan can escape them. Curtain)

END OF PLAY

CONTEMPORARY PLAYWRIGHTS SERIES

Christopher Durang Vol. I: 27 Short Plays

Christopher Durang Vol. II: Complete Full-Length Plays, 1975-1995

Horton Foote Vol. I: 4 New Plays

Horton Foote Vol. II: Collected Plays

John Guare: The War against the Kitchen Sink

A.R. Gurney Vol. I: 9 Early Plays

A.R. Gurney Vol. II: Collected Plays, 1977-1985

Israel Horovitz Vol. I: 16 Short Plays

Romulus Linney: 17 Short Plays

Jane Martin: Collected Plays, 1980-1995

Terrence McNally Vol. I: 15 Short Plays

Terrence McNally Vol.II: Collected Plays

William Mastrosimone: Collected Plays

Marsha Norman: Collected Plays

Eric Overmyer: Collected Plays

Lanford Wilson: 21 Short Plays

Lanford Wilson: Collected Plays, 1965-1970

20 One-Acts from 20 Years at the Humana Festival, 1975-1995

Humana Festival '93: The Complete Plays

Humana Festival '94: The Complete Plays

Humana Festival '95: The Complete Plays

Humana Festival '96: The Complete Plays

Women Playwrights: The Best Plays of 1992

Women Playwrights: The Best Plays of 1993

Women Playwrights: The Best Plays of 1994

Women Playwrights: The Best Plays of 1995

EST Marathon '94: One-Act Plays

EST Marathon '95: One-Act Plays

EST Marathon '96: One-Act Plays

Act One Festival '94: One-Act Plays

Act One Festival '95: One-Act Plays

If you require pre-publication information about upcoming Smith and Kraus books, you may receive our semi-annual catalogue, free of charge, by sending your name and address to *Smith and Kraus Catalogue, P.O. Box 127, One Main Street, Lyme, NH 03768. Or call us at (800) 895-4331, fax (603) 795-4427.***Smith and Kraus** *Books For Actors*